VISUAL QUICKSTART GUIDE

WORD 2002

FOR WINDOWS

Maria Langer

 Peachpit Press

Visual QuickStart Guide
Word 2002 for Windows
Maria Langer

Peachpit Press
1249 Eighth Street
Berkeley, CA 94710
510-524-2178 · 800-283-9444
510-524-2221 (fax)

Find us on the World Wide Web at: http://www.peachpit.com

Peachpit Press is a division of Pearson Education

Editor: Nancy Davis
Indexer: Emily Glossbrenner
Cover Design: The Visual Group
Production: Maria Langer, Connie Jeung-Mills

Colophon

This book was produced with Adobe PageMaker 6.5 on a Power Macintosh G3/300. The fonts used were Kepler Multiple Master, Meta Plus, and PIXymbols Command. Screenshots were created using Capture and Grabber2K on a Dell Dimension L933r.

Notice of Rights

Notice of Liability

Trademarks

ISBN 0-201-75845-8

9 8 7 6 5 4 3 2 1

Printed and bound in the United States of America.

Dedication

In memory of
Matt Rebholz
1929 - 2001

Thanks!

To Nancy Davis, once again, for her editing skills. Nancy finds even the tiniest mistakes in my manuscript.

To Connie Jeung-Mills, for her sharp eyes and gentle layout editing.

To Nancy Ruenzel, Marjorie Baer, and the other powers-that-be at Peachpit Press, for keeping me so darn busy.

To the rest of the folks at Peachpit Press— especially Gary-Paul, Mimi, Trish, Hannah, Paula, Zigi, Jimbo, and Keasley—for doing what they do so well.

To Microsoft Corporation for continuing to improve the best word processing program on earth.

And to Mike, for the usual reasons.

www.theflyingm.com

TABLE OF CONTENTS

TABLE OF CONTENTS

INTRODUCTION TO WORD 2002

Introduction

Microsoft Word 2002, a component of Microsoft Office XP, is the latest version of Microsoft's powerful word processing application for Windows users. Now more powerful and user friendly than ever, Word enables users to create a wide variety of documents, ranging in complexity from simple, one-page letters to complex, multi-file reports with figures, table of contents, and index.

This Visual QuickStart Guide will help you learn Word 2002 by providing step-by-step instructions, plenty of illustrations, and a generous helping of tips. On these pages, you'll find everything you need to know to get up and running quickly with Word—and more!

This book was designed for page flipping. Use the thumb tabs, index, or table of contents to find the topics for which you need help. If you're brand new to Word or word processing, however, I recommend that you begin by reading at least the first two chapters. **Chapter 1** provides basic information about Word's interface while **Chapter 2** introduces word processing concepts and explains exactly how they work in Word.

If you've used other versions of Word and are interested in information about new Word 2002 features, be sure to browse through this **Introduction**. It'll give you a good idea of the new things Word has in store for you.

New & Improved Features in Word 2002

Word 2002 includes many brand new features, as well as major improvements to some existing features. Here's a list.

✔ Tip

■ This book covers many of these features.

Interface features

◆ Task panes offer an easy-to-use interface for working with specific Word features:

▲ **New Document (Figure 1)** enables you to create new documents or open existing documents.

▲ **Clipboard** enables you to store multiple items on the clipboard and paste them as desired in your document.

▲ **Search** enables you to search for documents on your hard disk or network.

▲ **Styles and Formatting** enables you to view, apply, and modify styles.

▲ **Insert Clip Art** enables you to insert clip art into documents.

▲ **Reveal Formatting** displays the formatting for selected text in a document.

▲ **Mail Merge** offers access to the improved Mail Merge Wizard for merging Word documents with list of information.

▲ **Translate** offers access to Word's translation features.

◆ You can now hide the empty white space at the top and bottom of each page in Print Layout view. This eliminates wasted screen space.

Figure 1
The New Document task pane is one of several new task panes available in Word 2002.

Figure 2 When you paste text into a document, a Paste Smart Tag appears, offering options for working with the pasted in text.

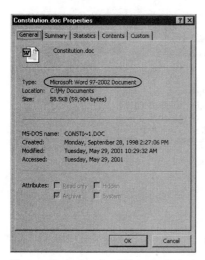

Figure 3 The Properties dialog now includes information about a document's format.

Figure 4 You can now add watermarks to printed documents.

◆ Smart Tags display pop-up menus beside various items that you type or paste:

▲ **AutoCorrect** Smart Tags enable you to work with Word's AutoCorrect feature after Word automatically corrects something you type.

▲ **Name, Address, and Date** Smart Tags offer options related to names, addresses, or dates you type, such as scheduling meetings and adding individuals to your address book.

▲ **Paste** Smart Tags (**Figure 2**) offer options for working with text or objects you paste into a document.

Formatting features

◆ Word now allows you to select multiple blocks of text at the same time.

◆ The new Clear Formatting feature enables you to remove all formatting from selected text.

◆ Word's new Check Format feature can find 10 different inconsistencies in formatting so you can fix them and have a more consistently formatted document.

◆ Word now enables you to create styles for lists and tables.

◆ The General tab of the Properties dialog now includes information about a document's format (**Figure 3**).

◆ You can now include a picture, logo, or text as a background "watermark" when printing Word documents (**Figure 4**).

◆ Word's new Drawing Canvas enables you to create a drawing area within a Word document and place objects on it. This makes it easier to position graphic objects in your document.

NEW & IMPROVED FEATURES IN WORD 2002

Document tool features

◆ The new Word Count toolbar (**Figure 5**) enables you to update a document's word count quickly and easily.

◆ Word now supports speech commands and dictation.

◆ Word enables you to translate words in your document based on installed language dictionaries or a Web-based translation service.

◆ Word supports more languages than ever before.

Collaboration features

◆ The new Send for Review command turns on the track changes feature when a document is e-mailed to someone else.

◆ The new Markup feature can display tracked changes as callouts in the right margin of the document.

◆ Word now supports editing by multiple users at the same time.

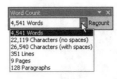

Figure 5 The Word Count toolbar makes it quick and easy to count the words, characters, lines, pages, and paragraphs in a document.

NEW & IMPROVED FEATURES IN WORD 2002

THE WORD WORKPLACE

Meet Microsoft Word

Microsoft Word is a full-featured word processing application that you can use to create all kinds of text-based documents—letters, reports, form letters, mailing labels, envelopes, flyers, and even Web pages.

Word's interface combines common Windows screen elements with buttons, commands, and controls that are specific to Word. To use Word effectively, you must have at least a basic understanding of these elements.

This chapter introduces the Word workplace by illustrating and describing the following elements:

◆ The Word screen, including window elements

◆ Menus, shortcut keys, toolbars, palettes, and dialogs

◆ Views and document navigation techniques

◆ Word's Help feature, including the Office Assistant

✔ Tip

■ If you've used previous versions of Word, browse through this chapter to learn about some of the interface elements that are new to this version of Word.

The Word Screen

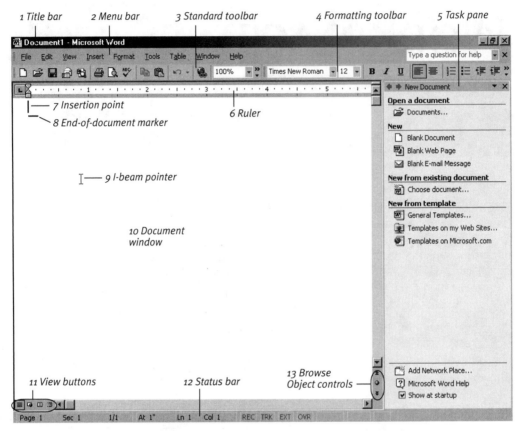

Figure 1 The Word screen displaying a document in Normal view.

Key to the Word screen

1 Title bar

The title bar displays the document's title. You can drag the title bar to move the window.

2 Menu bar

The menu bar appears at the top of the screen and offers access to Word's commands.

3 Standard toolbar

The Standard toolbar offers buttons for basic Word commands.

4 Formatting toolbar

The Formatting toolbar offers buttons and other controls for applying formatting to document contents.

5 Task pane

The task pane offers a quick way to access common Word tasks.

6 Ruler

Word's ruler enables you to set paragraph formatting options such as tabs and indentation.

7 Insertion point

The blinking insertion point indicates where text will appear when typed or inserted with the Paste command.

8 End-of-document marker

The end-of-document marker indicates the end of the document.

9 I-beam pointer

The Click and Type pointer, enables you to position the insertion point or select text. This pointer, which is controlled by the mouse, turns into various other pointers depending on its position and the Word view.

10 Document window

The document window is where you create, edit, and view Word documents.

11 View buttons

View buttons enable you to switch between various Word views.

12 Status bar

The status bar displays information about the document, such as the current page number and section and insertion point location.

13 Browse Object controls

These buttons enable you to navigate among various document elements.

✔ Tips

■ **Figure 1** shows the Word screen in Normal view. Other elements that appear in other views are discussed later in this chapter and throughout this book. Word's views are covered later in this chapter.

■ Standard Windows window elements are not discussed in detail in this book. For more information about how to use standard window elements such as the Close button, Minimize button, Maximize button, Restore button, and scroll bars, consult the documentation that came with your computer or Windows online help.

THE WORD SCREEN

The Mouse

As with most Windows programs, you use the mouse to select text, activate buttons, and choose menu commands.

Mouse pointer appearance

The appearance of the mouse pointer varies depending on its location and the item to which it is pointing. Here are some examples:

◆ In the document window, the mouse pointer usually looks like an I-beam pointer (**Figure 1**).

◆ On a menu name, the mouse pointer appears as an arrow pointing up and to the left (**Figure 2**).

◆ In the selection bar between the left edge of the document window and the text, the mouse pointer appears as an arrow pointing up and to the right (**Figure 3**).

◆ On selected text, the mouse pointer appears as an arrow pointing up and to the left (**Figure 4**).

To use the mouse

There are four basic mouse techniques:

◆ **Pointing** means to position the mouse pointer so that its tip is on the item to which you are pointing (**Figure 2**).

◆ **Clicking** means to press the mouse button once and release it. You click to position the insertion point or to activate a button.

◆ **Double-clicking** means to press the mouse button twice in rapid succession. You double-click to open an item or to select a word.

◆ **Dragging** means to press the mouse button down and hold it while moving the mouse. You drag to resize windows, select text, choose menu commands, or draw shapes.

Figure 2
Pointing to a menu name.

Figure 3
The mouse pointer in the selection bar.

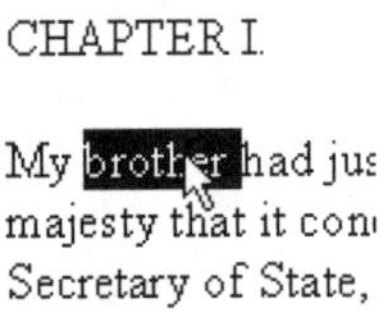

CHAPTER I.

My brother had jus majesty that it con Secretary of State,

CHAPTER I.

Figure 4
The mouse pointer pointing to a word.

My brother had jus majesty that it con Secretary of State,

✔ Tip

■ Throughout this book, when I instruct you to simply *click*, press the left mouse button. When I instruct you to *right-click*, press the right mouse button.

Figure 5
A personalized version of the Edit menu.

Figure 6
The Edit menu with all commands displayed.

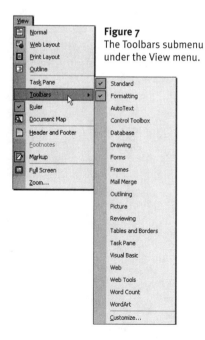

Figure 7
The Toolbars submenu under the View menu.

Menus

All of Word's commands are accessible through its menus. Word has three types of menus:

◆ **Personalized menus** appear on the menu bar near the top of the window. These menus automatically track and display only the commands you use most (**Figure 5**).

◆ **Full menus** also appear on the menu bar near the top of the winodw, but only when you either double-click the menu name, pause while displaying the menu, or click the arrows at the bottom of the menu. **Figure 6** shows the menu in **Figure 5** as a full menu with all commands displayed.

◆ **Shortcut menus** appear at the mouse pointer when you right-click on an item (**Figure 8**).

Here are some rules to keep in mind when working with menus:

◆ A menu command that appears in gray cannot be selected.

◆ A menu command followed by an ellipsis (...) displays a dialog.

◆ A menu command followed by a triangle has a submenu. The submenu displays additional commands when the main command is highlighted (**Figure 7**).

◆ A menu command followed by one or more keyboard characters can be chosen with a shortcut key.

◆ A menu command preceded by a check mark has been "turned on" (**Figure 7**). To toggle the command from on to off or off to on, choose it from the menu.

✔ Tip

■ Dialogs and shortcut keys are covered later in this chapter.

MENUS

To choose a menu command

1. Click the name of the menu from which you want to choose the command. The personalized version of the menu appears (**Figure 5**).

2. If necessary, click the menu name again to display the full menu version of the menu (**Figure 6**).

3. Click the command you want.

   or

   If the command is on a submenu, click on the submenu to display it (**Figure 7**) and then click on the command you want.

✔ Tips

■ This book uses the following notation to indicate menu commands: *Menu Name > Submenu Name* (if necessary) *> Command Name*. For example, "choose View > Toolbars > Standard" instructs you to choose the Standard command from the Toolbars submenu under the View menu.

■ You can also use mouseless menus. Press Alt, then use the letter and arrow keys to display and select menus and commands. Press Enter to activate a selected command.

To use a shortcut menu

1. Point to the item on which you want to use the shortcut menu.

2. Hold down Ctrl and press the mouse button down. The shortcut menu appears (**Figure 8**).

3. Choose the command that you want.

✔ Tips

■ The shortcut menu only displays the commands that can be applied to the item to which you are pointing.

■ Shortcut menus are sometimes referred to as *context-sensitive* or *contextual menus*.

Figure 8 A shortcut menu appears at the mouse pointer when you right-click on an item—in this case, selected text.

Shortcut Keys

Shortcut keys are combinations of keyboard keys that, when pressed, choose a menu command without displaying the menu. For example, the shortcut key for the Copy command under the Edit menu (**Figures 5** and **6**) is Ctrl C. Pressing this key combination chooses the command.

✔ Tips

- All shortcut keys use at least one of the following modifier keys:

Key Name	Keyboard Key
Control	Ctrl
Shift	⇧ Shift
Alt	Alt

- A menu command's shortcut key is displayed to its right on the menu (**Figures 5** and **6**).

- Many shortcut keys are standardized from one application to another. The Save and Print commands are good examples; they're usually Ctrl S and Ctrl P.

- **Appendix A** includes a list of Word's shortcut keys.

To use a shortcut key

1. Hold down the modifier key for the shortcut (normally Ctrl).

2. Press the letter or number key for the shortcut.

For example, to choose the Copy command, hold down Ctrl and press the C key.

Toolbars

Word includes a number of toolbars for various purposes. Each one includes buttons or menus that activate menu commands or set options.

By default, Word automatically displays two toolbars when you launch it:

◆ The Standard toolbar (**Figure 9**) offers buttons for a wide range of commonly used commands.

◆ The Formatting toolbar (**Figure 10**) offers buttons and menus for formatting selected items.

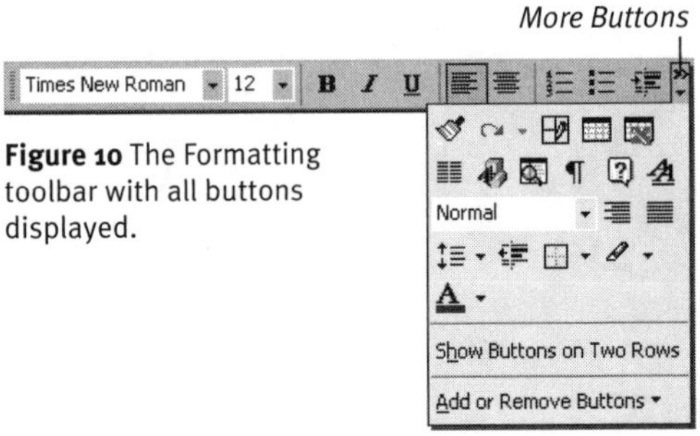

✔ Tips

■ Other toolbars may appear automatically depending on the task you are performing with Word.

■ Toolbar buttons with faint icon images (for example, Cut in **Figure 9**) cannot be selected.

■ Toolbar buttons with a blue border around them (for example, Align Left in **Figure 10**) are "turned on."

■ You can identify a button by its ScreenTip (**Figure 11**).

■ A toolbar can be *docked* or *floating*. A docked toolbar (**Figures 9** and **10**) is positioned against any edge of the screen. A floating toolbar can be moved anywhere within the screen.

More Buttons

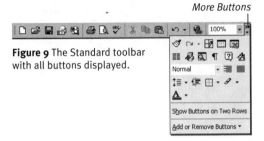

Figure 9 The Standard toolbar with all buttons displayed.

More Buttons

Figure 10 The Formatting toolbar with all buttons displayed.

TOOLBARS

Figure 11
A ScreenTip appears when you point to a button.

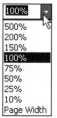

Figure 12
Click the triangle beside the menu to display the menu.

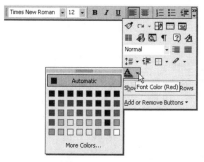

Figure 13 The Font Color menu appears when you click the Font Color button.

Figure 14
The menu appears as a floating menu or palette.

Figure 15 Select the current value,...

Figure 16 ...enter a new value, and press Enter.

To view more buttons

Click the More Buttons button at the far right end of the toolbar. Additional buttons for the toolbar appear (**Figures 9** and **10**).

To view ScreenTips

Point to a toolbar or palette button. A tiny yellow box containing the name of the button appears (**Figure 11**).

To use a toolbar button

1. Point to the button for the command or option that you want (**Figure 11**).

2. Click once.

To use a toolbar menu

1. Click on the triangle beside the menu to display the menu and its commands (**Figure 12**).

2. Click a command or option to select it.

✔ Tips

- Button menus that display a gray move handle along the top edge (**Figure 13**) can be "torn off" and used as floating menus or palettes. Simply display the menu and drag it away from the toolbar. When the palette appears, release the mouse button. The menu is displayed as a floating menu with a title bar that displays its name (**Figure 14**).

- Menus that display text boxes (**Figure 12**) can be changed by typing a new value into the box. Just click the contents of the box to select it (**Figure 15**), then type in the new value and press Enter (**Figure 16**).

To display or hide a toolbar

Choose the name of the toolbar that you want to display or hide from the Toolbars submenu under the View menu (**Figure 7**).

If the toolbar name has a check mark beside it, it is displayed and will be hidden.

or

If the toolbar name does not have a check mark beside it, it is hidden and will be displayed.

✔ Tip

■ You can also hide a floating toolbar by clicking its close button.

To float a docked toolbar

Drag the toolbar's move handle (**Figure 17**) away from the toolbar's docked position (**Figure 18**).

✔ Tip

■ Floating a docked toolbar will change the appearance and position of other toolbars docked in the same row (**Figure 18**).

To dock a floating toolbar

Drag the toolbar's titled bar to the edge of the screen (**Figure 19**).

✔ Tip

■ You can dock a toolbar against the top (**Figure 17**), either side (**Figure 19**), or the bottom of the screen. Buttons may change appearance when the toolbar is docked on the side of the screen.

To move a floating toolbar

Drag the title bar for the toolbar to reposition it on screen.

To resize a floating toolbar

Drag the edge of the toolbar (**Figure 20**).

Move handles

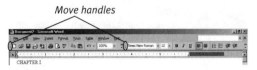

Figure 17 By default, the Standard and Formatting toolbars are docked.

Figure 18 Drag the toolbar into the document window to float it. When you float the Standard toolbar, the Formatting toolbar expands to occupy some of the vacated space.

Figure 19
When you drag a toolbar to the edge of the screen, it becomes docked there. In this example, the Standard toolbar is docked on the left side of the screen.

Figure 20 Drag the edge of a floating toolbar to resize it.

Figure 21
The New Document task pane.

Close button

Figure 22
To display a different task pane, choose its name from the pop-up menu in the task pane's title bar.

Figure 23
You can display the task pane by choosing Task Pane from the View menu.

The Task Pane

Microsoft Office XP introduces *task panes*, which appear in all Office applications, including Word. Each task pane includes a number of clickable links and other options to perform common tasks. For example, the New Document task pane (**Figure 21**), which appears when you run Word, enables you to open recent documents and create new documents.

✔ Tip

■ Although the task pane is a handy way to access commonly used commands and features without the use of dialogs that block your work, you may find that it takes up too much space on screen. If you prefer to use all screen real estate for your documents, you can close the task pane, as discussed below.

To perform a task pane task

Click the underlined link for the task you want to perform.

To display a different task pane

Choose the name of the task pane you want to display from the pop-up menu in the currently displayed task pane's title bar (**Figure 22**).

To close the task pane

Click the task pane's close button (**Figure 22**).

To open the task pane

Choose View > Task Pane (**Figure 23**).

To prevent the task pane from appearing when you run Word

Turn off the Show at startup check box at the bottom of the task pane (**Figure 21**).

THE TASK PANE

Dialogs

Like most other Windows programs, Word uses *dialogs* to communicate with you.

Word can display many different dialogs, each with its own purpose. There are two basic types of dialogs:

◆ Dialogs that simply provide information (**Figure 24**).

◆ Dialogs that offer options to select (**Figure 25**) before Word completes the execution of a command.

✔ Tip

■ Often, when a dialog appears, you must dismiss it by clicking OK or Cancel before you can continue working with Word.

Anatomy of a Word dialog

Here are the components of many Word dialogs, along with information about how they work.

◆ **Tabs** (**Figure 25**), which appear at the top of some dialogs, let you move from one group of dialog options to another. To switch to another group of options, click its tab.

◆ **Text boxes** or **entry fields** (**Figures 25** and **26**) let you enter information from the keyboard. You can press Tab to move from one box to the next or click in a box to position the insertion point within it. Then enter a new value.

◆ **List boxes** (**Figure 25**) offer a number of options to choose from. Use the scroll bar to view options that don't fit in the list window. Click an option to select it; it becomes highlighted and appears in the text box.

◆ **Check boxes** (**Figure 25**) let you turn options on or off. Click in a check box to toggle it. When a check mark or X appears in the check box, its option is turned on.

Figure 24
The Word Count dialog just displays information.

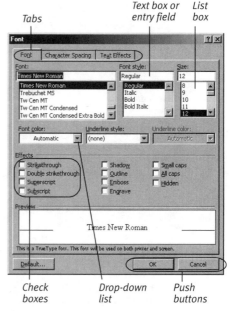

Figure 25 The Font dialog.

Option buttons

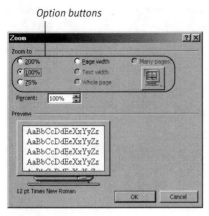

Figure 26 The Zoom dialog.

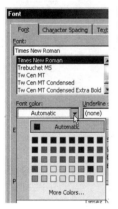

Figure 27
Displaying a
drop-down list.

◆ **Option buttons** (**Figure 26**) let you select only one option from a group. Click on an option to select it; the option that was selected before you clicked is deselected.

◆ **Drop-down lists** (**Figure 25**) also let you select one option from a group. Display a list as you would a menu (**Figure 27**), then choose the option that you want.

◆ **Preview areas** (**Figures 25** and **26**), when available, illustrate the effects of your changes before you finalize them by clicking the OK button.

◆ **Push buttons** (**Figures 24**, **25**, and **26**) let you access other dialogs, accept the changes and close the dialog (OK), or close the dialog without making changes (Cancel). To choose a button, click it once.

✔ Tips

■ When the contents of a text box are selected, whatever you type will replace the selection.

■ Word often uses text boxes and list boxes together (**Figure 25**). You can use either one to make a selection.

■ If a pair of tiny triangles appears to the right of an edit box (**Figure 26**), you can click a triangle to increase or decrease the value in the edit box.

■ In some list boxes, double-clicking an option selects it and dismisses the dialog.

■ You can turn on any number of check boxes in a group, but you can select only one option button in a group.

■ Pressing (Enter) while a push button is active "clicks" that button.

■ You can usually "click" the Cancel button by pressing (Esc).

DIALOGS

Views

Word offers several different ways to view the contents of a document window.

◆ **Normal view** (**Figure 28**), which is the default view, shows continuously scrolling text. It is the fastest view for entering and editing text but does not show page layout elements.

◆ **Web Layout view** (**Figure 29**) displays the contents of a document so they are easier to read on screen. Text appears in a larger font size and wraps to fit the window rather than margins or indentations.

◆ **Print Layout view** (**Figure 30**) displays the objects on a page positioned as they will be when the document is printed. This is a good view for working with documents that include multiple column text or positioned graphics, such as a newsletter or flyer.

◆ **Outline view** (**Figure 31**) displays the document's structure—headings and body text—in a way that makes it easy to rearrange the document. Headings can be collapsed to hide detail and simplify the view. Working with Outline view is discussed in **Chapter 8**.

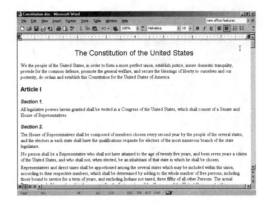

Figure 28 Normal view.

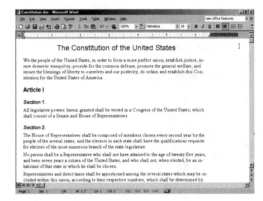

Figure 29 Web Layout view.

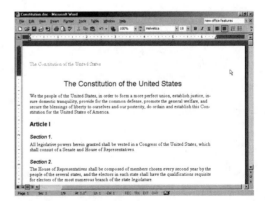

Figure 30 Print Layout view.

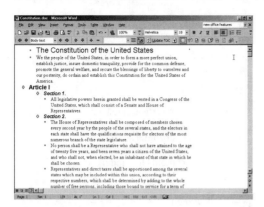

Figure 31 Outline view.

Figure 32
The View menu.

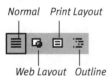

Normal   Print Layout

Web Layout   Outline

Figure 33 View buttons at the bottom of the document window. The currently selected option has a blue box around it.

✔ Tips

■ Although each view is designed for a specific purpose, you can use almost any view to work with a document.

■ The illustrations throughout this book display windows in Normal view, unless otherwise indicated.

To switch to another view

Choose the desired option from the View menu (**Figure 32**).

or

Click the appropriate view button at the bottom of the window (**Figure 33**).

✔ Tip

■ By default, the Outline View command appears only on the full version of the View menu (**Figure 32**). If you use it often enough, however, it should switch to the personalized version of the menu. Full and personalized menus are discussed earlier in this chapter.

VIEWS

Document Navigation

Word offers a variety of ways to view different parts of a document.

◆ Use **scroll bars** to shift the contents of the document window.

◆ Use the **Go To command** to view a specific document element, such as a certain page.

◆ Use **Browse Object buttons** to browse a document by its elements.

◆ Use the **Document Map** to move quickly to a specific heading.

✔ Tip

■ Although some keyboard keys change the portion of the document being viewed, they also move the insertion point. I tell you about these keys in **Chapter 2**.

To scroll the contents of the document window

Click the scroll arrow (**Figure 34**) for the direction that you want to view. For example, to scroll down to view the end of a document, click the down arrow.

or

Drag the scroll box (**Figure 34**) in the direction that you want to view. As you drag, a yellow box appears on screen (**Figure 35**). It indicates the page and, if applicable, the heading that you are scrolling to.

or

Click in the scroll bar above or below the scroll box (**Figure 34**). This shifts the window contents one screenful at a time.

✔ Tip

■ Having trouble remembering which scroll arrow to click? Just remember this: click up to see up, click down to see down, click left to see left, and click right to see right.

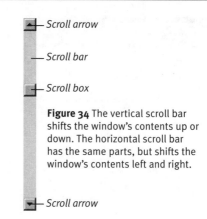

Scroll arrow

Scroll bar

Scroll box

Figure 34 The vertical scroll bar shifts the window's contents up or down. The horizontal scroll bar has the same parts, but shifts the window's contents left and right.

Scroll arrow

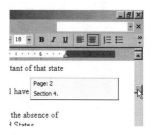

Figure 35 When you drag the scroll box, a yellow box with the page number and heading appears.

Figure 36 The Go To tab of the Find and Replace dialog.

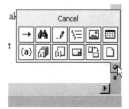

Figure 37 The Browse Object buttons at the bottom of the vertical scroll bar.

Figure 38
This menu pops up when you click the Select Browse Object button.

To use the Go To command

1. Choose Edit > Go To (**Figure 6**). The Find and Replace dialog appears with its Go To tab displayed (**Figure 36**).

2. In the Go to what list box, select the type of document element that you want to view.

3. Enter the appropriate reference in the text box.

4. Click the Next button to go to the next reference.

5. Click the dialog box's Close button to dismiss it.

For example, to go to page 5 of a document, select Page in step 2 and enter the number 5 in step 3.

To browse a document by its elements

1. Point to the Select Browse Object button (**Figure 37**).

2. Click to display the Select Browse Object pop-up menu.

3. Choose the element by which you want to browse (**Figure 38**).

4. Use the Next and Previous navigation buttons to view the next or previous element.

✔ Tips

- The name of the object that a button represents appears at the top of the Select Browse Object pop-up menu when you point to the button (**Figure 38**).

- Some of the buttons on the Select Browse Object pop-up menu (**Figure 38**) display dialogs that you can use for browsing.

BROWSING BY DOCUMENT ELEMENT

To use the Document Map

1. Choose View > Document Map (**Figure 32**).

   The Document Map appears in a narrow pane on the left side of the window (**Figure 39**).

2. Click the heading that you want to view. The main window pane's view shifts to show the heading that you clicked (**Figure 40**).

✔ Tips

- The Document Map is a good way to navigate documents that use Word's heading styles. I explain how to use headings in **Chapter 8** and styles in **Chapter 5**.

- Navigating with the Document Map also moves the insertion point. Moving the insertion point is discussed in **Chapter 2**.

- You can change the width of the Document Map's pane by dragging the border between it and the main window pane (**Figure 41**). When you release the border, both panes resize.

- You can collapse and expand the headings displayed in the Document Map by clicking the triangles to the left of the heading names (**Figure 42**).

- To hide the Document Map when you are finished using it, choose View > Document Map or double-click the border between the Document Map and the main window pane.

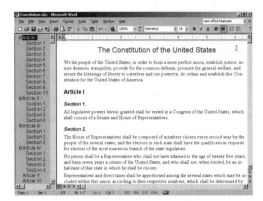

Figure 39 The Document Map in Normal view.

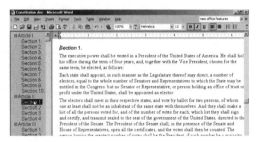

Figure 40 Clicking a heading in the Document Map shifts the document view to display that part of the document.

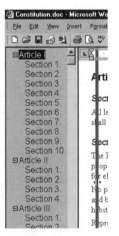

Figure 41 You can resize the Document Map's pane by dragging its right border.

Figure 42 Click the box beside a heading to hide or show its subheadings.

Figure 43
The Window menu.

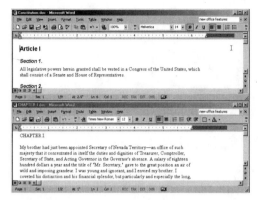

Figure 44 Arranged windows.

Figure 45
The File menu.

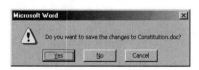

Figure 46 The dialog that appears when you close a window that contains unsaved changes.

Windows

Word allows you to open more than one document window at a time.

✔ Tips

- The active window is the one with the colored title bar. (If the window is maximized, it will be the only one that is visible.)

- **Chapter 2** explains how to open and create documents.

To activate a different window

Choose the name of the window that you want to view from the list on the Window menu (**Figure 43**).

To neatly arrange windows

Choose Window > Arrange All (**Figure 43**).

The windows are resized and repositioned so you can see into each one (**Figure 44**).

To close a window

1. If necessary, activate the window that you want to close.

2. Choose File > Close (**Figure 45**) or click the window's close button.

✔ Tips

- If the document contains unsaved changes, Word warns you and gives you a chance to save it (**Figure 46**). Saving documents is covered in **Chapter 2**.

- Closing all Word document windows also exits Word.

WORKING WITH DOCUMENT WINDOWS

The Office Assistant

The Office Assistant is an animated character (**Figure 47**) that appears onscreen to provide tips and assistance while you work. While enabled, it is the main interface for working with Word's onscreen Help feature.

Figure 47
The Office Assistant.

To display the Office Assistant

Choose Help > Show the Office Assistant.

Figure 48
Word's Help menu.

To hide the Office Assistant

1. Choose Help > Hide the Office Assistant (**Figure 48**).

2. If a balloon like the one in **Figure 49** appears, click No, just hide me.

✔ Tip

■ Hiding the Office Assistant temporarily removes it from screen; turning off or disabling it permanently removes it. Disabling the Office Assistant is discussed later in this section.

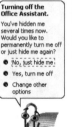

Figure 49
Sometimes the Office Assistant will ask if you want to hide it or turn it off.

To move the Office Assistant

Drag the Office Assistant to a new position on the screen.

✔ Tip

■ The Office Assistant will automatically move out of the way if necessary as you work.

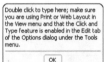

Figure 50
An Office Assistant tip.

To get tips

1. Click the light bulb that appears near Office Assistant's head (**Figure 47**) when the Office Assistant has a tip for you. The tip appears in a balloon beside the Office Assistant (**Figure 50**).

2. When you are finished reading the tip, click its OK button.

Figure 51 Get the Office Assistant's attention,...

Figure 52 ...then type in your question.

Figure 53
A list of possible topics appears in a balloon.

To ask the Office Assistant a question

1. Click the Office Assistant to get its attention. A balloon with instructions appears (**Figure 51**).

2. Type your question into the edit box (**Figure 52**) and click the Search button. A list of possible topics appears in another balloon (**Figure 53**).

3. Click a topic that interests you. A Microsoft Word Help window like the one in (**Figure 54**) appears beside your document.

4. Read the information on the right side of the window. You can click underlined links in the right side of the window or click topics in the left side of the window to get more information.

5. When you are finished reading help information, click the Microsoft Word Help window's close button to dismiss it.

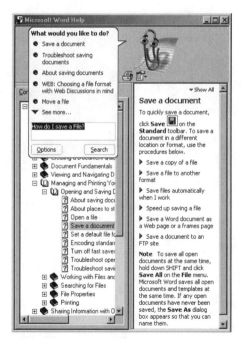

Figure 54 Detailed information and a list of help topics appears in the Microsoft Word Help window beside your document.

To disable the Office Assistant

1. Display the Office Asistant and click it to display its balloon (**Figure 51**).

2. Click the Options button.

3. In the Office Assistant dialog that appears (**Figure 55**), turn off the Use the Office Assistant check box.

4. Click OK. The Office Assistant disappears.

✔ Tips

■ Another way to disable the office Assistant is to click the Yes, turn me off option in the balloon that may appear when you hide it (**Figure 49**). It is impossible to predict, however, when or if this balloon will appear.

■ Once the Office Assistant has been disabled, it will not reappear unless you choose Help > Show the Office Assistant (**Figure 48**).

■ You can also use the Office Assistant dialog (**Figure 55**) to customize the way the Office Assistant looks and works.

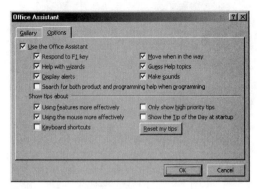

Figure 55 The Office Assistant dialog enables you to set its options — and disable it.

Show /Hide button

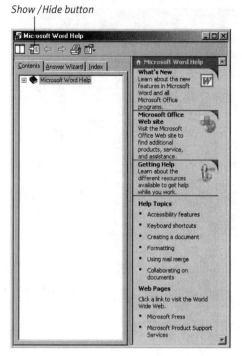

Figure 56 The Microsoft Word Help window's main page.

Word Help

Word has an extensive onscreen Help feature that provides information about using Word to complete specific tasks. You access Word Help via the Office Assistant (as discussed on the previous pages) or commands under the Help menu (**Figure 48**).

To open Microsoft Word Help

If the Office Assistant is enabled, follow the steps on the previous page to display the Microsoft Help window (**Figure 54**).

or

If the Office Assistant is disabled, choose Help > Microsoft Word Help (**Figure 48**), press F1, or click the Microsoft Word Help button 🔍 on the Standard toolbar to display the Microsoft Word Help window (**Figure 56**).

✔ Tips

■ The Microsoft Word Help window includes hyperlinks—blue words and phrases that, when clicked, display related information. The link for the Microsoft Office Web site (**Figure 56**) requires Internet access to use.

■ You can show or hide the help tabs on the left side of the Microsoft Word Help window by clicking the Show or Hide button at the top of the window. **Figures 54** and **56** illustrates the Microsoft Word Help window with help tabs shown.

USING WORD HELP

To ask a question

1. Open the Microsoft Word Help window as instructed on the previous page.

2. If necessary, click the Answer Wizard tab (**Figure 57**).

3. Enter your question in the text box at the top of the tab and click Search. A list of help topics appears in the Select topic to display box.

4. Click a topic that interests you. Detailed information and instructions appear on the right side of the window (**Figure 58**).

✔ Tip

■ You can also access the Answer Wizard feature by entering your question in the text box on the far right end of the menu bar (**Figure 59**). When you press (Enter), a menu of possible topics appears (**Figure 60**). Click the topic that interests you to display it in the Microsoft Word Help window.

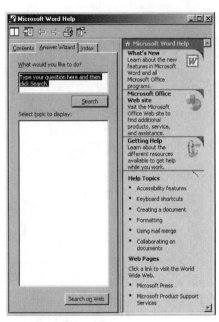

Figure 57 The Answer Wizard tab of the Microsoft Word Help window.

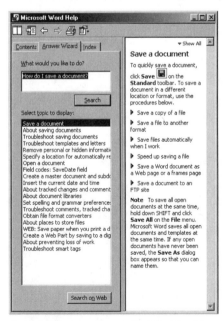

Figure 58 Topics appear on the left side of the window. Clicking a topic displays information on the right side of the window.

How do I save a document:

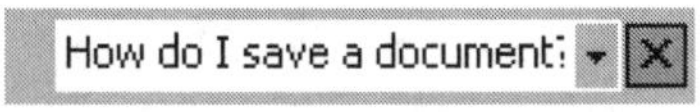

Figure 59 You can also enter your question in the box on the menu bar.

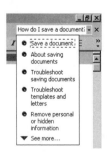

Figure 60 Pressing (Enter) displays a list of possible topics.

ASKING A QUESTION

Microsoft Word Help
Contents
Answer Wizard
Index
Show All
About page margins
Page margins are the blank space around the edges of the page. In general, you insert text and graphics in the printable area inside the margins. However, you can position some items in the margins — for example, headers, footers, and page numbers.
Microsoft Word offers several page margin options. You can:
Use the default page margins or specify your own.
Add margins for binding. Use a gutter margin to add extra space to the side or top margin of a document you plan to bind. A gutter margin ensures that text isn't obscured by the binding.
Microsoft Word Help
Document Fundamentals
Page Setup
Headers and Footers
Entering Text
Copying and Pasting
Formatting Text
Find and Replace
Tables
Linked Text Boxes
Word Count

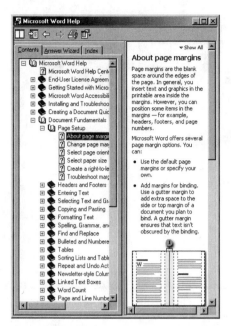

Figure 61 Navigate through Help by expanding topic outlines and clicking blue links.

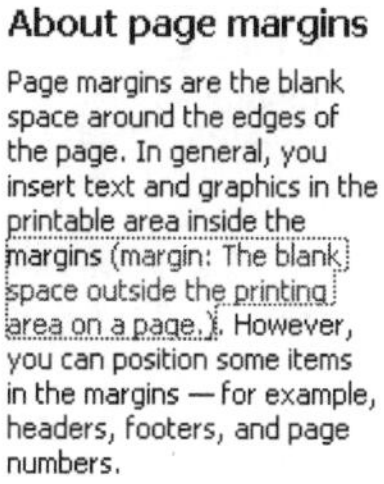

About page margins
Page margins are the blank space around the edges of the page. In general, you insert text and graphics in the printable area inside the margins (margin: The blank space outside the printing area on a page.). However, you can position some items in the margins — for example, headers, footers, and page numbers.

Figure 62 Sometimes, clicking a colored link expands the help topic to display additional information, such as definitions, in green.

To browse Help

1. Open the Microsoft Word Help window as instructed earlier in this section.
2. If necessary, click the Contents tab (**Figure 56**).
3. Navigate through topics and information as follows (**Figure 61**):
   - ▲ To expand a topic in the left side of the window, click the plus sign beside it. Subtopics appear beneath it.
   - ▲ To display information about a topic listed in the left side of the window, click the topic name. (Topics appear with question mark icons beside them.) The informaiton appears in the right side of the window.
   - ▲ To display information that is related to an item in the right side of the window, click a blue link. The information appears either as a new topic or as green text beside the link you clicked (**Figure 62**).

✔ Tip

- ■ You can click the left arrow button at top of the Microsoft Word Help window to browse topics you browsed earlier in the help session.

To use the Help Index

1. Open the Microsoft Word Help window as instructed earlier in this section.

2. If necessary, click the Index tab (**Figure 63**).

3. Type one or more keywords in the text box near the top of the window. Then click Search.

   or

   Type one or more keywords in the text box near the top of the window. Then scroll through the keywords list beneath it (**Figure 64**) and double-click one that interests you.

   A list of topics appears in the Choose a topic box (**Figure 65**).

4. Click a topic. Detailed information and instructions appear in the right side of the window.

Figure 63 The Index tab of the Microsoft Word Help window.

Figure 64 Enter a keyword and a list of keywords appears beneath it.

Figure 65 Clicking search or double-clicking a keyword displays a list of clickable topics.

WORD BASICS

Word Processing Basics

Word processing software has revolutionized the way we create text-based documents. Rather than committing each character to paper as you type—as you would do with a typewriter—word processing enables you to enter documents on screen, edit and format them as you work, and save them for future reference or revision. Nothing appears on paper until you use the Print command.

If you're brand new to word processing, here are a few concepts you should understand before you begin working with Microsoft Word or any other word processing software:

◆ Words that you type that do not fit at the end of a line automatically appear on the next line. This feature is called *word wrap*.

◆ Do not press Enter at the end of each line as you type. Doing so inserts a Return character, which signals the end of a paragraph, not the end of a line. Press Enter only at the end of a paragraph or to skip a line between paragraphs.

◆ Do not use Spacebar to indent text or position text in simple tables. Instead, use Tab in conjunction with tab settings on the ruler.

◆ Text can be inserted or deleted anywhere in the document.

✔ Tip

■ I tell you more about all of these concepts in this chapter and throughout this book.

Running Word

To use Word, you must run the Word program.

To run Word from the Taskbar

Click Start > Programs > Microsoft Word.

The Word splash screen appears briefly (**Figure 1**), then an empty document window named Document 1 appears, along with the New Document task pane (**Figure 2**).

✔ Tip

- You can disable the display of the New Document task pane at startup by turning off the Show at startup check box at the bottom of its window (**Figure 2**). Task panes are discussed in **Chapter 1** and elsewhere throughout this book.

To run Word by opening a Word document

1. In Windows Explorer, locate the icon for the document that you want to open (**Figure 3**).

2. Double-click the icon.

   The Word splash screen appears briefly (**Figure 1**), then a document window containing the document you opened appears (**Figure 4**).

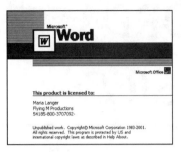

Figure 1 The Word 2002 splash screen.

Figure 2 When you run Word from the Taskbar, it displays a blank document window and the New Document task pane.

Figure 3
A Word
document icon.

CHAPTER
I.doc

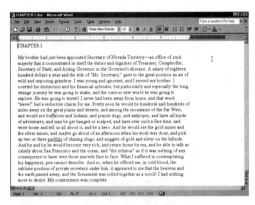

Figure 4 When you run Word by opening a Word document, it displays the document you opened.

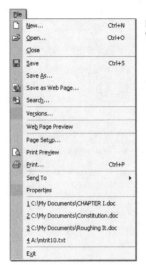

Figure 5
Word's File menu.

Figure 6 A dialog like this appears when a document with unsaved changes is open when you quit Word.

Exiting Word

When you're finished using Word, you should use the Exit command to close the application.

✔ Tip

■ Exiting Word also instructs Word to save preference settings and any changes to the Normal template.

To exit Word

Choose File > Exit (**Figure 5**). Here's what happens:

▲ If any documents are open, they close.

▲ If an open document contains unsaved changes, a dialog appears (**Figure 6**) so you can save the changes. Saving documents is discussed later in this chapter.

▲ The Word application closes.

✔ Tips

■ Closing all Word document windows also exits Word. Closing document windows is discussed in **Chapter 1**.

■ As you've probably guessed, Word automatically exits when you restart or shut down your computer.

Word Documents, Templates, & Wizards

The documents you create and save using Word are Word document files. These files contain all the information necessary to display the contents of the document as formatted using Microsoft Word.

All Word document files are based on *templates*. A template is a collection of styles and other formatting features that determines the appearance of a document. Templates can also include default text, macros, and custom toolbars.

For example, you can create a letterhead template that includes your company's logo and contact information or is designed to be printed on special paper. The template can include styles that utilize specific fonts. It can also include custom toolbars with buttons for commands commonly used when writing letters.

Wizards take templates a step further. They are special Word document files that include Microsoft Visual Basic commands to automate the creation of specific types of documents. Word comes with many wizards, some of which are covered in this book.

Figure 7
A Word template icon.

Memo
Wizard.wiz

Figure 8
A Word wizard icon.

Memo
Wizard.wiz

✔ Tips

- A Word document icon (**Figure 3**), template icon (**Figure 7**), and wizard icon (**Figure 8**) are very similar in appearance.

- Word can open and save files in formats other than Word document format. I tell you more about file formats later in this chapter.

- When no other template is specified for a document, Word applies the default template, *Normal*.

- I cover styles in **Chapter 4**. Macros, custom toolbars, and Visual Basic, however, are advanced features that are beyond the scope of this book.

Figure 9 A blank document window based on the Normal template.

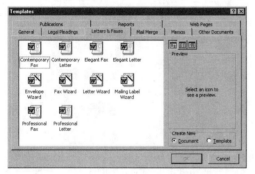

Figure 10 The Letters & Faxes tab of the Templates dialog.

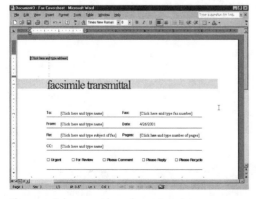

Figure 11 A document based on a template.

Creating Documents

You can create a new document with the New Document task pane.

To create a blank document

1. If the New Document task pane is not displayed, choose File > New (**Figure 5**) to display it.

2. In the New area (**Figure 2**), click Blank Document.

or

Press Ctrl N.

or

Click the New Blank Document button 🗋 on the Standard toolbar.

A blank document based on the Normal template appears (**Figure 9**). If the New Document task pane was showing, it disappears.

To create a document based on a template other than Normal

1. If the New Document task pane is not displayed, choose File > New (**Figure 5**) to display it.

2. In the New from template area (**Figure 2**), click General Templates to display the Templates dialog.

3. Click the tab for the category of template you want to use (**Figure 10**).

4. Select the icon for the template you want to use. A preview of the template may appear in the Preview area.

5. Click OK.

A document based on the template that you selected appears (**Figure 11**). Follow the instructions in the template to replace place-holder text with your text.

To create a document with a wizard

1. If the New Document task pane is not displayed, choose File > New (**Figure 5**) to display it.

2. In the New from template area (**Figure 2**), click General Templates to display the Templates dialog.

3. Click the tab for the category of wizard you want to use (**Figure 10**).

4. Select the icon for the wizard you want to use. A preview of the wizard may appear in the Preview area.

5. Click OK.

6. A document window appears, along with a series of Wizard dialogs (**Figures 12** and **13**). Enter appropriate information as prompted in each dialog of the Wizard to create the document.

7. When you've finished entering information, click Finish to dismiss the Wizard. The document you created remains open (**Figure 14**) so you can continue to work with it.

✔ Tip

■ When the wizard is finished, you can customize the document it creates (**Figure 14**) to meet your specific needs.

Figure 12 The first dialog of the Letter Wizard looks like this.

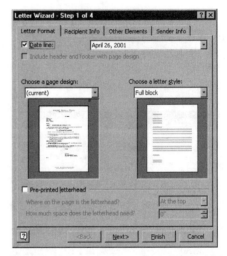

Figure 13 If you're sending only one letter with the Letter Wizard, the first tab of its main dialog looks like this.

Figure 14 A document created with a template and wizard.

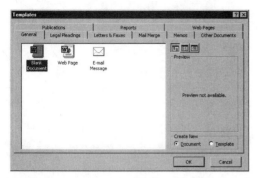

Figure 15 Like any other template, the Normal template (for creating a Blank Document) is included in the Templates dialog.

Figure 16 Use the Create New option buttons to specify whether you want to create a regular document or a template.

To create a template

1. If the New Document task pane is not displayed, choose File > New (**Figure 5**) to display it.

2. In the New from template area (**Figure 2**), click General Templates to display the Templates dialog.

3. To create a new blank template, select the Blank Document icon in the General tab (**Figure 15**).

   or

   To create a template based on another template, click the tab for a specific category of template and select the icon for the template you want to use.

4. Select the Template option in the Create New area (**Figure 16**) at the bottom of the Templates dialog.

5. Click OK.

6. A new document window appears. Add text, styles, or other features to the document as discussed throughout this book.

✔ Tip

■ When you save the document, it is automatically saved as a template. Saving documents and templates is covered later in this chapter.

CREATING TEMPLATES

Opening Existing Documents

Once a document has been saved, you can reopen it to read it, modify it, or print it.

To open an existing document

1. Choose File > Open (**Figure 5**) or press Ctrl O.

   or

   Click the Open button 🖼 on the Standard toolbar.

2. Use the Open dialog that appears (**Figure 17**) to locate the file that you want to open:

   ▲ Use the Look in drop-down list near the top of the dialog (**Figure 18**) to go to another location.

   ▲ Double-click a folder to open it.

3. Select the file that you want to open and click the Open button.

   or

   Double-click the file that you want to open.

✔ Tips

■ You can also navigate within the Open dialog by using the Places bar along the left side of the Open dialog. Consult the documentation that came with Windows to learn more about using these buttons.

■ To view only specific types of files in the Open dialog, select a format from the Files of type drop-down list at the bottom of the dialog (**Figure 19**).

■ If you select All Files from the Files of type drop-down list (**Figure 19**), you can open just about any kind of file. Be aware, however, that a document in an incompatible format may not appear the way you expect when opened.

Figure 17 The Open dialog.

Figure 18
The Look in drop-down list enables you to look in other locations.

Figure 19 The Files of type drop-down list includes file formats that can be read by Word.

■ You can open a recent file by selecting it from the list of recently opened files at the bottom of the File menu (**Figure 5**) or by clicking its name in the Open a Document area of the New Document task Pane (**Figure 2**).

OPENING EXISTING DOCUMENTS

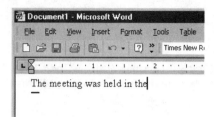

Figure 20 Text characters appear at the blinking insertion point as you type.

Figure 21 Word wrap automatically occurs when the text you type won't fit on the current line.

Figure 22 Press Enter to start a new paragraph.

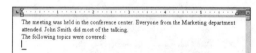

Figure 23 Press Shift Enter to start a new line in the same paragraph.

✔ Tip

- Use a line break instead of a paragraph break if you want to begin a new line without beginning a new paragraph. This makes it easy to apply paragraph formatting to a group of lines that belong together. Paragraph formatting is covered in **Chapters 4** and **5**.

Entering Text

In most cases, you will enter text into a Word document using the keyboard.

✔ Tip

- A wavy red or green line appearing beneath the text you type indicates that the text has a possible spelling or grammar error. The spelling and grammar checking features of Word are covered in **Chapter 5**.

To type text

Type the characters, words, or sentences that you want to enter into the document. Text appears at the blinking insertion point as you type it (**Figure 20**).

✔ Tips

- I explain how to move the insertion point a little later in this chapter.

- Do not press Enter at the end of a line. A new line automatically begins when a word can't fit on the current line (**Figure 21**).

To start a new paragraph

At the end of a paragraph, press Enter. This inserts a paragraph break or return character that ends the current paragraph and begins a new one (**Figure 22**).

To start a new line

To end a line without ending the current paragraph, press Shift Enter. This inserts a line break character within the current paragraph (**Figure 23**).

Formatting Marks

Every character you type is entered into a Word document—even characters that normally can't be seen, such as space, tab, return, line break, and optional hyphen characters.

Word enables you to display these *formatting marks* (**Figure 24**), making it easy to see all the characters in a document.

Figure 24 Text with formatting marks displayed. This example shows space, return, and line break characters.

✔ Tips

- Formatting marks are sometimes referred to as *nonprinting* or *invisible characters*.

- By displaying formatting marks, you can get a better understanding of the structure of a document. For example, **Figure 24** clearly shows the difference between the return and line break characters entered in **Figure 23**.

Figure 25
Choose Options from the Tools menu.

To show or hide formatting marks

Click the Show/Hide ¶ button 【¶】 on the Standard toolbar. This toggles the display of formatting marks.

To specify which formatting marks should be displayed

1. Choose Tools > Options (**Figure 25**).

2. Click the View tab in the Options dialog that appears (**Figure 26**).

3. Turn on the check boxes in the Formatting marks area of the dialog to specify which characters should appear.

4. Click OK.

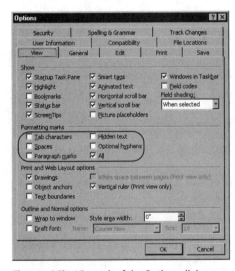

Figure 26 The View tab of the Options dialog.

✔ Tips

- To display all formatting marks, turn on the All check box in step 3.

- Word's options are discussed in detail in **Chapter 15**.

Table 1

Keystrokes for Moving the Insertion Point	
PRESS:	TO MOVE THE INSERTION POINT:
→	one character to the right
←	one character to the left
↑	one line up
↓	one line down
Ctrl →	one word to the right
Ctrl ←	one word to the left
Ctrl ↑	one paragraph up
Ctrl ↓	one paragraph down
End	to the end of the line
Home	to the beginning of the line
Ctrl End	to the end of the document
Ctrl Home	to the beginning of the document
Page Up	up one screen
Page Down	down one screen
Ctrl Page Up	to the top of the previous page
Ctrl Page Down	to the top of the next page
Ctrl Alt Page Up	to the top of the window
Ctrl Alt Page Down	to the bottom of the window
Shift F5	to the previous edit

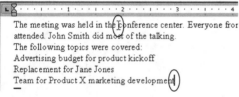

Figure 27 Position the mouse's I-beam pointer where you want the insertion point to move.

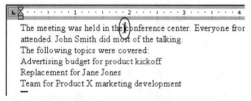

Figure 28 Click to move the insertion point.

The Insertion Point

The blinking insertion point indicates where the information you type or paste will be inserted. There are two main ways to move the insertion point: with the keyboard and with the mouse.

✔ Tip

- The insertion point also moves when you use the Document Map to navigate within a document. The Document Map is discussed in **Chapter 1**.

To move the insertion point with the keyboard

Press the appropriate keyboard key(s) (**Table 1**).

✔ Tip

- There are additional keystrokes that work within cell tables. I tell you about them in **Chapter 9**, where I discuss tables.

To move the insertion point with the mouse

1. Position the mouse's I-beam pointer where you want to move the insertion point (**Figure 27**).

2. Click once. The insertion point moves (**Figure 28**).

✔ Tips

- Simply moving the I-beam pointer is not enough. You must click to move the insertion point.

- Do not move the mouse while clicking. Doing so will select text.

Inserting & Deleting Text

You can insert or delete characters at the insertion point at any time.

◆ When you insert characters, any text to the right of the insertion point shifts to the right to make room for new characters (**Figures 29** and **30**).

◆ When you delete text, any text to the right of the insertion point shifts to the left to close up space left by deleted characters (**Figures 31** and **32**).

◆ When you insert or delete text, word wrap adjusts if necessary to comfortably fit characters on each line (**Figures 30** and **32**).

To insert text

1. Position the insertion point where you want to insert the text (**Figure 29**).

2. Type the text you want to insert (**Figure 30**).

✔ Tip

■ You can also insert text by pasting the contents of the Clipboard at the insertion point. Using the Clipboard to copy and paste text is covered later in this chapter.

To delete text

1. Position the insertion point to the right of the character(s) you want to delete (**Figure 31**).

2. Press ⟨Backspace⟩ to delete the character to the left of the insertion point (**Figure 32**).

or

1. Position the insertion point to the left of the character(s) you want to delete.

2. Press ⟨Delete⟩ to delete the character to the right of the insertion point.

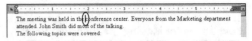

Figure 29 Position the insertion point.

Figure 30 Type the text that you want to insert.

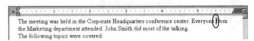

Figure 31 Position the insertion point to the right of the character(s) you want to delete.

Figure 32 Press ⟨Backspace⟩ to delete the characters, one at a time.

✔ Tip

■ You can also delete text by selecting it and pressing ⟨Backspace⟩ or ⟨Delete⟩. Selecting text is discussed a little later in this chapter.

Figure 33
The Click and Type pointer.

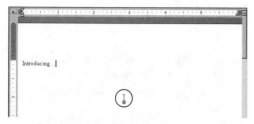

Figure 34 Position the Click and Type pointer where you want to enter text.

Figure 35 Double-click to position the insertion point.

Figure 36 Type the text you want to appear.

Click and Type

Click and Type is a feature that makes it easier to position text in a blank area of a page. You simply double-click with the Click and Type pointer (**Figure 33**) and enter the text you want to appear there. Word automatically applies necessary formatting to the text to position it where you want it.

✔ Tip

- Click and Type works only in Print Layout and Web Layout views. Word's views are discussed in **Chapter 1**.

To enter text with Click and Type

1. If necessary, switch to Print Layout or Web Layout view.

2. Position the mouse pointer in an empty area of the document window. The mouse pointer should turn into a Click and Type pointer (**Figure 34**).

3. Double-click. The insertion point appears at the mouse pointer (**Figure 35**).

4. Type the text you want to enter. (**Figure 36**).

✔ Tips

- The appearance of the Click and Type pointer indicates how it will align text at the insertion point. For example, the pointer shown in **Figures 33** and **34** indicates that text will be centered (**Figure 36**). I tell you more about alignment, including how to change it, in **Chapter 3**.

- There are some limitations to where you can use the Click and Type feature. Generally speaking, if the Click and Type pointer does not appear, you cannot use it to position text.

Selecting Text

You can select one or more characters to delete, replace, copy, cut, or format it. Selected text appears with a colored background or in inverse type.

✔ Tips

- There are many ways to select text. This section provides just a few of the most useful methods.

- Word 2002 enables you to select multiple blocks of text. To do this, down (Ctrl) while selecting each block, using any of the techniques discussed in this chapter.

To select text by dragging

1. Position the mouse I-beam pointer at the beginning of the text.

2. Press the mouse button down and drag to the end of the text you want to select (**Figure 37**).

3. Release the mouse button.

   All characters between the starting and ending points are selected.

✔ Tips

- This is the most basic text selection technique. It works for any amount of text.

- By default, Word automatically selects entire words when you drag through more than one word. To disable this feature, choose Tools > Options (**Figure 25**), click the Edit tab in the Options dialog that appears (**Figure 38**), and turn off the check box for When selecting, automatically select entire word.

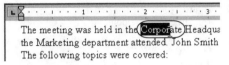

The meeting was held in the Corporate Headqua the Marketing department attended. John Smith The following topics were covered:

Figure 37 Drag over text to select it.

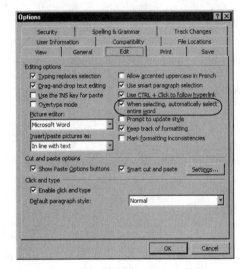

Figure 38 The Edit tab of the Options dialog.

Table 2

Techniques for Selecting Text by Clicking	
TO SELECT:	DO THIS:
a word	double-click the word
a sentence	hold down Ctrl and click in the sentence
a line	click in the selection bar to the left of the line (**Figure 39**)
a paragraph	triple-click in the paragraph or double-click in the selection bar to the left of the paragraph
the document	hold down Ctrl and double-click in the selection bar to the left of any line
any text	position the insertion point at the beginning of the text, then hold down Shift and click at the end of the text

Figure 39 Click in the selection bar beside a line to select the line.

Figure 40
The Edit menu.

To select text by clicking

Click as instructed in **Table 2** to select specific amounts of text.

✔ Tips

- You can combine techniques in **Table 2** with dragging to select multiple lines and paragraphs.

- When you select an entire word by double-clicking it, Word also selects any spaces after it.

To select the contents of a document

Choose Edit > Select All (**Figure 40**).

or

Press Ctrl A.

Editing Selected Text

Once you select text, you can delete it or replace it with other text.

To delete selected text

Press Backspace or Delete. The selected text disappears.

To replace selected text

With text selected, type the replacement text. The selected text disappears and the replacement text is inserted in its place.

Copying & Moving Text

Word offers two ways to copy or move text:

◆ Use the Copy, Cut, and Paste commands (or their shortcut keys) to place text on the Clipboard and then copy it from the Clipboard to another location.

◆ Use drag-and-drop editing to copy or move selected text.

You can copy or move text to:

◆ A different location within the same document.

◆ A different document.

◆ A document created with a program other than Word.

✔ Tips

■ Copying and moving text make it possible to reuse text and reorganize a document without a lot of retyping.

■ The Clipboard is a place in your computer's memory (RAM) that is used to temporarily store selected items that are copied or cut. Word supports two Clipboards:

▲ The *Windows Clipboard* is shared among all Windows applications that support the copy and paste commands.

▲ The *Office Clipboard* is shared among all Microsoft Office applications. It offers additional features, which are discussed later in this chapter.

■ Text copied or cut to the Clipboard remains on the Clipboard until you use the Copy or Cut command again or restart your computer. This makes it possible to use Clipboard contents over and over in any document created with Word or another application.

■ These techniques also work with objects such as graphics. I tell you more about working with objects in **Chapter 7**.

June 30, 2001

Mr. R.H. Andersen
125 West Grand Avenue
Surprise, AZ 85365

Dear Mr. Andersen,

Thanks for your very kind letter regarding Alphabet Squares, the newest addition to our Alphabet Soup Product line. We're glad to know that there are many hungry soup eaters out there who appreciate the variety of letters we include in every can. Your report that you use our soup to help you solve crossword puzzles is fascinating!

I've included a coupon for 75¢ off your next purchase of Alphabet Squares. Please enjoy your next can "on us"!

I'll send your comments regarding the overabundance of Qs and Zs to our production department. They'll make the appropriate adjustments to assure that these letters are more properly represented.

Sincerely,

John Aabbott
Product Manager

Figure 41 Select the text that you want to copy.

Sincerely,

John Aabbott
Product Manager

Figure 42
Position the insertion point where you want the copied text to appear.

Sincerely,

John Aabbott
Product Manager
Alphabet Soup

Figure 43
When you use the Paste command, the contents of the Clipboard appear at the insertion point, along with the Paste Options button.

Thanks for your very kind letter regarding Alphabet Squares, the newest addition to our Alphabet Soup product line. We're glad to know that there are many hungry soup eaters out there who appreciate the variety of letters we include in every can. Your report that you use our soup to help you solve crossword puzzles is fascinating!

I've included a coupon for 75¢ off your next purchase of Alphabet Squares. Please enjoy your next can "on us"!

I'll send your comments regarding the overabundance of Qs and Zs to our production department. They'll make the appropriate adjustments to assure that these letters are more properly represented.

Sincerely,

Figure 44 Select the text that you want to move.

Thanks for your very kind letter regarding Alphabet Squares, the newest addition to our Alphabet Soup product line. We're glad to know that there are many hungry soup eaters out there who appreciate the variety of letters we include in every can. Your report that you use our soup to help you solve crossword puzzles is fascinating!

I'll send your comments regarding the overabundance of Qs and Zs to our production department. They'll make the appropriate adjustments to assure that these letters are more properly represented.

Sincerely,

Figure 45 The text you cut disappears.

Thanks for your very kind letter regarding Alphabet Squares, the newest addition to our Alphabet Soup product line. We're glad to know that there are many hungry soup eaters out there who appreciate the variety of letters we include in every can. Your report that you use our soup to help you solve crossword puzzles is fascinating!

I'll send your comments regarding the overabundance of Qs and Zs to our production department. They'll make the appropriate adjustments to assure that these letters are more properly represented.

Sincerely,

Figure 46 Position the insertion point where you want the cut text to appear.

Thanks for your very kind letter regarding Alphabet Squares, the newest addition to our Alphabet Soup product line. We're glad to know that there are many hungry soup eaters out there who appreciate the variety of letters we include in every can. Your report that you use our soup to help you solve crossword puzzles is fascinating!

I'll send your comments regarding the overabundance of Qs and Zs to our production department. They'll make the appropriate adjustments to assure that these letters are more properly represented.

I've included a coupon for 75¢ off your next purchase of Alphabet Squares. Please enjoy your next can "on us"!

Sincerely,

Figure 47 The contents of the Clipboard appear at the insertion point, along with the Paste Options button.

To copy text with Copy & Paste

1. Select the text that you want to copy (**Figure 41**).

2. Choose Edit > Copy (**Figure 40**), press Ctrl C, or click the Copy button 📋 on the Standard toolbar.

   The selected text is copied to the Clipboard. The document does not change (**Figure 41**).

3. Position the insertion point where you want the text copied (**Figure 42**).

4. Choose Edit > Paste (**Figure 40**), press Ctrl V, or click the Paste button 📋 on the Standard toolbar.

   The text in the Clipboard is copied into the document at the insertion point (**Figure 43**).

To move text with Cut & Paste

1. Select the text that you want to move (**Figure 44**).

2. Choose Edit > Cut (**Figure 40**), press Ctrl X, or click the Cut button ✂ on the Standard toolbar.

   The selected text is copied to the Clipboard and removed from the document (**Figure 45**).

3. Position the insertion point where you want the cut text to appear (**Figure 46**).

4. Choose Edit > Paste (**Figure 40**), press Ctrl V, or click the Paste button 📋 on the Standard toolbar.

   The text in the Clipboard is copied into the document at the insertion point (**Figure 47**).

To copy text with drag-and-drop editing

1. Select the text that you want to copy (**Figure 41**).

2. Position the mouse pointer on the selected text (**Figure 48**).

3. Hold down Ctrl, press the mouse button down, and drag. As you drag, a tiny box and vertical line move with the mouse pointer, which has a plus sign beside it to indicate that it is copying (**Figure 49**).

4. When the vertical line at the mouse pointer is where you want the text copied to, release the mouse button and Ctrl. The selected text is copied (**Figure 43**).

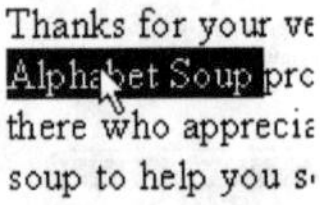

To move text with drag-and-drop editing

1. Select the text that you want to move (**Figure 44**).

2. Position the mouse pointer on the selected text (**Figure 50**).

3. Press the mouse button down and drag. As you drag, a box and vertical line move with the mouse pointer (**Figure 51**).

4. When the vertical line at the mouse pointer is where you want the text moved to, release the mouse button. The selected text is moved (**Figure 47**).

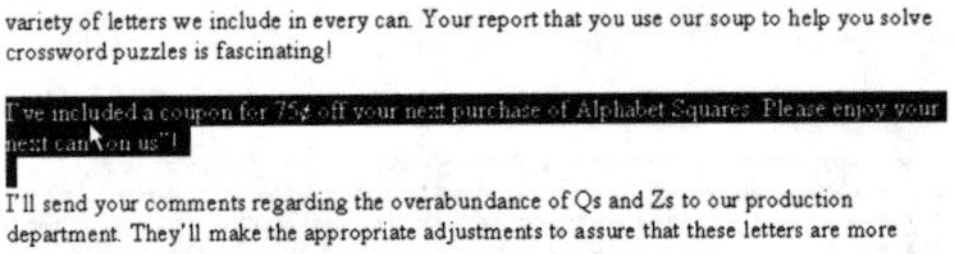

Thanks for your ve
Alphabet Soup pro
there who apprecia
soup to help you s

Figure 48 Point to the selection.

Sincerely,

John Aabbott
Product Manager

Figure 49 Hold down Ctrl and drag to copy the selection.

variety of letters we include in every can. Your report that you use our soup to help you solve crossword puzzles is fascinating!

I've included a coupon for 75¢ off your next purchase of Alphabet Squares. Please enjoy your next can on us"!

I'll send your comments regarding the overabundance of Qs and Zs to our production department. They'll make the appropriate adjustments to assure that these letters are more

Figure 50 Point to the selection.

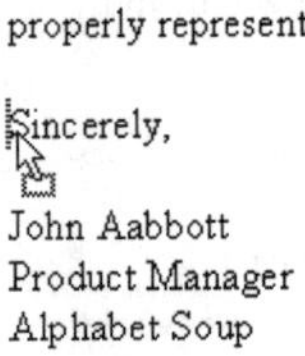

properly represented.

Sincerely,

John Aabbott
Product Manager
Alphabet Soup

Figure 51 Drag to move the selection.

DRAG-AND-DROP EDITING

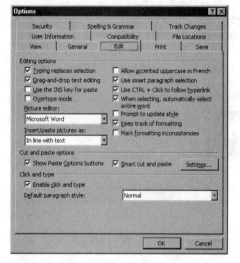

Figure 52 Clicking the Paste Options smart tag displays a menu of formatting options for the pasted in item.

Figure 53 You can disable the Paste Options feature in the Edit tab of the Options dialog.

Paste Options

When you use the Paste command or drag and drop text to copy or move it, the Paste Options button appears beside the item you copied or moved (**Figures 43** and **47**). Clicking this icon displays a pop-up menu of formatting options for the item (**Figure 52**):

◆ **Keep source formatting** retains the formatting applied to the original item.

◆ **Match destination formatting** changes the formatting to match the new location.

◆ **Keep text only** removes all formatting.

◆ **Apply Style or Formatting** displays the Styles and Formatting task pane so you can apply different formatting to the item.

✔ Tips

■ You do not have to use the Paste Options feature when you copy or move text. Use it only when the formatting of the option you copied or moved needs to be changed.

■ The Paste Options button automatically disappears as you work with Word.

■ Formatting text is discussed in detail in **Chapters 3** and 4.

To set formatting options with the Paste Options pop-up menu

1. Click the Paste Options button to display the Paste Options menu (**Figure 52**).

2. Click to select the option you want.

To disable the Paste Options feature

1. Choose Tools > Options (**Figure 25**).

2. Click the Edit tab in the Options dialog that appears (**Figure 53**).

3. Turn off the check box for Show Paste Options buttons.

4. Click OK.

PASTE OPTIONS

The Office Clipboard

The Office Clipboard enables you to "collect and paste" multiple items. You simply display the Office Clipboard task pane, then copy text or objects as usual. But instead of the Clipboard contents being replaced each time you use the Copy or Cut command, all items are stored on the Office Clipboard (**Figure 54**). You can then paste any of the items on the Office Clipboard into your Word document.

✔ Tips

■ The Office Clipboard works with all Microsoft Office applications—not just Word—so you can store items from different types of Office documents.

■ This feature was referred to as *Collect and Paste* in previous versions of Microsoft Office for Windows.

To display the Office Clipboard

Choose Edit > Office Clipboard (**Figure 40**). The Office Clipboard appears as a task pane beside the document window.

✔ Tip

■ The Office Clipboard automatically appears when you copy two items in a row.

To add an item to the Office Clipboard

1. If necessary, display the Office Clipboard (**Figure 54**).

2. Select the text or object you want to copy (**Figure 55**).

3. Choose Edit > Copy (**Figure 40**), press Ctrl C, or click the Copy button 🖺 on the Standard toolbar. The selection appears on the Office Clipboard (**Figure 56**).

Figure 54 The Office Clipboard appears as a task pane beside the document window.

Figure 55 Select the item you want to add to the Office Clipboard.

Figure 56 The item you copied is added to the Office Clipboard.

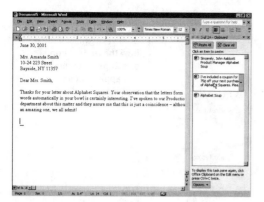

Figure 57 Position the insertion point where you want the item to appear, then click the item in the Office Clipboard.

Figure 58 The item you clicked is pasted in at the insertion point.

Figure 59 Click the button to display a pop-up menu.

Figure 60 The item is removed from the Office Clipboard.

To use Office Clipboard items

1. If necessary, display the Office Clipboard.

Then:

2. In the document window, position the insertion point where you want to place the Office Clipboard item (**Figure 57**).

3. In the Office Clipboard task pane, click on the item you want to paste into the document (**Figure 57**).

Or then:

2. Drag the item you want to use from the Office Clipboard window into the document window.

The item you pasted or dragged appears in the document window (**Figure 58**).

✔ Tip

■ Clicking the Paste All button at the top of the Office Clipboard (**Figure 58**) pastes all items into the document in the order in which they were added to the Office Clipboard.

To remove Office Clipboard items

1. In the Office Clipboard window, point to the item you want to remove (**Figure 57**). A blue border appears around it and a pop-up menu button appears beside it.

2. Click the pop-up menu button to display a menu of two options (**Figure 59**).

3. Choose Delete. The item is removed from the Office Clipboard (**Figure 60**).

or

Click the Clear All button at the top of the Office Clipboard (**Figure 60**) to remove all items.

Undoing, Redoing, & Repeating Actions

Word offers a trio of commands that enable you to undo, redo, or repeat the last thing you did.

◆ **Undo** reverses your last action. Word supports multiple levels of undo, enabling you to reverse more than just the very last action.

◆ **Redo** reverses the Undo command. This command is only available if the last thing you did was use the Undo command.

◆ **Repeat** performs your last action again. This command is only available when you performed any action other than use the Undo or Redo command.

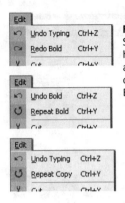

Figures 61, 62, & 63
Some examples of how the Undo, Redo, and Repeat commands can appear under the Edit menu.

✔ Tips

■ The exact wording of these commands on the Edit menu varies depending on the last action performed. The Undo command is always the first command under the Edit menu; the Redo or Repeat command (whichever appears on the menu) is always the second command under the full Edit menu. **Figures 61**, **62**, and **63** show some examples.

■ By default, the Redo and Repeat commands do not appear on personalized menus. Full and personalized menus are discussed in **Chapter 1**.

■ The Redo and Repeat commands are never both available at the same time.

■ Think of the Undo command as the Oops command—anytime you say "Oops," you'll probably want to use it.

■ The Repeat command is especially useful for applying formatting to text scattered throughout your document. I tell you more about formatting in **Chapters 3** and **4**.

Figure 64 Use the Undo pop-up menu to select actions to undo.

Figure 65 Use the Redo pop-up menu to select actions to redo.

To undo the last action

Choose Edit > Undo (**Figures 61**, **62**, or **63**), press Ctrl Z, or click the Undo button on the Standard toolbar.

To undo multiple actions

Choose Edit > Undo (**Figures 61**, **62**, or **63**) or press Ctrl Z repeatedly.

or

Click the triangle beside the Undo button on the Standard toolbar to display a pop-up menu of recent actions. Drag down to select all the actions that you want to undo (**Figure 64**). Release the mouse button to undo all selected actions.

To reverse the last undo

Choose Edit > Redo (**Figure 61**), press Ctrl Y, or click the Redo button on the Standard toolbar.

To reverse multiple undos

Choose Edit > Redo (**Figure 61**) or press Ctrl Y repeatedly.

or

Click the triangle beside the Redo button on the Standard toolbar to display a pop-up menu of recently undone actions. Drag down to select all the actions that you want to redo (**Figure 65**). Release the mouse button to reverse all selected undos.

To repeat the last action

Choose Edit > Repeat (**Figures 62** and **63**) or press Ctrl Y.

UNDOING, REDOING, & REPEATING ACTIONS

Find & Replace

Word has a very powerful find and replace feature. With it, you can search a document for specific text strings and, if desired, replace them with other text.

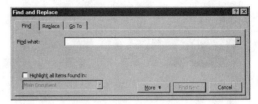

Figure 66 The Find tab of the Find and Replace dialog.

✔ Tip

- By default, the Find and Replace commands search the entire document, beginning at the insertion point.

To find text

1. Choose Edit > Find (**Figure 40**) or press Ctrl F.

2. In the Find tab of the Find and Replace dialog that appears (**Figure 66**), enter the text that you want to find.

3. Click the Find Next button. One of two things happens:

   ▲ If Word finds the search text, it selects the first occurrence that it finds (**Figure 67**). Repeat step 3 to find all occurrences, one at a time. When the last occurrence has been found, Word tells you with a dialog (**Figure 68**).

   ▲ If Word does not find the search text, it tells you with a dialog (**Figure 69**). Repeat steps 2 and 3 to search for different text.

4. When you're finished, dismiss the Find and Replace dialog by clicking its close button.

✔ Tip

- If desired, you can fine-tune search criteria. I tell you how a little later in this chapter.

Figure 67 Word selects each occurrence of the text that it finds.

Figure 68 When Word has finished showing all occurrences of the search text, it tells you.

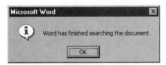

Figure 69 Word also tells you when it can't find the search text at all.

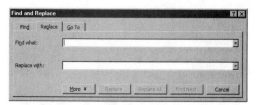

Figure 70 The Replace tab of the Find and Replace dialog.

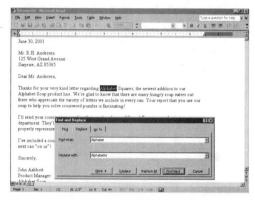

Figure 71 Word selects each occurrence of the search text that it finds.

Figure 72 Clicking the Replace button replaces the selected occurrence and finds the next one.

Figure 73 Clicking the Replace All button replaces all occurrences. Word tells you how many replacements it made.

To replace text

1. Choose Edit > Replace (**Figure 40**) or press Ctrl H. The Replace tab of the Find and Replace dialog appears (**Figure 70**).

2. Enter the text that you want to find in the Find what text box.

3. Enter the text that you want to replace the found text with in the Replace with text box.

4. Click the Find Next button to start the search. One of two things happens:

   ▲ If Word finds the search text, it selects the first occurrence that it finds (**Figure 71**). Continue with step 5.

   ▲ If Word does not find the search text, it tells you with a dialog (**Figure 69**). You can repeat steps 2 and 4 to search for different text.

5. Do one of the following:

   ▲ To replace the selected occurrence and automatically find the next occurrence, click the Replace button (**Figure 72**). You can repeat this step until Word has found all occurrences (**Figure 68**).

   ▲ To replace all occurrences, click the Replace All button. Word tells you how many changes it made (**Figure 73**).

   ▲ To skip the current occurrence and move on to the next one, click the Find Next button. You can repeat this step until Word has found all occurrences (**Figure 68**).

6. When you're finished, dismiss the Find and Replace dialog by clicking its close button.

✔ Tip

■ If desired, you can fine-tune search criteria. I tell you how on the next page.

REPLACING TEXT

To fine-tune search criteria

1. In the Find or Replace tab of the Find and Replace dialog, click the More button (**Figure 70**). The dialog expands to show additional search criteria options (**Figure 74**).

2. Click in the Find what or Replace with text box to indicate which criterion you want to fine-tune.

3. Set search criteria options as desired:

   ▲ The **Search** pop-up menu (**Figure 75**) lets you specify whether you want to search the current document or all documents and which direction you want to search.

   ▲ The **Match case** check box exactly matches capitalization.

   ▲ The **Find whole words only** check box finds the search text only when it is a separate word or phrase.

   ▲ The **Use wildcards** check box lets you include wildcard characters (such as ? for a single character and * for multiple characters).

   ▲ The **Sounds like** check box finds homonyms—words that sound alike but are spelled differently.

   ▲ The **Find all word forms** check box searches for all verb, noun, or adjective forms of the search text.

4. Set search or replace critera options as desired:

   ▲ The **Format** pop-up menu (**Figure 76**) lets you specify formatting options. Choosing one of these options displays the corresponding dialog. I explain how to use these dialogs in **Chapters 3** and **4**.

   ▲ The **Special** pop-up menu (**Figure 77**) lets you find and replace special characters.

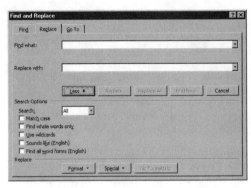

Figure 74 The Replace tab of the Find and Replace dialog expanded to show additional search criteria options.

Figure 75
The Search pop-up menu in the Find and Replace dialog.

Figure 76
The Format pop-up menu in the Find and Replace dialog.

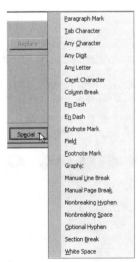

Figure 77
The Special pop-up menu in the Find and Replace dialog.

Figure 78 The Save As dialog.

Figure 79
The Save in pop-up menu at the top of the Save As dialog.

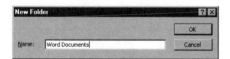

Figure 80 The New Folder dialog.

Figure 81 The name you give a document appears in its title bar after you save it.

Saving Documents

When you save a document, you put a copy of it on disk.

✔ Tips

- Until you save a document, its information is stored only in your computer's RAM. Your work on the document could be lost in the event of a power outage or system crash.

- It's a good idea to save documents frequently as you work. This ensures that the most recent versions are always saved to disk.

To save a document for the first time

1. Choose File > Save or File > Save As (**Figure 5**), press Ctrl S, or click the Save button ▣ on the Standard toolbar.

2. Use the Save As dialog that appears (**Figure 78**) to navigate to the folder in which you want to save the file:

   ▲ Use the Save in menu near the top of the dialog (**Figure 79**) to go to another location.

   ▲ Double-click a folder to open it.

   ▲ Click the Create New Folder button on the command bar to create a new folder within the current folder. Enter the name for the folder in the New Folder dialog (**Figure 80**) and click OK.

3. Enter a name for the file in the File name box.

4. Click Save.

   The file is saved to disk. Its name appears on the window's title bar (**Figure 81**).

To save changes to a document

Choose File > Save (**Figure 5**), press Ctrl S, or click the Save button on ▣ the Standard toolbar.

The document is saved with the s ame name in the same location on disk.

To save a document with a different name or in a different disk location

1. Choose File > Save As (**Figure 5**).

2. Follow steps 2 and/or 3 on the previous page to select a new disk location and/or enter a different name for the file.

3. Click the Save button.

✔ Tips

- You can use the Save as type pop-up menu at the bottom of the Save As dialog (**Figure 82**) to specify a different format for the file. This enables you to save the document in a format that can be opened and read by other versions of Word or other applications.

- If you save a file with the same name and same disk location as another file, a dialog offering three options (**Figure 83**):

  ▲ **Replace existing file** replaces the file already on disk with the file you are saving.

  ▲ **Save changes with a different name** redisplays the Save As dialog box so you can change the name or location of the file you are saving.

  ▲ **Merge changes into existing file** uses Word's collaboration features to add the current file's contents to the one already on disk. This is an advanced feature of Word that is discussed briefly in **Chapter 12**.

Figure 82 You can use the Save as type pop-up menu to specify a file format.

Figure 83 This dialog appears when you attempt to save a file with the same name and same disk location as another file.

Figure 84 The Save As dialog when you save a document as a template.

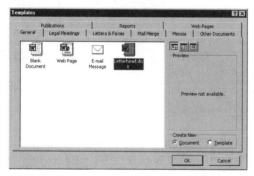

Figure 85 When a file has been saved as a template, it appears in the Templates dialog.

To save a document as a template

1. Choose File > Save As (**Figure 5**).

2. Enter a name for the file in the Name box.

3. Choose Document Template from the Save as type pop-up menu (**Figure 82**). The file list portion of the dialog automatically displays the contents of the Templates folder (**Figure 84**).

4. Click the Save button.

   The file is saved as a template. Its name appears in the document title bar.

✔ Tips

- To begin using a template right after you created it, close it, then follow the instructions near the beginning of this chapter to open a new file based on a template. The template appears in the General tab of the Templates dialog (**Figure 85**).

- I tell you more about templates in the beginning of this chapter.

FORMATTING BASICS

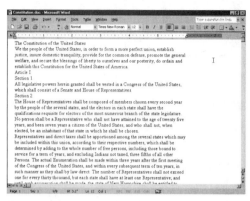

Figure 1 A document with no formatting.

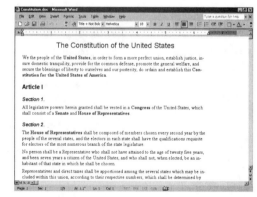

Figure 2 The same document with font and paragraph formatting applied.

Formatting Basics

Microsoft Word offers a wide range of formatting options that you can use to make your documents more interesting and readable. Most formatting can be broken down into three types:

◆ **Font** or **character formatting** applies to individual characters of text. Examples include bold, italic, underline, and font color. The actual font or typeface used to display characters is also a part of font formatting.

◆ **Paragraph formatting** applies to entire paragraphs of text. Examples are indentation, justification, and line spacing.

◆ **Page formatting** applies to entire documents or sections of documents. Examples include margins and vertical alignment of text on the page.

This chapter introduces basic formatting options—the formatting you'll use most often.

✔ Tips

■ When properly applied, formatting can make the document easier to read, as illustrated in **Figures 1** and **2**.

■ Don't get carried away with formatting—especially font formatting. Too much formatting distracts the reader, making the document difficult to read.

■ Page formatting is sometimes referred to as *section* or *document formatting* because it can be applied to a document section or the entire document.

Revealing Formatting

Word offers an easy way to see what kind of formatting is applied to text: the Reveal Formatting command (**Figure 3**). This command displays a task pane window that tells you exactly what kind of formatting is applied to the text characters on which you click (**Figures 4 and 5**).

To reveal formatting

1. Choose Format > Reveal Formatting (**Figure 3**). The Reveal Formatting task pane appears to the right of the document window. It lists all of the formatting applied to the character you clicked (**Figures 4 and 5**).

2. To learn about the formatting applied to a character, click on the character.

3. Repeat step 2 for each character for which you want to reveal formatting.

✔ Tips

- The Reveal Formatting feature shows the formatting applied to the paragraph in which a character resides as well as the character itself.

- You can also reveal formatting by choosing Help > What's This? or pressing Shift F1 and then using the help pointer that appears (**Figure 6**) to click on the character for which you want to learn about formatting.

- When you're finished using the Reveal Formatting feature, you can click the task pane's close button to dismiss it.

Figure 3
The full Format menu.

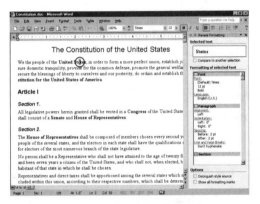

Figure 4 One example of revealing formatting.

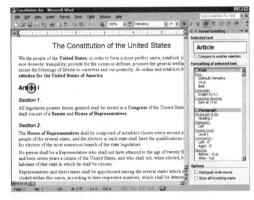

Figure 5 Another example of revealing formatting.

Figure 6 The help pointer appears when you choose What's This? from the Help menu.

REVEALING FORMATTING

Arial
Bookman Old Style
Century Gothic
Courier New
Forte
Garamond
Impact
Σψμβολ
Verdana
Times New Roman
✳●□✦✣✶■✕✢●▼▲

Figure 7
Some font examples using some of the fonts installed on my system. Your system's fonts may differ.

Regular
Bold
Italic
Bold Italic

Figure 8
The font styles offered by Word.

10 points
12 points
14 points
18 points
24 points
36 points

Figure 9
Examples of font sizes. This illustration is not at actual size.

No underline
Words Only
Underline Example
Underline Example
Underline Example
Underline Example
Underline Example
Underline Example
Underline Example
Underline Example
Underline Example
Underline Example
Underline Example
Underline Example
Underline Example
Underline Example
Underline Example
Underline Example
Underline Example
Underline Example

Figure 10
Examples of underlines offered by Word.

Strikethrough
Double Strikethrough
Superscript
Subscript
Shadow
Outline
Emboss
Engrave
SMALL CAPS
ALL CAPS

Figure 11
Examples of effects.

Font Formatting

Font formatting, which is sometimes referred to as *character formatting*, can be applied to individual characters of text. Word offers a wide variety of options.

◆ **Font** (**Figure 7**) is the typeface used to display characters.

◆ **Font style** (**Figure 8**) is the appearance of font characters: regular, italic, bold, or bold italic.

◆ **Size** (**Figure 9**) is the size of characters, expressed in points.

◆ **Font Color** is the color applied to text characters.

◆ **Underline style** (**Figure 10**) options allow you to apply a variety of underlines beneath characters.

◆ **Underline color** is the color of the applied underline. This is a new feature in Word 2001.

◆ **Effects** (**Figure 11**) are special effects that change the appearance of characters. Options include strikethrough, double strikethrough, superscript, subscript, shadow, outline, emboss, engrave, small caps, all caps, or hidden.

✔ Tips

■ Although some fonts come with Microsoft Office, Word enables you to apply *any* font that is properly installed in your system.

■ A *point* is 1/72 inch. The larger the point size, the larger the characters.

■ Hidden characters do not show onscreen unless formatting marks are displayed. Formatting marks are covered in **Chapter 2**.

■ Word offers additional font formatting options not covered here; I tell you about them in **Chapter 4**.

Applying Font Formatting

Font formatting is applied to selected characters or, if no characters are selected, to the characters you type at the insertion point after setting formatting options. Here are two examples:

◆ To apply a bold font style to text that you have already typed, select the text (**Figure 12**), then apply the formatting. The appearance of the text changes immediately (**Figure 13**).

◆ To apply a bold font style to text that you have not yet typed, position the insertion point where the text will be typed (**Figure 14**), apply the bold formatting, and type the text. The text appears in bold (**Figure 15**). You must remember, however, to "turn off" bold formatting before you continue to type (**Figure 16**).

Word offers several methods of applying font formatting:

◆ The Formatting toolbar enables you to apply font, size, some font styles, and font color formatting.

◆ Shortcut keys enable you to apply some font formatting.

◆ The Font dialog enables you to apply all kinds of font formatting.

✔ Tips

■ In my opinion, it's easier to type text and apply formatting later than to format as you type.

■ I explain how to select text in **Chapter 2**.

We the people of the United States, in domestic tranquility, provide for the co blessings of liberty to ourselves and or

Figure 12 Select the text that you want to format,...

We the people of the **United States**, in domestic tranquility, provide for the com blessings of liberty to ourselves and our r

Figure 13 ...then apply the formatting.

We the people of the |

Figure 14 Position the insertion point where you want the formatted text to appear,...

We the people of the **United States**|

Figure 15 ...then "turn on" the formatting and type the text.

We the people of the **United States**, in order to|

Figure 16 Be sure to "turn off" the formatting before continuing to type.

Figure 17
The Font menu on the Formatting toolbar.

Figure 18
The Font Size menu on the Formatting toolbar.

Figure 19 Select the contents of the Font box.

Figure 20 Enter the name of the font that you want to apply.

Figure 21 The Font Color menu on the Formatting toolbar.

Figure 22 The Highlight Color menu on the Formatting toolbar.

Figure 23 Word tells you when you've entered a font that isn't installed.

To apply font formatting with the Formatting toolbar

Choose the font or size that you want to apply from the Font or Font Size menu (**Figures 17** and **18**).

or

1. Click the Font (**Figure 19**) or Font Size text box to select its contents.

2. Enter the name of the font (**Figure 20**) or the size that you want to apply.

3. Press [Enter].

or

Click the button for the font style you want to apply: Bold **B**, Italic **I**, or Underline **U**.

or

Click the Font Color button **A** to apply the currently selected color or choose another color from the Font Color toolbar menu (**Figure 21**).

Click the Highlight button to apply the currently selected color or choose another color from the Highlight Color toolbar menu (**Figure 22**).

✔ Tips

- Font names appear on the Font menu in their typefaces (**Figure 17**).

- Recently applied fonts appear at the top of the Font menu (**Figure 17**).

- If you enter the name of a font that is not installed on your system, Word warns you (**Figure 23**). If you use the font anyway, the text appears in the document in the default paragraph font. The text will appear in the applied font after the font is installed on your system or when the document is opened on a system on which the font is installed.

APPLYING FONT FORMATTING

To apply font formatting with shortcut keys

Press the shortcut key combination (**Table 1**) for the formatting that you want to apply.

✔ Tip

■ The shortcut key to change the font requires that you press the first key combination, enter the name of the font desired, then press Enter. This command activates the Name edit box on the Formatting Palette.

To apply font formatting with the Font dialog

1. Choose Format > Font (**Figure 3**) or press Ctrl D.

2. Set formatting options as desired in the Font tab of the Font dialog that appears (**Figure 24**).

3. Click OK.

✔ Tip

■ The Preview area of the Font dialog illustrates what text will look like with the selected formatting applied.

Table 1

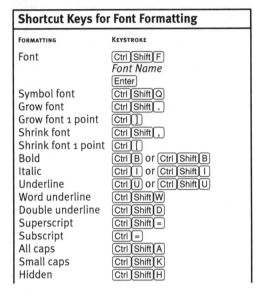

Shortcut Keys for Font Formatting	
FORMATTING	KEYSTROKE
Font	Ctrl Shift F *Font Name* Enter
Symbol font	Ctrl Shift Q
Grow font	Ctrl Shift .
Grow font 1 point	Ctrl]
Shrink font	Ctrl Shift ,
Shrink font 1 point	Ctrl [
Bold	Ctrl B or Ctrl Shift B
Italic	Ctrl I or Ctrl Shift I
Underline	Ctrl U or Ctrl Shift U
Word underline	Ctrl Shift W
Double underline	Ctrl Shift D
Superscript	Ctrl Shift =
Subscript	Ctrl =
All caps	Ctrl Shift A
Small caps	Ctrl Shift K
Hidden	Ctrl Shift H

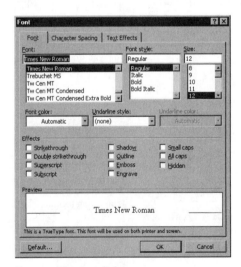

Figure 24 The Font dialog.

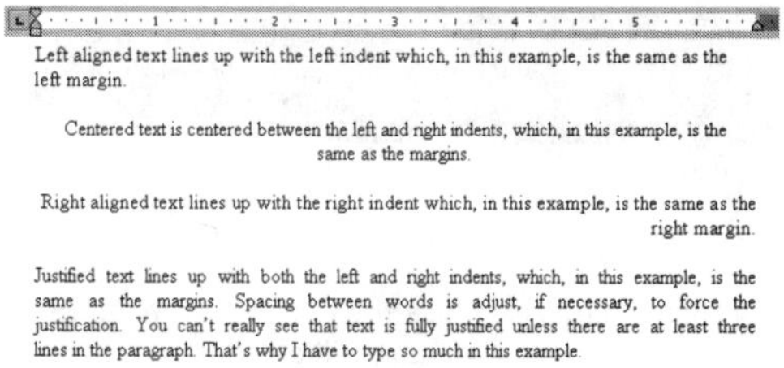

Paragraph Formatting

Paragraph formatting is applied to entire paragraphs of text. Word offers a variety of paragraph formatting options:

◆ **Alignment (Figure 25)** is the way lines of text line up between the indents.

◆ **Indentation (Figure 26)** is the spacing between text and margins. Word allows you to set left and right margins, as well as special indentations for first line and hanging indents.

◆ **Line spacing (Figure 27)** is the amount of space between lines. Spacing can be set as single, 1.5 lines, double, at least a certain amount, exactly a certain amount, or multiple lines.

◆ **Paragraph spacing (Figure 28)** is the amount of space before and after the paragraph.

✔ Tip

■ Word offers additional paragraph formatting options not covered here. I tell you about tabs later in this chapter and about other paragraph formatting options in **Chapter 4**.

Left aligned text lines up with the left indent which, in this example, is the same as the left margin.

Centered text is centered between the left and right indents, which, in this example, is the same as the margins.

Right aligned text lines up with the right indent which, in this example, is the same as the right margin.

Justified text lines up with both the left and right indents, which, in this example, is the same as the margins. Spacing between words is adjust, if necessary, to force the justification. You can't really see that text is fully justified unless there are at least three lines in the paragraph. That's why I have to type so much in this example.

Figure 25 Examples of alignment options.

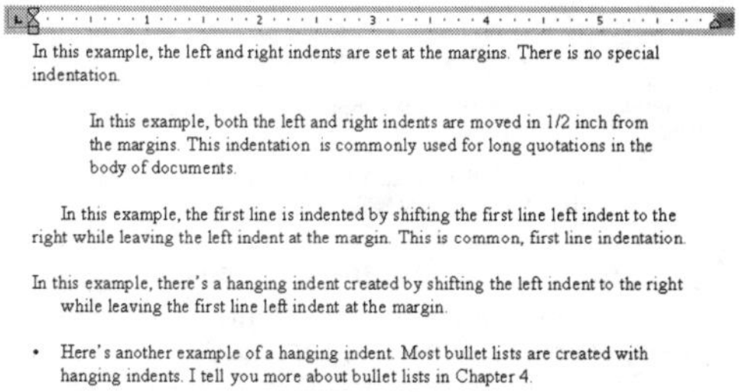

In this example, the left and right indents are set at the margins. There is no special indentation.

In this example, both the left and right indents are moved in 1/2 inch from the margins. This indentation is commonly used for long quotations in the body of documents.

In this example, the first line is indented by shifting the first line left indent to the right while leaving the left indent at the margin. This is common, first line indentation.

In this example, there's a hanging indent created by shifting the left indent to the right while leaving the first line left indent at the margin.

• Here's another example of a hanging indent. Most bullet lists are created with hanging indents. I tell you more about bullet lists in Chapter 4.

Figure 26 Examples of indentation options. The ruler in this illustration shows the indent markers set for the first sample paragraph.

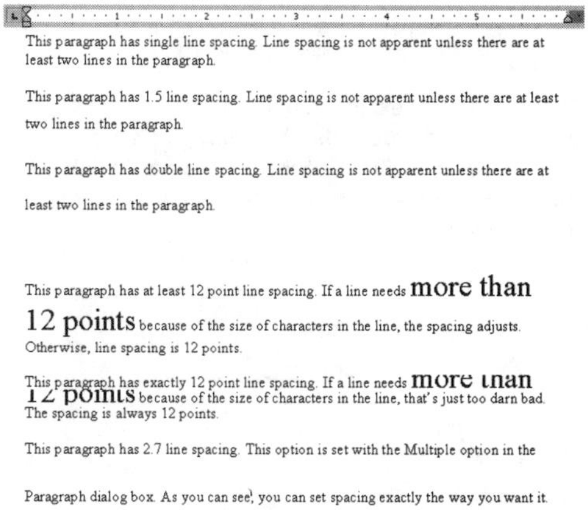

This paragraph has single line spacing. Line spacing is not apparent unless there are at least two lines in the paragraph.

This paragraph has 1.5 line spacing. Line spacing is not apparent unless there are at least two lines in the paragraph.

This paragraph has double line spacing. Line spacing is not apparent unless there are at least two lines in the paragraph.

This paragraph has at least 12 point line spacing. If a line needs more than 12 points because of the size of characters in the line, the spacing adjusts. Otherwise, line spacing is 12 points.

This paragraph has exactly 12 point line spacing. If a line needs more than 12 points because of the size of characters in the line, that's just too darn bad. The spacing is always 12 points.

This paragraph has 2.7 line spacing. This option is set with the Multiple option in the Paragraph dialog box. As you can see, you can set spacing exactly the way you want it.

Figure 27 Examples of line spacing options.

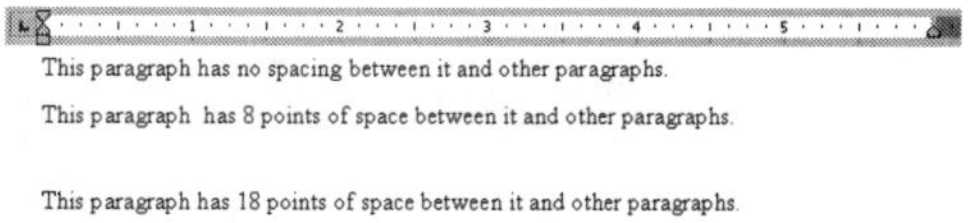

This paragraph has no spacing between it and other paragraphs.

This paragraph has 8 points of space between it and other paragraphs.

This paragraph has 18 points of space between it and other paragraphs.

Figure 28 Paragraph spacing options.

Applying Paragraph Formatting

Paragraph formatting is applied to selected paragraphs (**Figure 29**) or, if no paragraphs are selected, to the paragraph in which the insertion point is blinking (**Figure 30**).

Word offers several methods of applying paragraph formatting:

- The Formatting toolbar enables you to apply some paragraph formatting.
- Shortcut keys enable you to apply some paragraph formatting.
- The ruler enables you to apply indentation and tab formatting.
- The Paragraph dialog enables you to apply most kinds of paragraph formatting.

✔ Tips

- Paragraph formatting applies to the entire paragraph, even if only part of the paragraph is selected (**Figure 31**).
- A *paragraph* is the text that appears between paragraph marks. You can see paragraph marks when you display formatting marks (**Figures 29** through **31**). Formatting marks are discussed in **Chapter 2**.
- When you press Enter, the paragraph formatting of the current paragraph is carried forward to the new paragraph.
- Selecting paragraphs is explained in **Chapter 2**.

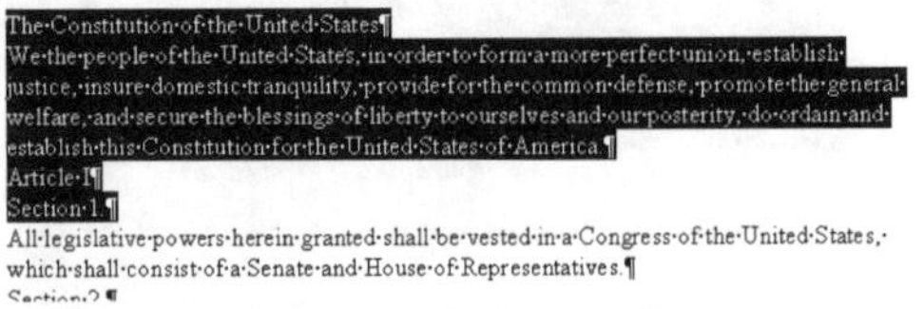
The·Constitution·of·the·United·States¶
We·the·people·of·the·United·States,·in·order·to·form·a·more·perfect·union,·establish·justice,·insure·domestic·tranquility,·provide·for·the·common·defense,·promote·the·general·welfare,·and·secure·the·blessings·of·liberty·to·ourselves·and·our·posterity,·do·ordain·and·establish·this·Constitution·for·the·United·States·of·America.¶
Article·I¶
Section·1.¶
All·legislative·powers·herein·granted·shall·be·vested·in·a·Congress·of·the·United·States,·which·shall·consist·of·a·Senate·and·House·of·Representatives.¶

Figure 29 In this example, the first four paragraphs are completely selected and will be affected by any paragraph formatting applied.

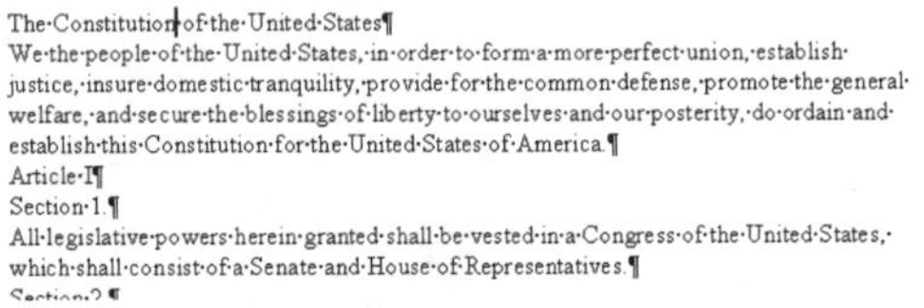
The·Constitution·of·the·United·States¶
We·the·people·of·the·United·States,·in·order·to·form·a·more·perfect·union,·establish·justice,·insure·domestic·tranquility,·provide·for·the·common·defense,·promote·the·general·welfare,·and·secure·the·blessings·of·liberty·to·ourselves·and·our·posterity,·do·ordain·and·establish·this·Constitution·for·the·United·States·of·America.¶
Article·I¶
Section·1.¶
All·legislative·powers·herein·granted·shall·be·vested·in·a·Congress·of·the·United·States,·which·shall·consist·of·a·Senate·and·House·of·Representatives.¶

Figure 30 In this example, the insertion point is in the first paragraph. That entire paragraph will be affected by any paragraph formatting applied.

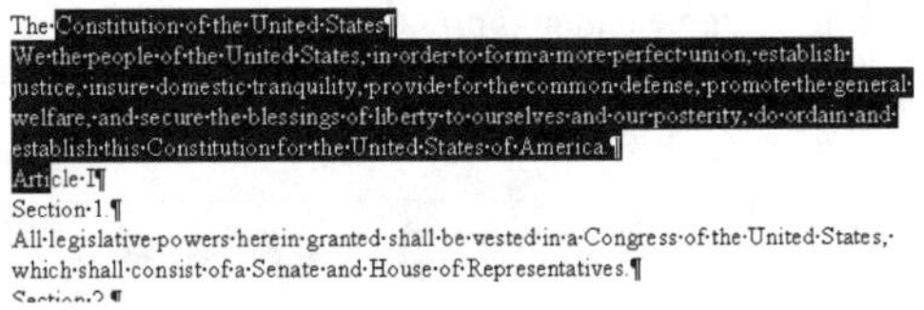
The·Constitution·of·the·United·States¶
We·the·people·of·the·United·States,·in·order·to·form·a·more·perfect·union,·establish·justice,·insure·domestic·tranquility,·provide·for·the·common·defense,·promote·the·general·welfare,·and·secure·the·blessings·of·liberty·to·ourselves·and·our·posterity,·do·ordain·and·establish·this·Constitution·for·the·United·States·of·America.¶
Article·I¶
Section·1.¶
All·legislative·powers·herein·granted·shall·be·vested·in·a·Congress·of·the·United·States,·which·shall·consist·of·a·Senate·and·House·of·Representatives.¶

Figure 31 In this example, only part of the first paragraph and part of the third paragraph are selected, along with all of the second paragraph. All three paragraphs will be affected by any paragraph formatting applied.

Table 2

Shortcut Keys for Paragraph Formatting	
FORMATTING	KEYSTROKE
Align left	Ctrl L
Center	Ctrl E
Align right	Ctrl R
Justify	Ctrl J
Indent	Ctrl M
Unindent	Ctrl Shift M
Hanging indent	Ctrl T
Unhang indent	Ctrl Shift T
Single line space	Ctrl 1
1.5 line space	Ctrl 5
Double line space	Ctrl 2
Open/Close Up Paragraph	Ctrl 0 (zero)

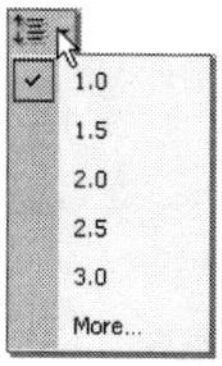

Figure 32
The Line Spacing
button's menu offers
a number of spacing
options.

To apply paragraph formatting with Formatting toolbar buttons

To set alignment, click Align Left ▦, Center ▦, Align Right ▦, or Justify ▦.

or

To set left indentation, click Decrease Indent ▦ or Increase Indent ▦.

or

To set line spacing, click the arrow beside the Line Spacing button ▦▾ and choose an option from the menu that appears (**Figure 32**).

✔ Tip

■ Choosing More from the Line Spacing button's menu (**Figure 32**) displays the Paragraph dialog, which is discussed on the next page.

To apply paragraph formatting with shortcut keys

Press the shortcut key combination (**Table 2**) for the formatting that you want to apply.

APPLYING PARAGRAPH FORMATTING

To set indentation with the ruler

Drag the indent markers (**Figure 33**) to set indentation as desired:

♦ **First Line Indent** sets the left boundary for the first line of a paragraph.

♦ **Hanging Indent** sets the left boundary for all lines of a paragraph other than the first line.

♦ **Left Indent** sets the left boundary for all lines of a paragraph. (Dragging this marker moves the First Line Indent and Hanging Indent markers.)

♦ **Right Indent** sets the right boundary for all lines of a paragraph.

✔ Tips

■ If the ruler is not showing, choose View > Ruler (**Figure 34**) to display it.

■ Dragging the First Line Indent marker to the right creates a standard indent.

■ Dragging the Hanging Indent marker to the right creates a hanging indent.

To apply paragraph formatting with the Paragraph dialog

1. Choose Format > Paragraph (**Figure 3**).

2. Set formatting options as desired in the Indents and Spacing tab of the Paragraph dialog that appears (**Figure 35**).

3. Click OK.

✔ Tip

■ The Preview area of the Paragraph dialog illustrates what text will look like with formatting applied.

First line indent

Hanging indent
Left indent

Right indent

Figure 33 Indent markers on the ruler.

Figure 34
To display the ruler, choose Ruler from the View menu.

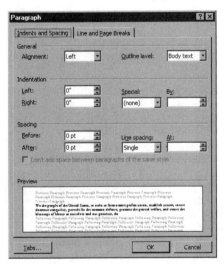

Figure 35 The Indents and Spacing tab of the Paragraph dialog.

Tab marker icon

Figure 36 Default tab stops appear as tiny gray lines on the ruler.

Figure 37 Word's five tab stops in action. In order, they are: left, bar, right, center, decimal. Examine the ruler to see how they're set.

Figure 38 Word's tab leader options: none, dotted, dashed, and underscore.

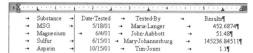

Figure 39 Displaying formatting marks enables you to see the tab characters.

Tabs

Tab stops determine the horizontal position of the insertion point when you press Tab.

By default, a blank document includes tab stops every half inch. They appear as gray marks on the bottom of the ruler (**Figure 36**). You can use the ruler or Tabs dialog to set tabs that override the defaults.

Word supports five kinds of tabs (**Figure 37**):

◆ **Left tab** aligns tabbed text to the left against the tab stop.

◆ **Center tab** centers tabbed text beneath the tab stop.

◆ **Right tab** aligns tabbed text to the right against the tab stop.

◆ **Decimal tab** aligns the decimal point (or period) of tabbed numbers beneath the tab stop. When used with text, a decimal tab works just like a right tab.

◆ **Bar tab** is a vertical line that appears beneath the tab stop.

Word also supports four types of tab leaders (**Figure 38**)—characters that appear in the space otherwise left by a tab: none, periods, dashes, and underscores.

✔ Tips

■ Tabs are a type of paragraph formatting; when set, they apply to an entire paragraph.

■ Tabs are often used to create simple tables.

■ When trying to align text in a simple table, use tabs, not spaces. Tabs always align to tab stops while text positioned with space characters may not align properly due to the size and spacing of characters in a font.

■ It's a good idea to display formatting marks when working with tabs (**Figure 39**) so you can distinguish tabs from spaces. Formatting marks are discussed in **Chapter 2**.

TABS

To set tab stops with the ruler

1. Click the tab marker icon at the far-left end of the ruler (**Figure 36**) until it displays the icon for the type of tab stop that you want to set (**Figure 40**).

2. Click on the ruler where you want to position the tab stop to set it there.

3. Repeat steps 1 and 2 until all desired tab stops have been set (**Figure 37**).

✔ Tip

■ When you set a tab stop, all default tab stops to its left disappear (**Figures 37** and **39**).

To move a tab stop with the ruler

1. Position the mouse pointer on the tab stop that you want to move.

2. Press the mouse button and drag the tab stop to its new position.

✔ Tip

■ Don't click on the ruler anywhere except on the tab stop that you want to move. Doing so will set another tab stop.

To remove a tab stop from the ruler

1. Position the mouse pointer on the tab stop that you want to remove.

2. Press the mouse button and drag the tab stop down into the document. When you release the mouse button, the tab stop disappears.

Figure 40 The tab marker icons for left, center, right, decimal, and bar tabs.

Figure 41
The Tabs dialog.

Figure 42
When you add a tab, it appears in the list in the Tabs dialog.

Figure 43
The tab stop settings for **Figure 37**.

Figure 44
When you click Clear to remove a tab stop, it is removed from the tab list.

To open the Tabs dialog

Choose Format > Tabs (**Figure 3**).

or

Click the Tabs button in the Paragraph dialog (**Figure 35**).

or

Double-click a tab stop on the ruler.

To set tab stops with the Tabs dialog

1. Open the Tabs dialog (**Figure 41**).

2. In the Alignment area, select the option button for the type of tab that you want.

3. In the Leader area, select the option button for the type of leader that you want the tab stop to have.

4. Enter a ruler measurement in the Tab stop position box.

5. Click Set. The tab stop is added to the tab list (**Figure 42**).

6. Repeat steps 2 through 5 for each tab stop that you want to set (**Figure 43**).

7. Click OK.

To remove tab stops with the Tabs dialog

1. In the Tabs dialog, select the tab stop that you want to remove.

2. Click Clear. The tab stop is removed from the list and added to the list of Tab stops to be cleared in the dialog (**Figure 44**).

3. Repeat steps 1 and 2 for each tab stop that you want to remove.

4. Click OK.

✔ Tip

■ To remove all tab stops, click the Clear All button in the Tabs dialog (**Figure 44**) and then click OK.

SETTING TAB STOPS WITH THE TABS DIALOG

To change the default tab stops

1. In the Tabs dialog (**Figure 41**), enter a new value in the Default tab stops box.

2. Click OK.

✔ Tip

- Remember, tab stops that you set manually on the ruler or with the Tabs dialog override default tab stops to their left.

To create a simple table with tab stops

1. Position the insertion point in the paragraph in which you set tabs (**Figure 45**).

2. To type at a tab stop, press Tab, then type (**Figure 46**).

3. Repeat step 2 to type at each tab stop.

4. Press Enter or Shift Enter to end the paragraph or line and begin a new one. The tab stops in the paragraph are carried forward (**Figure 47**).

5. Repeat steps 2 through 4 to finish typing your table (**Figure 39**).

✔ Tips

- You can move tabs at any time—even after you have begun using them. Be sure to select all the paragraphs that utilize the tabs before you move them. Otherwise, you may only adjust tabs for part of the table.

- Another way to create tables is with Word's table feature, which is far more flexible than using tab stops. I tell you about it in **Chapter 9**.

Figure 45 Position the insertion point in the paragraph for which you have set tab stops.

Figure 46 Press Tab to type at the first tab stop, then type. In this example, text is typed at a right-aligned tab stop.

Figure 47 When you are finished typing a line press Enter to start a new paragraph with the same tab stops.

Figure 48 A margin is the space between the edge of the paper and the indent.

Figure 49 Examples of vertical alignment: top (top left), center (top right), justified (bottom left), and bottom (bottom right).

Page Formatting

Page formatting is applied to an entire document or section of a document. Word offers several options for page formatting, two of which are covered in this chapter:

◆ **Margins** are the spacing between the edge of the paper and the indents (**Figure 48**). **Gutter** is the amount of extra space on the inside margin of a document which is required for binding.

◆ **Vertical alignment** (**Figure 49**) is the vertical position of text on a page. Options include top, center, justified, and bottom.

✔ Tip

■ Word offers additional page formatting options not covered here. Working with header, footer, and section break options is covered in **Chapter 4**.

Applying Page Formatting

Page formatting can be applied four ways:

◆ To the entire document.

◆ To the document from the insertion point forward. This creates a section break at the insertion point.

◆ To selected text. This creates a section break before and after the selected text.

◆ To selected document sections. This requires that section breaks already be in place and that you either select the sections or position the insertion point in a section.

You format a page with the Page Setup dialog.

✔ Tip

■ Creating and using section breaks is covered in **Chapter 4**. Be sure to read about section breaks before using the Page Setup dialog to format a section.

To set margin options

1. Choose File > Page Setup (**Figure 50**) to display the Page Setup dialog.

2. If necessary, click the Margins tab to display its options (**Figure 51**).

3. Enter values in the Top, Bottom, Left, and Right boxes.

4. To set a gutter width, enter a value in the Gutter box.

5. To apply your changes to the entire document, make sure Whole document is selected from the Apply to drop-down list. Otherwise, choose the desired option from the Apply to drop-down list; I tell you more about that in **Chapter 4**.

6. Click OK.

✔ Tips

- You can select an option from the Multiple Pages drop-down list (**Figure 52**) to set up the document for special multiple-page printing.

- The Preview area of the Page Setup dialog illustrates all page formatting settings (**Figures 51** and **53**).

Figure 50 Choose Page Setup from the File menu.

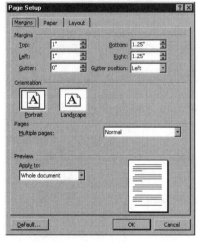

Figure 51 The Margins tab of the Page Setup dialog.

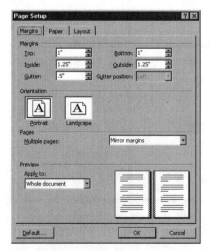

Figure 53 The Margins tab of the Page Setup dialog, set with Mirror margins and a half-inch gutter.

Figure 52 Use the Multiple Pages drop-down list to select a special multiple-page printing option.

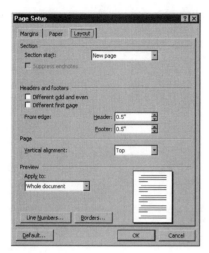

Figure 54 The Layout tab of the Page Setup dialog.

Figure 55 The Vertical alignment drop-down list in the Layout tab of the Page Setup dialog.

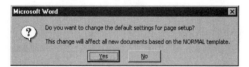

Figure 56 Word confirms that you really want to change the default page settings.

To set vertical alignment

1. Choose File > Page Setup (**Figure 50**) to display the Page Setup dialog.

2. If necessary, click the Layout tab to display its options (**Figure 54**).

3. Choose the alignment option that you want from the Vertical alignment drop-down list (**Figure 55**).

4. To apply your changes to the entire document, make sure Whole document is selected from the Apply to drop-down list. Otherwise, choose the desired option from the Apply to drop-down list; I tell you more about that in **Chapter 4**.

5. Click OK.

✔ Tips

- Vertical alignment is only apparent on pages that are less than a full page in length.

- On screen, you can only view vertical alignment in Web Layout view, Print Layout view, and Print Preview.

To set default page formatting

1. Choose File > Page Setup (**Figure 50**) to display the Page Setup dialog.

2. Set options as desired in the Margins and Layout tabs (**Figures 51** and **54**).

3. Click the Default button.

4. Word asks if you want to change the default settings for the document (**Figure 56**). Click Yes only if you want the settings to apply to all new documents that you create based on the Normal (Blank Document) template.

ADVANCED FORMATTING

Advanced Formatting

Microsoft Word offers a number of formatting options and techniques in addition to those discussed in **Chapter 3**:

- ◆ **Character spacing** includes the spacing, position, and kerning of characters.

- ◆ **Drop Caps** enlarges the first character(s) of a paragraph and wraps text around it.

- ◆ **Change Case** changes the case of typed characters.

- ◆ **Bullets and numbering** instructs Word to automatically insert bullet characters or numbers at the beginning of paragraphs.

- ◆ **Borders and shading** enable you to place borders around text, and color or shades of gray within text areas.

- ◆ **Format Painter** enables you to copy font and paragraph formats from one selection to another.

- ◆ **Styles** enables you to define and apply named sets of formatting options for individual characters or paragraphs.

- ◆ **AutoFormat** instructs Word to automatically format text you type.

- ◆ **Breaks** determines the end of a page, section, or column.

- ◆ **Multiple-column text** enables you to use newspaper-like columns in documents.

- ◆ **Headers and footers** enables you to specify text to appear at the top and bottom of every page in the document.

✔ Tip

- ■ It's a good idea to have a solid understanding of the concepts covered in **Chapter 3** before you read this chapter.

Character Spacing

Chapter 3 omitted a few more advanced font formatting options:

◆ **Scale** determines the horizonal size of font characters. Scale is specified as a percentage of normal character width (**Figure 1**).

◆ **Spacing** determines the amount of space between each character of text. Spacing can be normal or can be expanded or condensed by the number of points you specify (**Figure 2**).

◆ **Position** determines whether text appears above or below the baseline. Position can be normal or can be raised or lowered by the number of points you specify (**Figure 3**).

◆ **Kerning** determines how certain combinations of letters "fit" together (**Figure 4**).

✔ Tips

■ Like any other type of font formatting, you can apply character spacing to characters as you type them or to characters that have already been typed. Check **Chapter 3** for details.

■ The baseline is the invisible line on which characters sit.

■ Don't confuse character position with superscript and subscript. Although all three of these font formatting options change the position of text in relation to the baseline, superscript and subscript also change the size of characters. I tell you about superscript and subscript in **Chapter 3**.

■ The effect of kerning varies depending on the size and font applied to characters for which kerning is enabled. Kerning is more apparent at larger point sizes and requires that the font contain *kerning pairs*—predefined pairs of letters to kern. In many instances, you may not see a difference in spacing at all.

This is normal text.
This is text scaled to 120%.
This is text scaled to 80%.

Figure 1 Three examples of character scaling: 100% (top), 120% (middle), and 80% (bottom).

This is normal text.
This text is expanded by 1 point.
This text is condensed by 1 point.

Figure 2 Three examples of character spacing: normal (top), expanded by 1 point (middle), and condensed by 1 point (bottom).

This is an example of normal position.
This is an example of raised position.
This is an example of lowered position.

Figure 3 Three examples of character position: normal (top), raised 3 points (middle), and lowered 3 points (bottom).

To We
To We

Figure 4 Two common kerning pairs without kerning enabled (top) and with kerning enabled (bottom).

Figure 5
The Format menu.

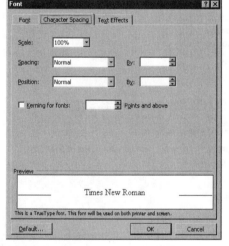

Figure 6 The Character Spacing tab of the Font dialog.

Figure 7
The Spacing
drop-down list.

Figure 8
The Position
drop-down list.

To apply character spacing

1. Choose Format > Font (**Figure 5**).

2. In the Font dialog that appears, click the Character Spacing tab to display its options (**Figure 6**).

3. Set options as desired:

   ▲ To change scale, enter a percentage value in the Scale box.

   ▲ To change spacing, choose an option from the Spacing drop-down list (**Figure 7**). Then enter a value in its By box.

   ▲ To change position, choose an option from the Position drop-down list (**Figure 8**). Then enter a value in its By box.

   ▲ To enable kerning, turn on the Kerning for fonts check box. Then enter a value in the Points and above box to specify the minimum point size of fonts to which kerning should be applied.

4. Click OK.

✔ Tip

■ The Preview area of the Font dialog (**Figure 6**) shows what selected characters will look like when you apply settings by clicking OK.

APPLYING CHARACTER SPACING

Drop Caps

A drop cap is an enlarged and/or repositioned character at the beginning of a paragraph. Word supports two types of drop caps (**Figure 9**):

- ◆ **Dropped** enlarges the character and wraps the rest of the text in the paragraph around it.

- ◆ **In Margin** enlarges the character and moves it into the margin.

✔ Tips

- ■ Word creates drop caps using frames, a feature that enables you to precisely position text on a page or in relation to a paragraph. Frames is an advanced feature of Word that is beyond the scope of this book.

- ■ To see drop caps, you must be in Print Layout view or Print Preview. A drop cap appears as an enlarged character in its own paragraph in Normal view (**Figure 10**).

- ■ A drop cap can consist of more than just the first letter of a paragraph (**Figure 11**).

Since Aramis' singular transformation into a confessor of the order, Baisemeaux was no longer the same man. Up to that period, the place in which Aramis had held in the worthy governor's estimation was that of a prelate whom he respected and a friend to whom he owed a debt of gratitude; but now he felt himself an inferior, and that Aramis was his master. He himself lighted a lantern, summoned a turnkey, and said, returning to Aramis:

Since Aramis' singular transformation into a confessor of the order, Baisemeaux was no longer the same man. Up to that period, the place in which Aramis had held in the worthy governor's estimation was that of a prelate whom he respected and a friend to whom he owed a debt of gratitude; but now he felt himself an inferior, and that Aramis was his master. He himself lighted a lantern, summoned a turnkey, and said, returning to Aramis:

Since Aramis' singular transformation into a confessor of the order, Baisemeaux was no longer the same man. Up to that period, the place in which Aramis had held in the worthy governor's estimation was that of a prelate whom he respected and a friend to whom he owed a debt of gratitude; but now he felt himself an inferior, and that Aramis was his master. He himself lighted a lantern, summoned a turnkey, and said, returning to Aramis:

Figure 9 The same paragraph three ways: without a drop cap (top), with a drop cap (middle), and with an in margin drop cap (bottom).

S

ince Aramis' singular transformation into a confessor of the order, Baisemeaux was no longer the same man. Up to that period, the place in which Aramis had held in the worthy governor's estimation was that of a prelate whom he respected and a friend to whom he owed a debt of gratitude; but now he felt himself an inferior, and that Aramis was his master. He himself lighted a lantern, summoned a turnkey, and said, returning to Aramis:

Figure 10 A paragraph with a drop cap when viewed in Normal view.

Since Aramis' singular transformation into a confessor of the order, Baisemeaux was no longer the same man. Up to that period, the place in which Aramis had held in the worthy governor's estimation was that of a prelate whom he respected and a friend to whom he owed a debt of gratitude; but now he felt himself an inferior, and that Aramis was his master. He himself lighted a lantern, summoned a turnkey, and said, returning to Aramis:

Figure 11 A drop cap can consist of more than just one character.

Figure 12
The Drop
Cap dialog.

To create a drop cap

1. Position the insertion point anywhere in the paragraph for which you want to create a drop cap.

2. Choose Format > Drop Cap (**Figure 5**).

3. In the Drop Cap dialog that appears (**Figure 12**), click the icon for the type of drop cap that you want to create.

4. Choose a font for the drop cap from the Font drop-down list.

5. Enter the number of lines for the size of the drop cap character in the Lines to drop box.

6. Enter a value for the amount of space between the drop cap character and the rest of the text in the paragraph in the Distance from text box.

7. Click OK.

✔ Tip

■ To create a drop cap with more than one character (**Figure 12**), select the characters that you want to appear as drop caps, then follow steps 2 through 7 above.

To remove a drop cap

Follow the steps above, but select the icon for None in step 3.

Changing Case

You can use the Change Case dialog (**Figure 13**) to change the case of selected characters. There are five options (**Figure 14**):

- **Sentence case** capitalizes the first letter of a sentence.

- **lowercase** changes all characters to lowercase.

- **UPPERCASE** changes all characters to uppercase.

- **Title Case** capitalizes the first letter of every word.

- **tOGGLE cASE** changes uppercase characters to lowercase and lowercase characters to uppercase.

✔ Tips

- Technically speaking, changing the case of characters with the Change Case dialog (**Figure 13**) does not format the characters. Instead, it changes the actual characters that were originally entered into the document.

- To change the case of characters without changing the characters themselves, use the All caps or Small caps option in the Font tab of the Font dialog (**Figure 15**). I tell you how in **Chapter 3**.

To change the case of characters

1. Select the characters whose case you want to change.

2. Choose Format > Change Case (**Figure 5**).

3. In the Change Case dialog that appears (**Figure 13**), select the option button for the option that you want.

4. Click OK.

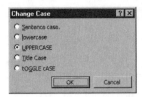

Figure 13
The Change Case dialog.

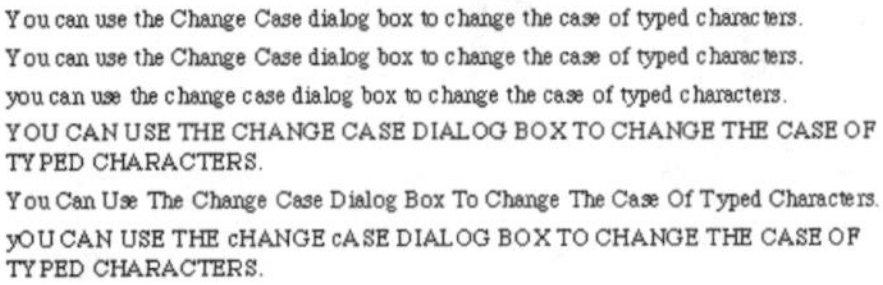

You can use the Change Case dialog box to change the case of typed characters.
You can use the Change Case dialog box to change the case of typed characters.
you can use the change case dialog box to change the case of typed characters.
YOU CAN USE THE CHANGE CASE DIALOG BOX TO CHANGE THE CASE OF TYPED CHARACTERS.
You Can Use The Change Case Dialog Box To Change The Case Of Typed Characters.
yOU CAN USE THE cHANGE cASE DIALOG BOX TO CHANGE THE CASE OF TYPED CHARACTERS.

Figure 14 Change Case in action—from top to bottom: original text, Sentence case, lowercase, UPPERCASE, Title Case, and tOGGLE cASE.

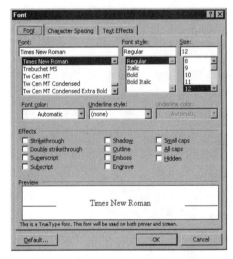

Figure 15 The Font tab of the Font dialog.

✔ Tip

- If you use the Change Case dialog to change the case of characters and get unexpected results, use the Undo command to reverse the action, then try the Change Case dialog again. I cover the Undo command in **Chapter 2**.

The following topics were covered:
* Advertising budget for product kickoff
* Replacement for Jane Jones
* Team for Product X marketing development

The following topics were covered:
1. Advertising budget for product kickoff
2. Replacement for Jane Jones
3. Team for Product X marketing development

Figure 16 Three paragraphs with bullets (top) and numbering (bottom) formats applied.

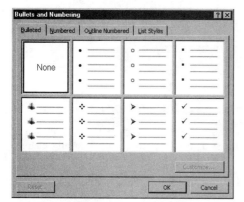

Figure 17 The Bulleted tab of the Bullets and Numbering dialog.

Bullets & Numbering

Word automatically includes bullets or numbers at the beginning of paragraphs to which you apply a bulleted or numbered list format (**Figure 16**).

✔ Tips

- You can apply list formats as you type or to paragraphs that have already been typed. Check **Chapter 3** for details.

- The bullet and number formats include hanging indents. I explain Word's indentation options in **Chapter 3**.

- If you use Word's numbering format, Word will automatically increment the number for each consecutive paragraph.

To apply bulleted list formatting

Click the Bullets button 📊 on the Formatting toolbar.

or

1. Choose Format > Bullets and Numbering (**Figure 5**).

2. In the Bullets and Numbering dialog that appears, click the Bulleted tab to display its options (**Figure 17**).

3. Click the box that displays the type of bullet character that you want.

4. Click OK.

✔ Tips

- Clicking the Bullet button on the Formatting toolbar applies the last style of bullet set in the Bullets and Numbering dialog (**Figure 17**) or Customize bulleted list dialog (**Figure 18**).

Continued on next page...

BULLETS & NUMBERING

Continued from previous page.

- To further customize a bullet list, after step 3 above, click the Customize button in the Bullets and Numbering dialog (**Figure 17**). Set options in the Customize bulleted list dialog that appears (**Figure 18**), and click OK.

- You can also use pictures for bullets. Click the Picture button in the Customize Bulleted List dialog (**Figure 18**). Then select one of the pictures in the Picture Bullet dialog that appears (**Figure 19**) and click OK. Word automatically uses the same picture for all bullets in the list.

To apply numbered list formatting

Click the Numbering button ▦ on the Formatting Palette.

or

1. Choose Format > Bullets and Numbering (**Figure 5**).

2. In the Bullets and Numbering dialog that appears, click the Numbered tab to display its options (**Figure 20**).

3. Click the box that displays the numbering format that you want.

4. Click OK.

✔ Tips

- Clicking the Numbering button on the Formatting toolbar applies the last style of numbering set in the Bullets and Numbering dialog (**Figure 20**) or Customize Numbered List dialog (**Figure 21**).

- To further customize a numbered list, after step 3 above, click the Customize button in the Bullets and Numbering dialog (**Figure 20**). Set options in the Customize Numbered List dialog that appears (**Figure 21**), and click OK.

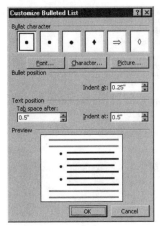

Figure 18
The Customize Bulleted List dialog.

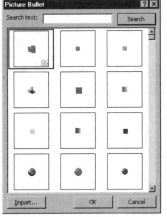

Figure 19
Use this dialog to locate and insert a picture to use as a bullet character.

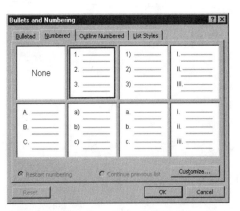

Figure 20 The Numbered tab of the Bullets and Numbering dialog.

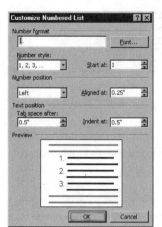

Figure 21
The Customize Numbered List dialog.

To remove bulleted or numbered list formatting

1. Choose Format > Bullets and Numbering (**Figure 5**).

2. In the Bullets and Numbering dialog (**Figure 17** or **20**), click the None box.

3. Click OK.

or

To remove bulleted list formatting from a selected paragraph, click the Bullet button 📇 on the Formatting toolbar.

or

To remove numbered list formatting from a selected paragraph, click the Numbering button 📇 on the Formatting toolbar.

BULLETS & NUMBERING

Borders & Shading

Borders and shading are two separate features that can work together to emphasize text:

- ◆ **Borders** enables you to place lines above, below, to the left, or to the right of selected characters or paragraphs (**Figure 22**).

- ◆ **Page borders** enables you to place simple or graphic borders at the top, bottom, left, or right sides of document pages (**Figure 23**).

- ◆ **Shading** enables you to add color or shades of gray to selected characters or paragraphs (**Figure 22**).

✔ Tips

- ■ How borders or shading are applied depends on how text is selected:

  - ▲ To apply borders or shading to characters, select the characters.

  - ▲ To apply borders or shading to a paragraph, click in the paragraph or select the entire paragraph.

  - ▲ To apply borders or shading to multiple paragraphs, select the paragraphs.

  - ▲ To apply page borders to all pages in a document, click anywhere in the document.

  - ▲ To apply page borders to a specific document section, click anywhere in that section.

- ■ When applying borders to selected text characters (as opposed to selected paragraphs), you must place a border around each side, creating a box around the text.

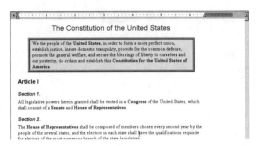

Figure 22 Borders and shading can emphasize text.

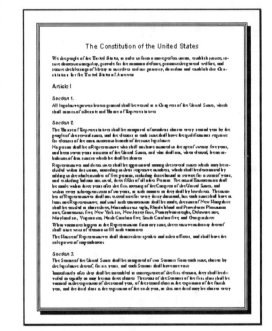

Figure 23 Page borders can make a page look fancy.

Figure 24
The Border pop-up
menu on the
Formatting toolbar.

To apply text borders with the Formatting toolbar

1. Select the text to which you want to apply borders.

2. Click the arrow beside the Border button ▣▾ to display a pop-up menu of border options (**Figure 24**).

3. Click the button for the border you want to apply.

✔ Tips

- You can apply more than one border to selected paragraphs. For example, if you want a top and bottom border, choose the top border option and then choose the bottom border option. Both are applied.

- Some border options apply more than one border. For example, the outside border option (top left button) applies the outside border as well as the top, bottom, left, and right borders.

To apply text borders with the Borders and Shading dialog

1. Select the text to which you want to apply borders.

2. Choose Format > Borders and Shading (**Figure 5**).

3. Click the Borders tab in the Borders and Shading dialog that appears to display its options (**Figure 25**).

4. Click a Setting icon to select the type of border. All options except None and Custom place borders around each side of the selected text.

5. Click a style in the Style list box to select a line style.

6. Choose a line color from the Color pop-up menu (**Figure 26**). If you choose Automatic, Word applies the color that is specified in the paragraph style that was applied to the text.

7. Choose a line thickness from the Width drop-down list (**Figure 27**).

8. If necessary, choose an option from the Apply to drop-down list (**Figure 28**). The Preview area changes accordingly.

9. To apply custom borders, click the buttons in the Preview area to add or remove a line using the settings in the dialog.

10. When the Preview area illustrates the kind of border that you want to apply, click OK.

✔ Tips

- You can repeat steps 5 through 7 and 9 to customize each border of a custom paragraph border.

- You can further customize a paragraph border by clicking the Options button to display the Border and Shading Options dialog (**Figure 29**). Set options as desired and click OK to return to the Borders and Shading dialog.

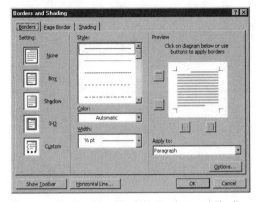

Figure 25 The Borders tab of the Borders and Shading dialog.

Figure 26 The Color pop-up menu.

Figure 27 The Width drop-down list.

Figure 28 The Apply to drop-down list.

APPLYING TEXT BORDERS

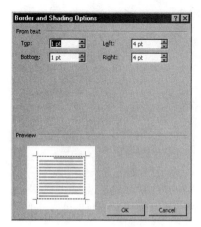

Figure 29 The Border and Shading Options dialog for paragraph borders.

To remove text borders

1. Select the text from which you want to remove borders.

2. Click the arrow beside the Border button ▣▾ to display a pop-up menu of border options (**Figure 24**).

3. Click the No Borders button (the second button on the bottom row).

or

1. Select the text from which you want to remove borders.

2. Choose Format > Borders and Shading (**Figure 5**) and click the Borders tab in the Borders and Shading dialog that appears (**Figure 25**).

3. Click the None icon.

4. Click OK.

REMOVING TEXT BORDERS

To apply page borders

1. If necessary, position the insertion point in the section of the document to which you want to apply page borders.

2. Choose Format > Borders and Shading (**Figure 5**).

3. Click the Page Border tab in the Borders and Shading dialog that appears to display its options (**Figure 30**).

4. Click a Setting icon to select the type of border. All options except None and Custom place borders around each side of the page.

5. Click a style in the Style scrolling list to select a line style. Then choose a line color from the Color pop-up menu (**Figure 26**) and a line thickness from the Width drop-down list (**Figure 27**).

   or

   Select a graphic from the Art drop-down list (**Figure 31**).

6. If necessary, choose an option from the Apply to drop-down list (**Figure 32**).

7. To apply custom borders, click the buttons in the Preview area to add or remove a line using the settings in the dialog.

8. When the Preview area illustrates the kind of border that you want to apply, click OK.

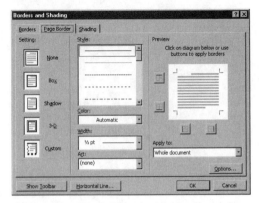

Figure 30 The Page Border tab of the Borders and Shading dialog.

Figure 31 The Art drop-down list.

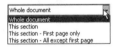

Figure 32 The Apply To drop-down list.

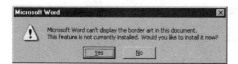

Figure 33 This dialog appears if the border art feature is not installed.

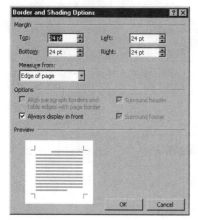

Figure 34 The Border and Shading Options dialog for page borders.

✔ Tips

■ If a dialog like the one in **Figure 33** appears when you attempt to select a graphic in step 5, the border art feature is not installed. To install it, click Yes and follow the prompts that appear onscreen. You will then be able to choose an option from the Art drop-down list.

■ You can repeat steps 5 and 7 to customize each border of a custom border.

■ You can further customize a border by clicking the Options button in the Borders and Shading dialog to display the Border and Shading Options dialog (**Figure 34**). Set options as desired and click OK to return to the Borders and Shading dialog.

To remove page borders

1. Position the insertion point in the section from which you want to remove borders.

2. Choose Format > Borders and Shading (**Figure 5**) and click the Page Border tab in the Borders and Shading dialog that appears (**Figure 30**).

3. Click the None icon.

4. Click OK.

APPLYING & REMOVING PAGE BORDERS

To apply shading

1. Select the text to which you want to apply shading.

2. Choose Format > Borders and Shading (**Figure 5**).

3. Click the Shading tab in the Borders and Shading dialog that appears to display its options (**Figure 35**).

4. Click a Fill color or shade to select it.

5. To create a pattern, choose an option from the Style drop-down list (**Figure 36**) and then choose a color from the Color pop-up menu (**Figure 26**).

6. If necessary, choose an option from the Apply to drop-down list (**Figure 28**). The Preview area changes accordingly.

7. When the Preview area illustrates the kind of shading that you want to apply, click OK.

✔ Tip

■ Use text shading with care. If overdone or if the pattern is too "busy," the text you have shaded may be impossible to read!

To remove shading

1. Select the text from which you want to remove shading.

2. Choose Format > Borders and Shading (**Figure 5**) and click the Shading tab in the Borders and Shading dialog that appears (**Figure 35**).

3. Click the No Fill button in the Fill area.

4. Choose Clear from the Style drop-down list (**Figure 36**).

5. Click OK.

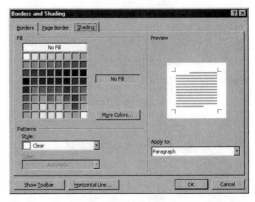

Figure 35 The Shading tab of the Borders and Shading dialog.

Figure 36
The Style drop-down list in the Patterns area.

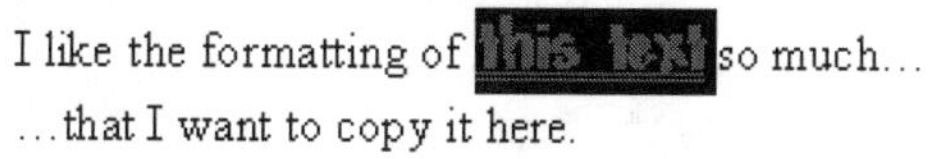

I like the formatting of ▇▇▇▇ ▇▇▇▇ so much...
...that I want to copy it here.

Figure 37 Select the text with the formatting you want to copy.

 Figure 38 When you click the Format Painter button, the mouse pointer turns into a Format Painter pointer.

I like the formatting of this text so much...
...that I want to copy it here.

Figure 39 Use the Format Painter pointer to select the text you want to apply the formatting to.

I like the formatting of this text so much...
...that I want to copy it here.

Figure 40 When you release the mouse button, the formatting is applied.

The Format Painter

The Format Painter enables you to copy the font or paragraph formatting of selected text and apply it to other text. This can save time and effort when applying the same formatting in multiple places throughout a document.

✔ Tip

■ Another way to apply the same formatting in various places throughout a document is with styles. I begin my discussion of Word's styles feature on the next page.

To use the Format Painter

1. Select the text whose formatting you want to copy (**Figure 37**).

2. Click the Format Painter button ▨ on the Standard toolbar. The Format Painter button becomes selected and the mouse pointer turns into an I-beam pointer with a plus sign beside it (**Figure 38**).

3. Use the mouse pointer to select the text to which you want to copy the formatting (**Figure 39**). When you release the mouse button, the formatting is applied (**Figure 40**) and the mouse pointer returns to normal.

✔ Tips

■ To copy paragraph formatting, be sure to select the entire paragraph in step 1, including the nonprinting Return character at the end of the paragraph. I tell you about nonprinting characters in **Chapter 2**.

■ To copy the same formatting to more than one selection, double-click the Format Painter button. The mouse pointer remains a Format Painter pointer (**Figure 38**) until you press Esc or click the Format Painter button ▨ again.

Styles

Word's styles feature enables you to define and apply sets of paragraph and/or font formatting to text throughout a document. This offers two main benefits over applying formatting using the basic techniques covered so far:

◆ **Consistency.** All text with a particular style applied will have the same formatting (**Figure 41**)—unless additional formatting has also been applied.

◆ **Flexibility.** Changing a style's definition is relatively easy. Once changed, the change automatically applies to all text formatted with that style (**Figure 42**).

Word 2002 supports four kinds of styles:

◆ **Character styles** affect the formatting of characters.

◆ **Paragraph styles** affect the formatting of entire paragraphs. The default paragraph style is called *Normal*.

◆ **Table styles** affect the formatting of tables.

◆ **List styles** affect the formatting of bulleted and numbered lists.

✔ Tips

■ Like font or paragraph formatting, you can apply styles as you type or to text that has already been typed. Check **Chapter 3** for details.

■ Styles are sometimes known as *style sheets*.

■ Word includes a number of predefined styles that you can apply to text.

■ Word's outline feature automatically applies predefined Heading styles as you create an outline. You can learn more about outlines in **Chapter 8**.

■ Tables are covered in **Chapter 9**.

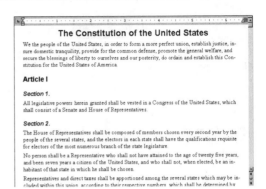

Figure 41 In this example, styles are applied to all text for consistent formatting.

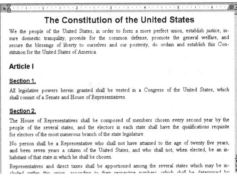

Figure 42 When two of the styles are modified, the formatting of text with those styles applied changes automatically. In this example, Normal style's paragraph formatting was changed from align left to justified and Heading 2 style's font formatting was changed from bold italic to regular with underline.

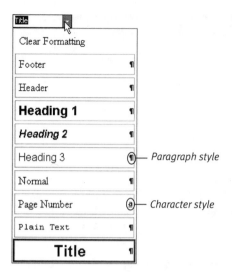

 — Paragraph style

 — Character style

Figure 43 The Style pop-up menu on the Formatting toolbar for the document shown in **Figure 41**.

Normal

Figure 44 Click the style name to select it.

Title

Figure 45 Type in the name of the style that you want to apply.

To apply a style with the Formatting toolbar

Choose a style from the Style pop-up menu on the Formatting toolbar (**Figure 43**).

or

1. Click the name of the style in the Style pop-up menu's text box to select it (**Figure 44**).

2. Type in the exact name of the style that you want to apply (**Figure 45**).

3. Press Enter.

✔ Tips

- The Style pop-up menu displays only the styles that have been applied in the document, the first three Heading styles, Normal, and the Clear Formatting option (**Figure 43**).

- To include all built-in template styles on the Style pop-up menu, hold down Shift while clicking to display the menu.

- The Style pop-up menu displays each style name using the formatting of that style (**Figure 43**).

- You can distinguish between character styles and paragraph styles in the Style pop-up menu by the symbol to the right of the style name (**Figure 43**).

- If you enter the name of a style that does not yet exist in the document in step 2 above, Word creates a new style for you, based on the selected paragraph. The formatting of the paragraph does not change, but the new style name appears on the Style pop-up menu.

APPLYING STYLES

To apply a style with the Styles and Formatting task pane

1. Choose Format > Styles and Formatting (**Figure 5**) or click the Styles and Formatting button on the Formatting toolbar. The Styles and Formatting task pane appears (**Figure 46**).

2. If necessary, use the Show drop-down list (**Figure 47**) to display a specific group of styles:

   ▲ **Available formatting** are the formats and styles that have been used in the document.

   ▲ **Formatting in use** are the styles applied within the document.

   ▲ **Available styles** are the styles that have been used in the document.

   ▲ **All styles** are all of the styles included within the template on which the document is based.

   ▲ **Custom** displays the Format Settings dialog (**Figure 48**), which you can use to specify which styles appear in the list.

3. Click the name of the style you want to apply.

✔ Tips

■ You can distinguish between character styles and paragraph styles in the Style dialog by the symbol to the left of the style name (**Figure 46**).

■ The name of the currently applied style appears in the box at the top of the Styles and Formatting task pane (**Figure 46**). In addition, a dark blue border appears around the name of the currently applied style in the list.

■ When you point to the name of a style in the Styles and Formatting task pane, a box with a description of the style appears (**Figure 49**).

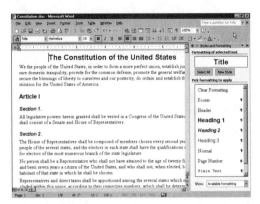

Figure 46 The Styles and Formatting task pane appears beside the document window.

Figure 47
The Show drop-down list in the Styles and Formatting task pane.

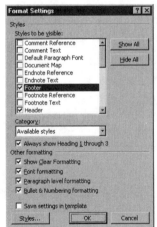

Figure 48
The Format Settings dialog enables you to customize the display of the Styles and Formatting task pane.

Figure 49
Pointing to a style displays a list of the formatting it includes.

APPLYING STYLES

Figure 50
Clicking the arrow beside a style name displays a menu of options for that style.

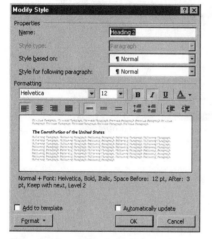

Figure 51 The Modify Style dialog.

Figure 52
The Format pop-up menu at the bottom of the Modify Style dialog.

To modify a style

1. If necessary, choose Format > Styles and Formatting (**Figure 5**) or click the Styles and Formatting button 🔲 on the Formatting toolbar to display the Styles and Formatting task pane (**Figure 46**).

2. If necessary, use the Show drop-down list (**Figure 47**) to display a specific group of styles.

3. Point to the name of the style you want to modify, and then choose Modify from its menu (**Figure 50**). The Modify Style dialog appears (**Figure 51**).

4. To change the style's name, enter a new name in the Name box.

5. To change basic style formatting options, use the drop-down lists and buttons in the Formatting area.

6. To change other formatting options, choose a type of formatting from the Format pop-up menu (**Figure 52**). Each option displays the appropriate formatting dialog. Make changes as desired in the dialog that appears and click OK.

7. Repeat step 6 as necessary to make all desired formatting changes.

8. To add the revised style to the template on which the document is based, turn on the Add to template check box.

9. To instruct Word to automatically update the style's definition whenever you apply manual formatting to text with the style applied, turn on the Automatically update check box.

10. Click OK.

MODIFYING STYLES

To create a new style

1. If necessary, choose Format > Styles and Formatting (**Figure 5**) or click the Styles and Formatting button 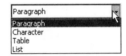 on the Formatting toolbar to display the Styles and Formatting task pane (**Figure 46**).

2. Click the New button to display the New Style dialog (**Figure 53**).

3. Enter a name for the style in the Name box.

4. Choose the type of style that you want to create from the Style type drop-down list (**Figure 54**).

5. To base the style on an existing style, choose the style from the Based on drop-down list. This menu lists all styles of the type you selected in step 4 that are included in the template on which the document is based.

6. To set basic style formatting options, use the drop-down lists and buttons in the Formatting area.

7. To set other formatting options, choose a type of formatting from the Format pop-up menu (**Figure 52**). Each option displays the appropriate formatting dialog. Set options as desired in the dialog that appears and click OK.

8. Repeat step 7 as necessary to set all desired formatting options.

9. To add the new style to the template on which the document is based, turn on the Add to template check box.

10. To instruct Word to automatically update the style whenever you apply manual formatting to text with the style applied, turn on the Automatically update check box.

11. Click OK.

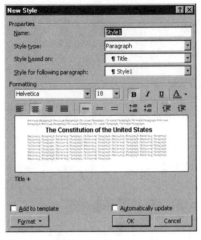

Figure 53 The New Style dialog.

Figure 54
The Style type
drop-down list.

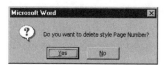

Figure 55 Word confirms that you want to delete a style.

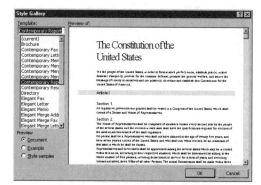

Figure 56 The Style Gallery showing a template's styles applied to the active document.

✔ Tips

- I tell you about Word's Themes feature in **Chapter 14**.

- If the template you select in step 3 has not yet been installed, a message will appear at the top of the Preview area. Click OK to install the template and apply it to your document.

To delete a style

1. If necessary, choose Format > Styles and Formatting (**Figure 5**) or click the Styles and Formatting button 🔳 on the Formatting toolbar to display the Styles and Formatting task pane (**Figure 46**).

2. If necessary, use the Show drop-down list (**Figure 47**) to display a specific group of styles.

3. Point to the name of the style you want to delete, and then choose Delete from its menu (**Figure 50**).

4. In the confirmation dialog that appears (**Figure 55**), click Yes.

✔ Tips

- When you delete a paragraph style, the default style (Normal) is applied to any text to which the deleted style was applied.

- Not all styles can be deleted. For example, you cannot delete the Heading styles that are predefined by Word.

To use the Style Gallery

1. Choose Format > Theme (**Figure 5**).

2. In the Theme dialog that appears, click the Style Gallery button to display the Style Gallery dialog.

3. Click the name of a template in the Template list to select it. An example of the document with the template's styles applied appears in the Preview area of the dialog (**Figure 56**).

4. To apply the styles of a selected template to the current document, click OK.

   or

   To close the Style Gallery dialog without changing styles, click Cancel.

DELETING STYLES, USING THE STYLE GALLERY

To attach a template to a document

1. Choose Tools > Templates and Add-Ins (**Figure 57**) to display the Templates and Add-ins dialog (**Figure 58**).

2. To update the current document's styles with styles from the template you are attaching, turn on the Automatically update document styles check box.

3. Click the Attach button.

4. Use the Attach Template dialog that appears (**Figure 59**) to locate, select, and open the template you want to attach to the document.

5. Back in the Templates and Add-ins dialog, click OK.

✔ Tips

- You can attach any Word template to a Word document—not just one of the templates that came with Microsoft Word.

- When you attach a template to a document, you make all the styles stored in the template available for use in the document.

- Attaching a template to a document is a good way to get an existing document to use standard formatting stored in a template file, even if the template was not available when the document was originally created.

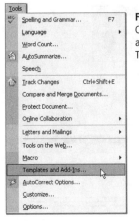

Figure 57
Choosing Templates and Add-Ins from the Tools menu.

Figure 58 The Templates and Add-ins dialog.

Figure 59 Use this dialog to locate, select, and open the template you want to attach.

Figure 60 The AutoFormat dialog.

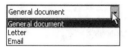

Figure 61 Use this drop-down list to tell Word what kind of document it must format.

AutoFormat

Word's AutoFormat feature can automatically format a document either as you type or when the document is finished. Word formats documents by applying appropriate styles to text based on how it is used in the document—for example, as titles, lists, headings, or body text. Word can also format Internet addresses as hyperlinks and replace typed symbols (such as --) with actual symbols (such as —).

✔ Tips

- AutoFormat As You Type is automatically turned on when you first use Word.

- I tell you more about Internet addresses and hyperlinks in **Chapter 14** and about symbols in **Chapter 7**.

To use AutoFormat on a completed document

1. Choose Format > AutoFormat (**Figure 5**) to display the AutoFormat dialog (**Figure 60**).

2. To use AutoFormat without reviewing changes, select the AutoFormat now option.

   or

   To review changes as you use AutoFormat, select the AutoFormat and review each change option.

3. Select the appropriate type of document from the drop-down list (**Figure 61**).

4. Click OK to begin the AutoFormat process.

   ▲ If you selected the AutoFormat now option in Step 2, Word formats the document and displays the changes. The AutoFormat process is complete; the rest of the steps do not apply.

continued on next page...

USING AUTOFORMAT

continued from previous page

▲ If you selected the AutoFormat and review each change option in step 2, Word formats the document. Continue with step 5.

5. A different AutoFormat dialog appears (**Figure 62**). Click one of its four buttons to proceed:

▲ **Accept All** accepts all changes to the document. The AutoFormat process is complete; the rest of the steps do not apply.

▲ **Reject All** rejects all changes to the document. The AutoFormat process is reversed; the rest of the steps do not apply.

▲ **Review Changes** enables you to review the changes one by one. The Review AutoFormat Changes dialog appears. Continue with step 6.

▲ **Style Gallery** displays the Style Gallery dialog (**Figure 56**) so you can select a different template's styles. I tell you how to use the Style Gallery earlier in this chapter. When you are finished using the Style Gallery, you will return to this dialog; click one of the other buttons to continue.

6. In the Review AutoFormat Changes dialog, click the second Find button (Find forward) to begin reviewing changes throughout the document (**Figure 63**):

▲ To accept a change, click the Find button again.

▲ To reject a change and move to the next change, click the Reject button.

7. Repeat step 6 until you have reviewed every change.

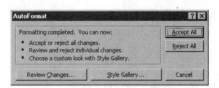

Figure 62 This AutoFormat dialog appears when Word has finished the AutoFormat process and is waiting for you to review its changes.

Figure 63 The Review AutoFormat Changes dialog lets you accept or reject each change as it is selected in the document window.

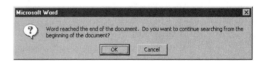

Figure 64 Word tells you when you reach the end of a document.

8. Word displays a dialog (**Figure 64**) when you reach the end of the document. Click Cancel to dismiss it.

9. Click Cancel again to return to the Auto-Format Dialog (**Figure 62**).

10. Click Accept All to accept all changes that you did not reject.

USING AUTOFORMAT

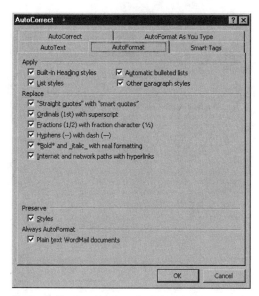

Figure 65 The AutoFormat tab of the AutoCorrect dialog.

▲ **Styles** prevents styles already applied in the document from being changed.

▲ **Plain text WordMail documents** enables you to format e-mail messages when you use Word as your e-mail editor.

4. Click OK to save your settings.

✔ Tips

■ To convert other characters to corresponding symbols, such as (tm) to ™ or (c) to ©, use the AutoCorrect feature, which I explain in **Chapter 5**.

■ I tell you about hyperlinks and other Internet-related features in **Chapter 14**.

To set AutoFormat options

1. Choose Format > AutoFormat (**Figure 5**) to display the AutoFormat dialog (**Figure 60**).

2. Click Options. The AutoFormat tab of the AutoCorrect dialog appears (**Figure 65**).

3. Set options as desired:

▲ **Built-in Heading styles** applies Word's Heading styles to heading text.

▲ **List styles** applies list and bullet styles to numbered, bulleted, and other lists.

▲ **Automatic bulleted lists** applies bulleted list formatting to paragraphs beginning with *, o, or - followed by a space or tab.

▲ **Other paragraph styles** applies other styles such as Body Text, Inside Address, and Salutation.

▲ **"Straight quotes" with "smart quotes"** replaces plain quote characters with curly quote characters.

▲ **Ordinals (1st) with superscript** formats ordinals with superscript. For example, 1st becomes 1st.

▲ **Fractions (1/2) with fraction characters ($^1/_2$)** replaces fractions typed with numbers and slashes with fraction characters.

▲ **Hyphens (- -) with dash (—)** replaces a single hyphen with an en dash (–) and a double hyphen with an em dash (—).

▲ ***Bold* and _italic_ with real formatting** formats text enclosed within asterisk characters (*) as bold and text enclosed within underscore characters as italic. For example, *hello* becomes **hello** and _goodbye_ becomes *goodbye*.

▲ **Internet and network paths with hyperlinks** formats e-mail addresses and URLs as clickable hyperlink fields.

To set automatic formatting options

1. Choose Format > AutoFormat (**Figure 5**) to display the AutoFormat dialog (**Figure 60**).

2. Click the Options button. The AutoFormat tab of the AutoCorrect dialog appears (**Figure 65**).

3. Click the AutoFormat As You Type tab to display its options (**Figure 66**).

4. Set options as desired. Most of the options are the same as those in the AutoFormat tab, which is discussed on the previous page. Here are the others:

   ▲ **Automatic numbered lists** applies numbered list formatting to paragraphs beginning with a number or letter followed by a space or tab.

   ▲ **Border lines** automatically applies paragraph border styles when you type three or more hyphens, underscores, or equal signs.

   ▲ **Tables** creates a table when you type a series of hyphens with plus signs to indicate column edges, such as +----------+-----+.

   ▲ **Format beginning of list item like the one before it** repeats character formatting that you apply to the beginning of a list item. For example, if the first word of the previous list item was formatted as bold, the first word of the next list item is automatically formatted as bold.

   ▲ **Set left- and first-indent with tabs and backspaces** sets left indentation on the ruler based on tabs and backspaces you type.

   ▲ **Define styles based on your formatting** automatically creates or modifies styles based on manual formatting that you apply in the document.

5. Click OK to save your settings.

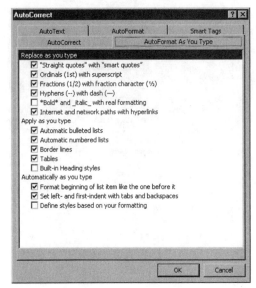

Figure 66 The AutoFormat As You Type tab of the AutoCorrect dialog.

✔ Tips

■ I tell you about borders, list formatting, and styles earlier in this chapter and about tables in **Chapter 9**.

■ Most AutoFormatting As You Type options are turned on by default. The only way to disable this feature is to turn off all options in the AutoFormat As You Type tab of the AutoCorrect dialog (**Figure 66**).

SETTING AUTOMATIC FORMATTING OPTIONS

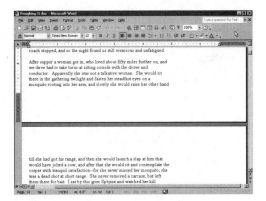

Figure 67 A page break in Print Layout view.

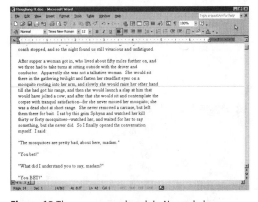

Figure 68 The same page break in Normal view.

Figure 69 A manual page break adjusts all the subsequent automatic page breaks.

Page, Section, & Column Breaks

As you work with a document, Word automatically sets page breaks based on page size, margins, and contents. A *page break* marks the end of a page; anything after the page break will appear on the next page when the document is printed. This is easy to see in Print Layout view (**Figure 67**). In Normal view, automatic page breaks appear as dotted lines across the document (**Figure 68**).

Although you cannot change an automatic page break directly, you can change it indirectly by inserting a manual page break before it (**Figure 69**). This forces the page to end where you specify and, in most cases, forces subsequent automatic page breaks in the document to change.

In addition to page breaks, Word also enables you to insert section and column breaks. A *section break* marks the end of a document section. Sections are commonly used to divide a document into logical parts, each of which can have its own settings in the Page Setup dialog. A *column break* marks the end of a column of text. Column breaks are usually used in conjunction with multi-column text.

✔ Tips

- Automatic page breaks do not appear in Web Layout or Outline view.

- As discussed in **Chapter 3**, section breaks may be automatically inserted by Word in a document when you change page formatting settings.

- Columns and multi-column text are discussed a little later in this chapter.

To insert a break

1. Position the insertion point where you want the break to occur (**Figure 70**).

2. Choose Insert > Break (**Figure 71**) to display the Break dialog (**Figure 72**).

3. Choose the option for the type of break you want to insert:

   ▲ **Page break** inserts a page break. **Figure 69** shows an inserted page break.

   ▲ **Column break** inserts a column break.

   ▲ **Text wrapping break** ends the current line and forces the text to continue after a picture or table.

   ▲ **Next page** inserts a section break that also acts as a page break.

   ▲ **Continuous** inserts a section break in the middle of a page.

   ▲ **Odd page** inserts a section break that also acts as a page break. The following page will always be odd-numbered.

   ▲ **Even page** inserts a section break that also acts as a page break. The following page will always be even-numbered.

   or

   Use one of the following shortcut keys:

   ▲ To insert a page break, press Shift Enter.

   ▲ To insert a column break, press Ctrl Shift Enter.

To remove a break

1. In Normal view, select the break by clicking in the selection bar to its left (**Figure 73**).

2. Press Backspace.

Insertion point

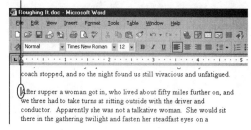

Figure 70 Position the insertion point where you want the break to occur.

Figure 71 Choose Break from the Insert menu.

Figure 72 Use the Break dialog to select the type of break to insert.

Figure 73 Click in the selection bar to the left of the break to select it.

Figure 74 Multi-column text in Print Layout view.

Figure 75 Multi-column text in Normal view.

Figure 76 Select the text for which you want to set columns.

Figure 77 Choose the number of columns from the Columns button menu on the Standard toolbar.

Figure 78 Word sets the columns for the selected text, inserting section breaks if necessary.

Columns

Word enables you to format text with multiple columns, like those in a newspaper.

✔ Tips

- Although you can edit multi-column text in any view, you must be in Print Layout view (**Figure 74**) to see the columns side by side. In Normal view, the text appears in the same narrow column (**Figure 75**).

- Column formatting applies to sections of text. You can insert section breaks as discussed on the previous page to set up various multi-column sections.

To set the number of columns

1. Select the text for which you want to set the number of columns (**Figure 76**).

2. Click the Columns button ▦ on the Standard toolbar to display a menu of columns and choose the number of columns (**Figure 77**).

If you are not in Print Layout view, Word switches to that view. The text is reformatted with the number of columns you specified (**Figure 78**).

✔ Tips

- To set the number of columns for an entire single-section document, in step 1 above, position the insertion point anywhere in the document.

- To set the number of columns for one section of a multi-section document, in step 1 above, position the insertion point anywhere in the section.

- If necessary, Word inserts section breaks to mark the beginning and end of multi-column text (**Figure 78**).

To set column options

1. Position the insertion point in the section for which you want to change column options.

   or

   Select the sections for which you want to change column options.

2. Choose Format > Columns (**Figure 5**) to display the Columns dialog (**Figure 79**).

3. To set the number of columns, click one of the icons in the Presets section or enter a value in the Number of columns box.

4. To set different column widths for each column, make sure the Equal column width check box is turned off, then enter values in the Width boxes for each column. You can also enter values in the Spacing boxes to specify the amount of space between columns.

5. To put a vertical line between columns, turn on the Line between check box.

6. To specify the part of the document that you want the changes to apply to, choose an option from the Apply to drop-down list (**Figure 80**).

   or

   To insert a column break at the insertion point, choose This point forward from the Apply to drop-down list (**Figure 80**), then turn on the Start new column check box.

7. When you are finished setting options, click OK to save them.

✔ Tip

- You can see the effect of your changes in the Preview area as you change settings in the Columns dialog.

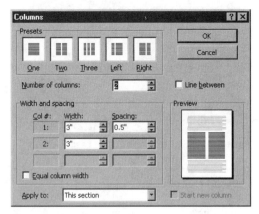

Figure 79 The Columns dialog.

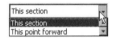

Figure 80 The Apply to drop-down list in the Columns dialog when the insertion point is in a section of a multi-section document. The options on this menu vary depending on the document and what is selected.

Figure 81
Choose Header and Footer from the View menu.

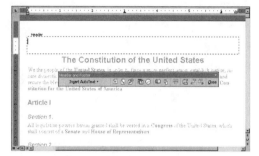

Figure 82 The Header area of a document window.

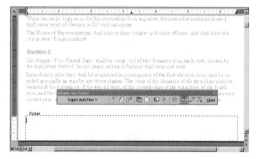

Figure 83 The Footer area of a document window.

Headers & Footers

A header is a part of the document that appears at the top of every page. A footer is a part of the document that appears at the bottom of every page. Headers and footers are commonly used to place page numbers, revision dates, or other document information on document pages.

To display a header or footer

Choose View > Header and Footer (**Figure 81**).

If necessary, Word switches to Print Layout view and displays the Header area of the current document section with the Header and Footer toolbar (**Figure 82**).

◆ To view the footer for the current section, click the Switch Between Header and Footer button 🔳 on the Header and Footer toolbar. The Footer area appears (**Figure 83**).

◆ To view the header or footer for the previous or next section of a multi-section document, click the Show Previous 🔳 or Show Next 🔳 button on the Header and Footer toolbar.

✔ Tip

■ If you are viewing a document in Print Layout view, you can view a header or footer by double-clicking in the header or footer area of a page.

To hide a header or footer

Click the Close button in the Header and Footer toolbar.

or

Double-click anywhere in the document window other than in the Header or Footer area.

The document returns to the view you were in before you viewed the header or footer. The Header and Footer toolbar disappears.

HEADERS & FOOTERS

To create a header or footer

1. Display the header or footer area (**Figure 82** or **83**) for the header or footer that you want to create.

2. Enter the header (**Figure 84**) or footer (**Figure 85**) information.

3. When you're finished, hide the header or footer area to continue working on the document.

✔ Tip

- You can format the contents of a header or footer the same way that you format any other part of the document. You can find detailed formatting instructions in **Chapter 3** and earlier in this chapter.

To edit a header or footer

1. Display the header (**Figure 84**) or footer (**Figure 85**) area for the header or footer that you want to change.

2. Edit the header or footer information.

3. When you're finished, hide the header or footer area to continue working on the document.

Figure 84 A simple header.

Figure 85 A simple footer.

Figure 86
The Insert AutoText menu on the Header and Footer toolbar.

Figure 87 The Header and Footer toolbar.

Figure 88 This footer example uses the "Author, Page #, Date" AutoText entry to insert Word fields.

To insert AutoText entries or Word fields in a header or footer

1. Position the insertion point in the Header or Footer area where you want the Auto-Text entry or field to appear.

2. To insert an AutoText entry, click the Insert AutoText button on the Header and Footer toolbar to display a menu of entries (**Figure 86**). Choose the one that you want to insert.

3. To insert a Word field, click the appropriate button on the Header and Footer toolbar (**Figure 87**) to insert the field.

✔ Tips

■ I tell you about AutoText entries and Word fields in **Chapter 7**.

■ To number pages, use the Insert Page Number button [#] on the Header and Footer toolbar or one of the first three options on the Insert AutoText button's menu (**Figure 86**) to insert a page number in the header or footer. **Figure 88** shows an example using the "Author, Page #, Date" AutoText Entry. In my opinion, using these options is the best way to number pages in a document. Using the Page Numbers command on the Insert menu inserts page numbers in frames that can be difficult to work with. The Page Numbers command is not covered in this book.

USING WORD FIELDS IN HEADERS & FOOTERS

To create a different first page or odd and even header and footer

1. Choose File > Page Setup (**Figure 89**) to display the Page Setup dialog. If necessary, click the Layout tab (**Figure 90**).

2. To create a different header and footer on odd- and even-numbered pages of the document, turn on the Different odd and even check box.

3. To create a different header and footer on the first page of the document or document section, turn on the Different first page check box.

4. Click OK.

5. Follow the instructions on the previous pages to create headers and footers as desired. Use the Show Previous [icon] and Show Next [icon] buttons on the Header and Footer toolbar to display and edit each header and footer.

To remove a header or footer

1. Display the Header or Footer area for the header or footer that you want to remove.

2. Select its contents and press (Backspace). The header or footer is removed.

3. Hide the header or footer area to continue working on the document.

Figure 89
Choose Page Setup from the File menu.

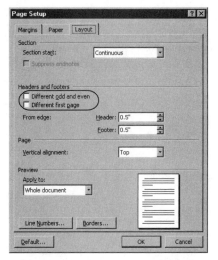

Figure 90 The Layout tab of the Page Setup dialog.

WRITING TOOLS

Word's Writing Tools

Microsoft Word includes a number of features to help you be a better writer. Some of these features can help you find and fix errors in your documents, while other features can help you fine tune your documents for publication.

Here are the writing tools covered in this chapter:

◆ The **spelling checker** compares words in your document to words in dictionary files to identify unknown words.

◆ The **grammar checker** checks sentences against a collection of grammar rules to identify questionable sentence construction.

◆ **AutoCorrect** automatically corrects common errors as you type.

◆ The **thesaurus** enables you to find synonyms or antonyms for words in your document.

◆ **Hyphenation** automatically hyphenates words based on hyphenation rules.

◆ **Word count** counts the words in a selection or the entire document.

✔ Tip

■ No proofing tool is a complete substitute for carefully rereading a document to manually check it for errors. Use Word's spelling and grammar checkers to help you find and fix errors, but don't depend on them to find all spelling or grammar errors in your documents.

The Spelling & Grammar Checkers

Word's spelling and grammar checkers help you to identify potential spelling and grammar problems in your documents. They can be set to check text automatically as you type or when you have finished typing.

The spelling checker compares the words in a document to the words in its main spelling dictionary, which includes many words and names. If it cannot find a match for a word, it then checks the active custom dictionaries—the dictionary files that you create. If Word still cannot find a match, it flags the word as unknown so you can act on it.

The grammar checker works in much the same way. It compares the structure of sentences in the document with predetermined rules for a specific writing style. When it finds a sentence or sentence fragment with a potential problem, it identifies it for you so you can act on it.

Both the spelling and grammar checkers are highly customizable so they work the way that you want them to.

✔ Tips

- The spelling checker cannot identify a misspelled word if it correctly spells another word. For example, if you type *from* when you meant to type *form*, the spelling checker would not find the error. The grammar checker, on the other hand, might find this particular error, depending on its usage.

- Do not add a word to a custom dictionary unless you *know* it is correctly spelled. Otherwise, the word will never be flagged as an error.

Figure 1
The Tools menu.

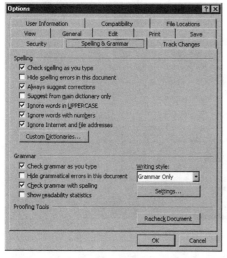

Figure 2 The default settings in the Spelling & Grammar tab of the Options dialog.

To enable or disable automatic spelling and/or grammar checking

1. Choose Tools > Options (**Figure 1**).

2. In the Options dialog that appears, click the Spelling & Grammar tab to display its options (**Figure 2**).

3. To enable automatic spelling checking, turn on the Check spelling as you type check box.

   or

   To disable automatic spelling checking, turn off the Check spelling as you type check box.

4. To enable automatic grammar checking, turn on the Check grammar as you type check box.

   or

   To disable automatic grammar checking, turn off the Check grammar as you type check box.

5. Click OK.

✔ Tips

- By default, Word is set up to automatically check spelling and grammar as you type.

- I explain how to set other spelling and grammar options in **Chapter 15**.

To check spelling as you type

1. Make sure that the automatic spelling checking feature has been enabled.

2. As you enter text into the document, a red wavy underline appears beneath each unknown word (**Figure 3**).

3. Right-click on a flagged word. The spelling shortcut menu appears (**Figure 4**).

4. Choose the appropriate option:

   ▲ Suggested spellings appear at the top of the shortcut menu. Choosing one of these spellings changes the word and removes the wavy underline.

   ▲ **Ignore All** tells Word to ignore the word throughout the document. Choosing this option removes the wavy underline from all occurrences of the word.

   ▲ **Add to Dictionary** adds the word to the current custom dictionary. The wavy underline disappears and the word is never flagged again as unknown.

   ▲ **AutoCorrect** enables you to create an AutoCorrect entry for the word using one of the suggested spellings (**Figure 5**). The word is replaced in the document and will be automatically replaced with the word you chose each time you type in the unknown word.

   ▲ **Language** enables you to set language options for the word.

   ▲ **Spelling** opens the Spelling dialog (**Figure 6**).

✔ Tips

■ As shown in **Figure 7**, Word's spelling checker also identifies repeated words and offers appropriate options.

■ AutoCorrect and the Spelling dialog are discussed later in this chapter. Language options are beyond the scope of this book.

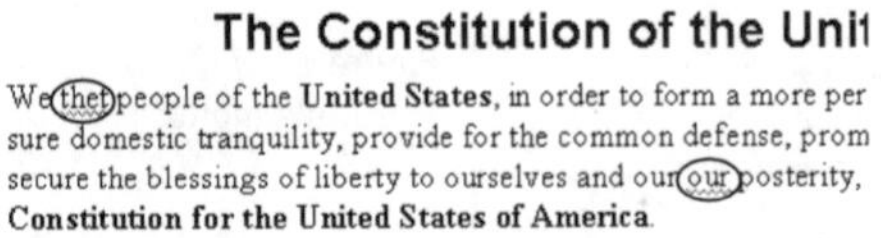

The Constitution of the Unit

We the people of the United States, in order to form a more per sure domestic tranquility, provide for the common defense, prom secure the blessings of liberty to ourselves and our our posterity, **Constitution for the United States of America**.

Figure 3 Two possible errors identified by the spelling checker.

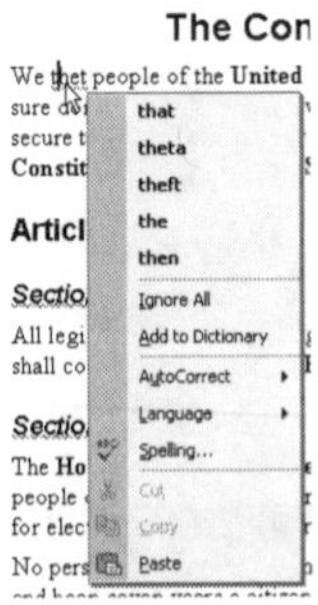

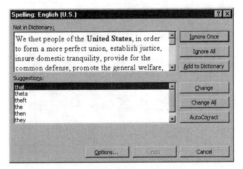

Figure 4 A shortcut menu displays options to fix a possible spelling problem.

Figure 5 The AutoCorrect option displays a submenu with the suggested words. Choose one to create an AutoCorrect entry.

Figure 6 The Spelling dialog offers additional options for dealing with possible spelling errors. This dialog is very similar to the Spelling and Grammar dialog shown in **Figures 13** and **14**.

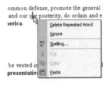

Figure 7 The shortcut menu offers different options for repeated words.

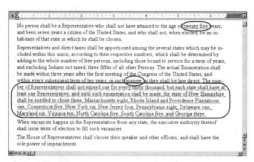

Figure 8 Three possible errors identified by the grammar checker.

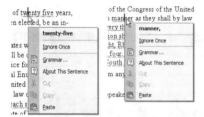

Figures 9 & 10 Using the grammar shortcut menu to correct possible grammar problems. (I wonder what our founding fathers would have thought of this!)

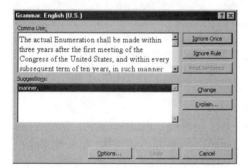

Figure 11 The Grammar dialog offers additional options for working with possible grammar problems. This dialog is very similar to the Spelling and Grammar dialog shown in **Figures 13** and **14**.

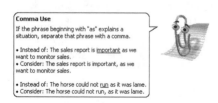

Figure 12 The Office Assistant can explain grammar rules.

To check grammar as you type

1. Make sure that the automatic grammar checking feature has been enabled.

2. As you enter text into the document, a green wavy underline appears beneath each questionable word, phrase, or sentence (**Figure 8**).

3. Right-click on a flagged problem. The grammar shortcut menu appears (**Figures 9** and **10**).

4. Choose the appropriate option:

   ▲ Suggested corrections appear near the top of the shortcut menu (**Figures 9** and **10**). Choosing one of these corrections changes the text and removes the wavy underline.

   ▲ **Ignore Once** tells Word to ignore the problem. Choosing this option removes the wavy underline.

   ▲ **Grammar** opens the Grammar dialog (**Figure 11**).

   ▲ **About this Sentence** provides information about the grammar rule that caused the sentence to be flagged (**Figure 12**). The Office Assistant must be enabled for this option to work.

✔ Tips

■ I tell you more about the Grammar dialog later in this chapter.

■ Word's grammar checker doesn't always have a suggestion to fix a problem.

■ Don't choose a suggestion without examining it carefully. The suggestion Word offers may not be correct.

To check spelling and grammar all at once

1. Choose Tools > Spelling and Grammar (**Figure 1**) or press F7.

   or

   Click the Spelling and Grammar button 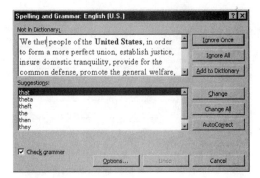 on the Standard toolbar.

   Word begins checking spelling and grammar. When it finds a possible error, it displays the Spelling and Grammar dialog (**Figures 13** and **14**).

Figure 13 The Spelling and Grammar dialog displaying options for a spelling problem.

2. For a spelling or grammar problem:

   ▲ To ignore the problem, click Ignore.

   ▲ To ignore all occurrences of the problem in the document, click Ignore All.

   ▲ To use one of Word's suggested corrections, click to select the suggestion and then click Change.

   ▲ To change the problem without using a suggestion, edit it in the top part of the Spelling and Grammar dialog. Then click Change.

   For a spelling problem only:

   ▲ To add the word to the current custom dictionary, click Add.

   ▲ To change the word throughout the document to one of the suggested corrections, click to select it and then click Change All.

   ▲ To create an AutoCorrect entry for the word, select one of the suggestions and click AutoCorrect.

3. Word continues checking. It displays the Spelling and Grammar dialog for each possible error. Repeat step 2 until the entire document has been checked.

Figure 14 The Spelling and Grammar dialog displaying options for a grammar problem.

✔ Tips

■ The Spelling and Grammar dialog contains elements found in both the Spelling dialog (**Figure 6**) and the Grammar dialog (**Figure 11**).

■ If the Office Assistant is open, it explains each grammar problem Word finds (**Figure 12**).

■ To disable grammar checking during a manual spelling check, turn off the Check grammar check box in the Spelling and Grammar dialog (**Figures 13** and **14**).

CHECKING SPELLING & GRAMMAR AT ONCE

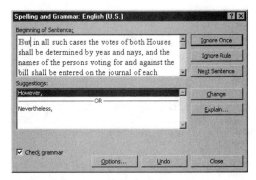

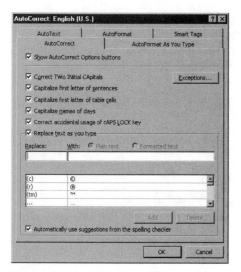

Figure 15 The AutoCorrect tab of the AutoCorrect dialog.

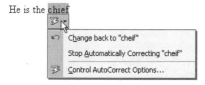

Figure 16 When Word makes an automatic correction, it displays a button you can click to display a menu of options.

AutoCorrect

Word's AutoCorrect feature can correct common typographical errors as you make them. You set up AutoCorrect entries by entering the incorrect and correct text in the AutoCorrect dialog (**Figure 15**). Then, each time you make an error for which an AutoCorrect entry exists, Word automatically corrects the error.

✔ Tips

- Word comes preconfigured with hundreds of AutoCorrect entries based on abbreviations, special symbols, and common errors.

- AutoCorrect is enabled by default.

To set AutoCorrect options

1. Choose Tools > AutoCorrect Options (**Figure 1**).

2. The AutoCorrect dialog appears. If necessary, click the AutoCorrect tab to display its options (**Figure 15**).

3. Set options as desired:

   ▲ **Show AutoCorrect Options buttons** displays a tiny blue button beside text that was automatically corrected when you point to it. Clicking this button displays a menu that you can use to reverse the correction or set Auto-Correct options (**Figure 16**).

   ▲ **Correct TWo INitial CApitals** changes the second letter in a pair of capital letters to lowercase.

   ▲ **Capitalize first letter of sentences** capitalizes the first letter following the end of a sentence.

   ▲ **Capitalize first letter of table cells** capitalizes the first letter of a word in a table cell.

Continued on next page...

Continued from previous page.

▲ **Capitalize names of days** capitalizes the names of the days of the week.

▲ **Correct accidental usage of cAPS LOCK key** corrects capitalization errors that occur when you type with [Caps Lock] down. (It also turns off [Caps Lock].)

▲ **Replace text as you type** enables the AutoCorrect feature for the AutoCorrect entries in the bottom of the dialog.

▲ **Automatically use suggestions from the spelling checker** tells Word to replace spelling errors with words from the dictionary as you type.

4. Click OK to save your settings.

Figure 17 Each AutoCorrect entry has two parts.

✔ Tip

■ To disable AutoCorrect, turn off all check boxes in the AutoCorrect tab of the Auto-Correct dialog.

To add an AutoCorrect entry

1. Choose Tools > AutoCorrect Options (**Figure 1**).

2. The AutoCorrect dialog appears. If neces-sary, click the AutoCorrect tab to display its options (**Figure 15**).

3. Type the text that you want to automati-cally replace in the Replace box.

4. Type the text that you want to replace it with in the With box (**Figure 17**).

5. Click the Add button.

6. Click OK.

✔ Tip

■ To add a formatted text entry, enter and format the replacement text in your docu-ment. Then select that text and follow the steps above. Make sure the Formatted text option button is selected before clicking the Add button in step 5.

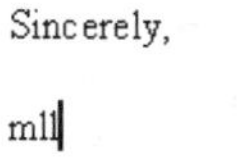

Sincerely,

mll|

Figure 18 To use an AutoCorrect entry, type the text from the Replace part of the entry...

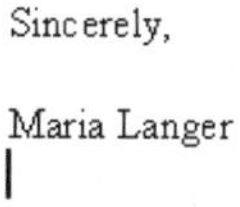

Sincerely,

Maria Langer
|

Figure 19 ...and the With part of the entry appears automatically as you continue typing.

To use AutoCorrect

In a document, type the text that appears on the Replace side of the AutoCorrect entries list (**Figure 18**). When you press ⟨Spacebar⟩, ⟨Enter⟩, ⟨Shift⟩⟨Enter⟩, or some punctuation, the text you typed changes to the corresponding text on the With side of the AutoCorrect entries list (**Figure 19**).

To delete an AutoCorrect entry

1. Choose Tools > AutoCorrect Options (**Figure 1**).

2. The AutoCorrect dialog appears. If necessary, click the AutoCorrect tab to display its options (**Figure 15**).

3. Scroll through the list of AutoCorrect entries in the bottom half of the dialog to find the entry that you want to delete and click it once to select it.

4. Click the Delete button.

5. Click OK.

USING AUTOCORRECT

The Thesaurus

Word's thesaurus enables you to find synonyms or antonyms for words in your document—without leaving Word.

To find a synonym quickly

1. Right-click on the word for which you want to find a synonym.

2. A shortcut menu appears. If the Synonyms option is available, highlight it to display a submenu of synonyms for the word (**Figure 20**).

3. To replace the word with one of the synonyms, choose it from the submenu.

To use the Thesaurus dialog

1. Select the word for which you want to find a synonym or antonym.

2. Choose Tools > Language > Thesaurus (**Figure 21**) to display the Thesaurus dialog (**Figure 22**).

3. Click to select a meaning in the Meanings list. A list of synonyms (or antonyms) appears on the right side of the dialog.

4. To replace the selected word, click to select the synonym or antonym with which you want to replace it. Then click Replace. The dialog disappears.

   or

   To look up a synonym or antonym, click it to select it and then click Look Up. Then repeat step 3.

✔ Tips

- The Looked Up drop-down list (**Figure 23**) keeps track of all the words you looked up while using the Thesaurus dialog. Choose a word from the menu to look it up again.

- To close the Thesaurus dialog without replacing a word, click its Cancel button.

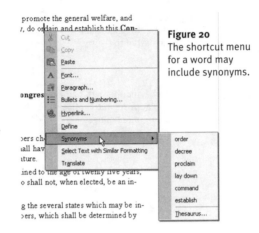

Figure 20
The shortcut menu for a word may include synonyms.

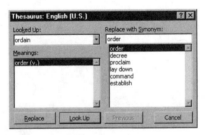

Figure 21
The Language submenu includes options for the Thesaurus and Hyphenation.

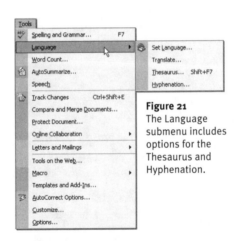

Figure 22 The Thesaurus dialog.

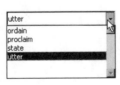

Figure 23
This drop-down list keeps track of all the words you've looked up.

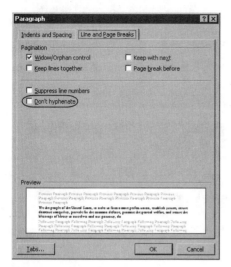

Figure 24 Use the Line and Page Breaks tab of the Paragraph dialog to prevent hyphenation in selected paragraphs.

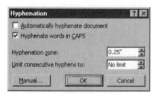

Figure 25 The default settings in the Hyphenation dialog.

✔ Tip

- To remove hyphenation inserted with the automatic hyphenation feature, turn off the Automatically hyphenate document check box in the Hyphenation dialog (**Figure 25**).

Hyphenation

Word's hyphenation feature can hyphenate words so they fit better on a line. Word can hyphenate the words in your documents automatically as you type or manually when you have finished typing.

✔ Tips

- Hyphenation helps prevent ragged right margins in left aligned text and large gaps between words in full justified text. I tell you about alignment in **Chapter 3**.

- To prevent text from being hyphenated, select it and then turn on the Don't hyphenate option in the Line and Page Breaks tab of the Paragraph dialog (**Figure 24**). I explain options in the Paragraph dialog in **Chapters 3** and **4**.

To set hyphenation options

1. Choose Tools > Language > Hyphenation (**Figure 21**) to display the Hyphenation dialog (**Figure 25**).

2. Set options as desired:
   - ▲ **Automatically hyphenate document** enables automatic hyphenation as you type. (By default, this option is turned off.)
   - ▲ **Hyphenate words in CAPS** hyphenates words entered in all uppercase letters, such as acronyms.
   - ▲ **Hyphenation zone** is the distance from the right indent within which you want to hyphenate the document. The lower the value you enter, the more words are hyphenated.
   - ▲ **Limit consecutive hyphens to** is the maximum number of hyphens that can appear in a row.

3. Click OK.

HYPHENATION

To manually hyphenate a document

1. Follow steps 1 and 2 on the previous page to open the Hyphenation dialog (**Figure 25**) and set options. Be sure to leave the Automatically hyphenate document check box turned off.

2. Click the Manual button. Word begins searching for hyphenation candidates. When it finds one, it displays the Manual Hyphenation dialog (**Figure 26**).

3. Do one of the following:

   ▲ To hyphenate the word at the recommended break, click Yes.

   ▲ To hyphenate the word at a different break, click the hyphen at the desired break and then click Yes. (The hyphen that you click must be to the left of the margin line.)

   ▲ To continue without hyphenating the word, click No.

4. Word continues looking for hyphenation candidates. It displays the Manual Hyphenation dialog for each one. Repeat step 3 until the entire document has been hyphenated.

✔ Tips

■ To hyphenate only part of a document, select the part that you want to hyphenate before following the above steps.

■ You can also manually insert two types of special hyphens within words:

   ▲ Press Ctrl - to insert an optional hyphen, which only breaks the word when necessary. Use this to manually hyphenate a word without using the Manual Hyphenation dialog.

   ▲ Press Shift Ctrl - to insert a non-breaking hyphen, which displays a hyphen but never breaks the word.

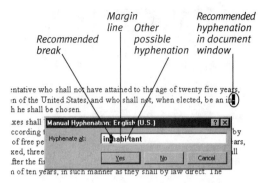

Recommended break / *Margin line* / *Other possible hyphenation* / *Recommended hyphenation in document window*

Figure 26 The Manual Hyphenation dialog.

Figure 27 The Word Count dialog.

Word Count

The word count feature counts the pages, words, characters, paragraphs, and lines in a selection or the entire document.

✔ Tip

■ The word count feature is especially useful for writers who often have word count limitations or get paid by the word.

To count pages, words, characters, paragraphs, & lines

1. If necessary, select the text that you want to count.

2. Choose Tools > Word Count (**Figure 1**) to display the Word Count dialog (**Figure 27**).

   After a moment, complete count figures appear.

3. To include footnotes and endnotes in the count, turn on the Include footnotes and endnotes check box.

4. When you are finished working with the count figures, click Close to dismiss the dialog.

PRINTING DOCUMENTS

Printing Documents

In most cases, when you've finished writing, formatting, and proofreading a document, you'll want to print it. This chapter tells you about the three parts of the printing process:

- ◆ **Page Setup** enables you to specify information about the paper size, print orientation, and paper source options.

- ◆ **Print Preview** enables you to view the document on screen before you print it. You can also use this view to set page breaks and margins to fine-tune printed appearance.

- ◆ **Print** enables you to specify the page range, number of copies, and other options for printing. It then sends the document to your printer.

✔ Tips

- ■ Although it's a good idea to go through all three parts of the printing process, you don't have to. You can just print. But as explained throughout this chapter, each part of the printing process may benefit a print job.

- ■ When you save a document, Microsoft Word saves many Page Setup and Print options with it.

- ■ This chapter assumes that your computer is already set up for printing. If it is not, consult the documentation that came with your printer for setup information.

- ■ Information about printing mailing labels, form letters, and envelopes is provided in **Chapters 10** and **11**.

Page Setup

The Page Setup dialog (**Figures 1** through **3**) enables you to set a number of options to be used when printing your document. The dialog offers three tabs of options:

- **Margins** (**Figure 1**) enables you to set margins, gutter, orientation, and multiple page options for a document. Many of these options are covered in **Chapter 3**.

- **Paper** (**Figure 2**) enables you to set the paper size and source for a print job.

- **Layout** (**Figure 3**) enables you to set section options, header and footer locations, and vertical alignment for a document or section. Most of these options are covered in **Chapters 3** and **4**.

This part of the chapter explains how to set the following options directly related to printing:

- **Orientation** is the direction of the page contents. Portrait is the default setting.

- **Paper Size** is the size of the paper. Options include standard US and European paper sizes, but you can also specify a custom paper size. US Letter is the default setting (in the US).

- **Paper Source** is the location of the paper to be used to print the first and subsequent pages of the document.

✔ Tips

- Some Page Setup options—such as paper size and orientation—affect a page's margins. If you plan to use non-standard Page Setup options, consider setting them before you create and format your document.

- Additional printing options that can be set in the Options dialog are discussed in **Chapter 15**.

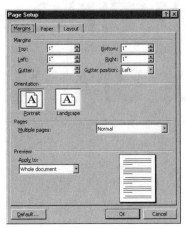

Figure 1
The Margins tab of the Page Setup dialog.

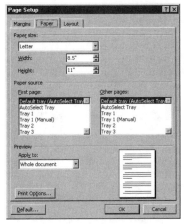

Figure 2
The Paper tab of the Page Setup dialog.

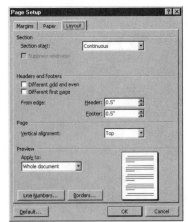

Figure 3
The Layout tab of the Page Setup dialog.

Figure 4
The File menu offers access to all three printing-related commands.

Figure 5
The Paper Size drop-down list includes many standard US and European paper sizes.

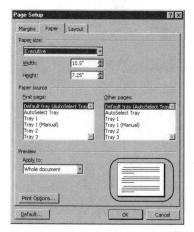

Figure 6 The Preview area of the Page Setup dialog changes when you make changes to paper size and orientation settings. In this example, Landscape orientation and Executive size paper have been selected.

To set orientation, paper size, & paper source

1. Choose File > Page Setup (**Figure 4**) to open the Page Setup dialog.

2. Click the Margins tab to display its options (**Figure 1**).

3. Select one of the two Orientation options: Portrait (the default option) or Landscape.

4. Click the Paper tab to display its options (**Figure 2**).

5. Choose one of the standard sizes from the Paper Size drop-down list (**Figure 5**).

   or

   Enter measurements in the Width and Height boxes to set a custom paper size.

6. Use the list boxes in the Paper source area to select the loading method for the first and subsequent (other) pages of the document. The options that appear here vary depending on your printer.

7. Click OK.

✔ Tip

■ The preview area in the Page Setup dialog will change to reflect changes you make to orientation and paper size settings (**Figure 6**).

PAGE SETUP

Print Preview

Word's Print Preview (**Figure 7**) displays one or more pages of a document exactly as they will appear when printed. It also enables you to make last-minute changes to margins and document contents before printing.

✔ Tip

■ Print Preview can save a lot of time and paper—it's a lot quicker to look at a document on screen than to wait for it to print, and it doesn't use a single sheet of paper!

To switch to Print Preview

Choose File > Print Preview (**Figure 4**).

or

Click the Print Preview button 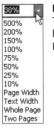 on the Standard toolbar.

✔ Tip

■ The Print Preview toolbar (**Figure 8**) appears automatically at the top of the screen when you switch to Print Preview.

To zoom in or out

1. Select the Magnifier button ![magnifier] on the Print Preview toolbar (**Figure 8**).

2. Click on the page that you want to zoom in or out on. With each click, the view toggles between 100% and the current Zoom percentage on the Print Preview toolbar.

or

Choose an option from the Zoom drop-down list on the Print Preview toolbar (**Figure 9**).

or

1. Click in the Zoom box on the Print Preview toolbar.

2. Enter a value.

3. Press (Enter).

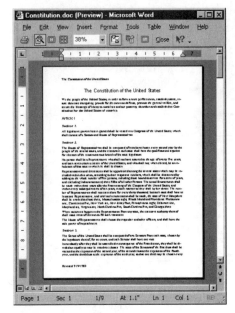

Figure 7 A single page of a document in Print Preview.

Figure 8 The Print Preview toolbar.

Figure 9
The Zoom drop-down list on the Print Preview toolbar.

Figure 10
Use the Multiple Pages button's menu to choose a layout for displaying multiple document pages.

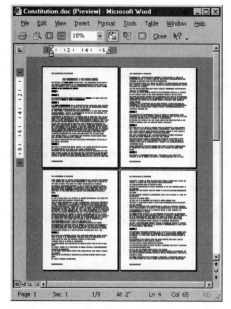

Figure 11 Four pages of a document displayed in Print Preview.

Figure 12
The mouse pointer changes when you position it on a margin on the ruler.

Figure 13
Drag to change the margin.

To view multiple pages

Click the Multiple Pages button 🔲 on the Print Preview toolbar to display a menu of page layouts and choose the one that you want (**Figure 10**).

The view and magnification change to display the pages as you specified (**Figure 11**).

✔ Tip

■ To return to a single-page view, click the One Page button 🔲 on the Print Preview toolbar.

To change margins

1. If necessary, click the View Ruler button 🔲 on the Print Preview toolbar to display the ruler in the Print Preview window (**Figure 7**).

2. Position the mouse pointer on the ruler in the position corresponding to the margin you want to change. The mouse pointer turns into a box with arrows on either end and a yellow box appears, identifying the margin (**Figure 12**).

3. Press the mouse button down and drag to change the margin. As you drag, a dotted line indicates the position of the margin (**Figure 13**). When you release the mouse button, the margin changes.

✔ Tips

■ A better way to change margins is with the Margins tab of the Page Setup dialog (**Figure 1**), which is covered in **Chapter 3**.

■ You can also use the ruler to change indentation for selected paragraphs. **Chapter 3** explains how.

To move from page to page

In Print Preview, click the Previous Page or Next Page button at the bottom of the vertical scroll bar (**Figure 14**).

To edit the document

1. If necessary, zoom in to get a better look at the text you want to edit.

2. Deselect the Magnifier button 🔍 on the Print Preview toolbar.

3. Click in the document window to position the insertion point.

4. Edit the document as desired.

To reduce the number of pages

Click the Shrink to Fit button 📑 on the Print Preview toolbar.

Word squeezes the document onto one less page by making minor adjustments to font size and paragraph spacing. It then displays the revised document.

✔ Tip

■ This feature is useful for squeezing a two-page letter onto one page when the second page only has a line or two.

To switch to a full-screen view

Click the Full Screen button 🔲 on the Print Preview toolbar.

The screen redraws to remove the status bar (**Figure 15**). This enables you to get a slightly larger view of the document page(s).

✔ Tip

■ To return to a regular Print Preview view, click the Close Full Screen button on the Full Screen toolbar.

To leave Print Preview

Click the Close button on the Print Preview toolbar (**Figure 8**).

Previous Page

Next Page

Figure 14 Use the Previous Page and Next Page buttons at the bottom of the vertical scroll bar to move from one page to another.

Full Screen toolbar

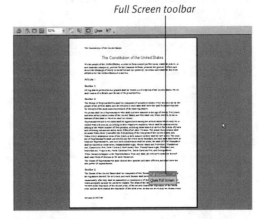

Figure 15 Full Screen view in Print Preview.

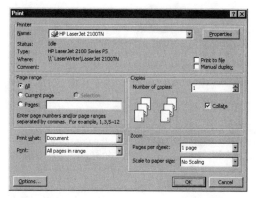

Figure 16 The Print dialog.

Printing

You use the Print dialog (**Figure 16**) to set a number of options for the print job, including:

◆ **Name** is the name of the printer to which you want to print.

◆ **Page Range** is the range of document pages you want to print.

◆ **Copies** is the number of copies of the document you want to print.

◆ **Zoom** is the number of pages to be printed per sheet and the magnification to be used for printing.

After setting options, clicking the Print button sends the document to the printer.

✔ Tip

■ These are just a few of the options offered in the Print dialog. I tell you about others on the next few pages.

To set print options & print

1. Choose File > Print (**Figure 4**), press Ctrl P, or click the Print button in the Page Setup dialog (**Figures 1** through **3**).

    The Print dialog appears (**Figure 16**).

2. If more than one printer is available to you, choose a printer from the Name drop-down list.

3. Select a Page range option:

    ▲ **All** prints all pages.

    ▲ **Current** page prints the currently selected page or the page in which the insertion point is blinking.

    ▲ **Pages** enables you to enter one or more page ranges. Separate first and last page numbers with a hyphen; separate multiple page ranges with a comma.

Continued on next page...

THE PRINT DIALOG

Continued from previous page.

4. Choose an option from the Print what drop-down list (**Figure 17**):

    ▲ **Document** prints the Word document.

    ▲ **Document properties** prints information about the document.

    ▲ **Document showing markup** prints the document with any revision marks.

    ▲ **List of markup** prints a list of document markups.

    ▲ **Styles** prints style information.

    ▲ **AutoText entries** prints a list of AutoText entries.

    ▲ **Key assignments** prints a list of shortcut keys available throughout Word.

5. If desired, choose an option from the Print drop-down list (**Figure 18**):

    ▲ **All pages in range** prints all pages in the range specified in step 3.

    ▲ **Odd pages** prints only the odd pages in the range specified in step 3.

    ▲ **Even pages** prints only the even pages in the range specified in step 3.

6. Enter the number of copies to print in the Copies box.

7. To print more than one page on each sheet of paper, choose an option from the Pages per sheet drop-down list (**Figure 19**).

8. To scale the printout so it fits on a specific paper size, choose an option from the Scale to paper size drop-down list (**Figure 20**).

9. Click OK to send the document to the printer.

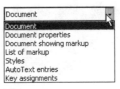

Figure 17
The Print what drop-down list enables you to specify what you want to print.

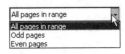

Figure 18
Use the Print drop-down list to specify which pages in the range to print.

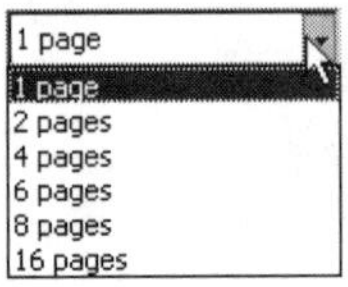

Figure 19
To print more than one page per sheet of paper, choose an option from the Pages per sheet drop-down list.

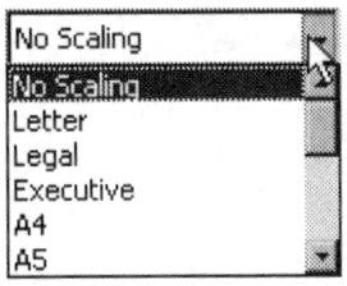

Figure 20
Set scaling options with the Scale to paper size drop-down list.

PRINTING

Figure 21 The Paper tab of the Properties dialog box is just one of four groups of printer-specific options you can set.

Figure 22 Use the Print to file dialog to name and save a document as a .PRN file.

✔ Tips

- Clicking the Print button 🖨 on the Standard or Print Preview toolbar sends the document directly to the printer without displaying the Print dialog.

- The options that vary on the Name menu in step 2 vary depending on the printers set up for your computer.

- Word's revision feature is covered in **Chapter 12**, styles are covered in **Chapter 4**, AutoText is covered in **Chapter 7**, and shortcut keys are covered in **Chapter 1**.

- If you enter a value greater than 1 in the Copies box in step 6, you can use the Collate check box to determine whether copies should be collated as they are printed.

- Clicking the Properties button displays the Properties dialog (**Figure 21**), which you can use to set printer-specific options.

- To print the document as a file on disk, turn on the Print to file check box in the Print dialog (**Figure 16**). When you click OK, you can use the Print to file dialog that appears (**Figure 22**) to save the document as a .PRN file.

PRINTING

133

INSERTING TEXT & GRAPHICS

Figure 1
The Insert menu.

Special Elements

Microsoft Word's Insert menu (**Figure 1**) includes a number of commands that you can use to insert special text and graphic elements into your documents:

- ◆ **AutoText** enables you to create and insert AutoText entries, which are commonly used text snippets, such as your name or the closing of a letter.

- ◆ **Field** enables you to insert Word fields, which are pieces of information that change as necessary, such as the date, file size, or page number.

- ◆ **Symbol** enables you to insert symbols and special characters such as bullets, smiley faces, and the registered trademark symbol (®).

- ◆ **Footnote** (on the Reference submenu) enables you to insert footnotes or end-notes, which are annotations that appear (and print) beneath text, at the bottom of the page, at the end of the section, or at the end of the document.

- ◆ **File** enables you to insert another file.

- ◆ **Picture** enables you to insert a variety of graphics, including clip art, AutoShapes, and WordArt.

✔ Tip

- ■ I discuss other Insert menu commands throughout this book:
  - ▲ Break, in **Chapter 4**
  - ▲ Comment, in **Chapter 12**
  - ▲ Index and Tables, in **Chapter 8**
  - ▲ Hyperlink, in **Chapter 14**
  - ▲ Object, in **Chapter 13**

AutoText & AutoComplete

Word's AutoText feature makes it quick and easy to insert text snippets that you use often in your documents. First, create the AutoText entry that you want to use. Then use one of two methods to insert it:

◆ Begin to type the entry or entry name. When an AutoComplete suggestion box appears (**Figure 7**), press Enter to enter the rest of the entry. This feature is known as AutoComplete.

◆ Use options on the AutoText submenu under the Insert menu (**Figure 3**) to insert the entry.

✔ Tip

■ Word comes preconfigured with dozens of AutoText entries.

To create an AutoText entry

1. Select the text that you want to use as an AutoText entry (**Figure 2**).

2. Choose Insert > AutoText > New (**Figure 3**).

3. The Create AutoText dialog appears (**Figure 4**). It displays a default name for the entry. If desired, change the name.

4. Click OK.

or

1. Choose Insert > AutoText > AutoText (**Figure 3**) to display the AutoText tab of the AutoCorrect dialog (**Figure 5**).

2. Enter the text that you want to use as an AutoText entry in the Enter AutoText entries here box.

3. Click Add. The entry appears in the scrolling list.

4. Repeat steps 2 and 3, if desired, to add additional entries.

5. When you are finished, click OK.

We the people of the United States, in sure domestic tranquility, provide for t

Figure 2 Select the text that you want to use as an AutoText entry.

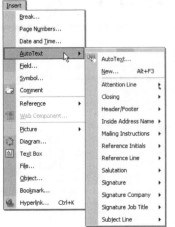

Figure 3 The AutoText submenu under the Insert menu.

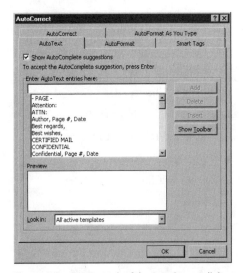

Figure 4 The Create AutoText dialog.

Figure 5 The AutoText tab of the AutoCorrect dialog.

CREATING AN AUTOTEXT ENTRY

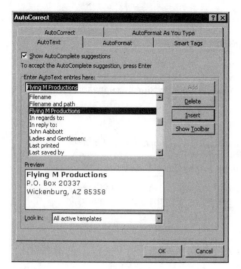

Figure 6 Selecting an AutoText entry.

To delete an AutoText entry

1. Choose Insert > AutoText > AutoText (**Figure 3**) to display the AutoText tab of the AutoCorrect dialog (**Figure 5**).

2. In the scrolling list of AutoText entries, click to select the entry that you want to delete (**Figure 6**). You can confirm that you have selected the correct entry by checking its contents in the Preview area.

3. Click Delete. The entry is removed from the scrolling list.

4. Repeat steps 2 and 3, if desired, to delete other entries.

5. When you are finished, click OK.

To enable or disable the AutoComplete feature

1. Choose Insert > AutoText > AutoText (**Figure 3**) to display the AutoText tab of the AutoCorrect dialog (**Figure 5**).

2. To enable the AutoComplete feature, turn on the Show AutoComplete suggestions check box.

   or

   To disable the AutoComplete feature, turn off the Show AutoComplete suggestions check box.

3. Click OK.

✔ Tip

■ The AutoComplete feature is turned on by default.

AUTOTEXT ENTRIES & AUTOCOMPLETE

To insert an AutoText entry with AutoComplete

1. Type text into your document.

2. When you type the first few characters of an AutoText entry, an AutoComplete suggestion box appears (**Figure 7**).

3. To enter the text displayed in the Auto-Complete suggestion, press Enter. The text you were typing is completed with the text from the AutoText entry (**Figure 8**).

    or

    To ignore the AutoComplete suggestion, keep typing.

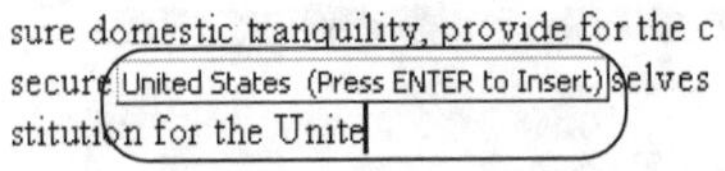

To insert an AutoText entry with the AutoText submenu

1. Position the insertion point where you want the AutoText entry to appear.

2. Use your mouse to display the AutoText submenu under the Insert menu (**Figure 3**).

3. Select the submenu option that contains the entry that you want (**Figure 9**) and select the entry. It is inserted into the document.

✔ Tip

■ The AutoText entries you create appear on the Normal submenu under the AutoText submenu.

sure domestic tranquility, provide for the c
secur[United States (Press ENTER to Insert)]elves
stitution for the Unite|

Figure 7 When you begin to type text for which there is an AutoText entry, an AutoComplete suggestion box appears.

sure domestic tranquility, provide for the c
secure the blessings of liberty to ourselves
stitution for the(United States)

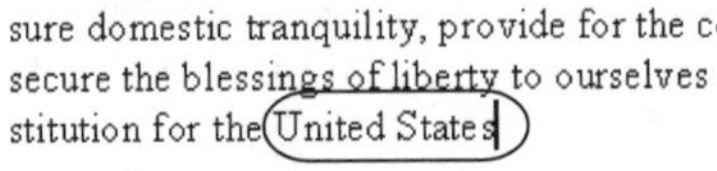

Figure 8 Press Enter to complete the text you are typing with the AutoText entry.

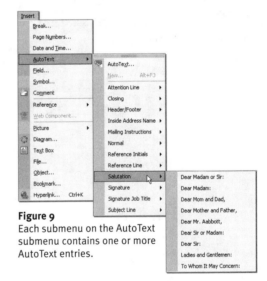

Figure 9
Each submenu on the AutoText submenu contains one or more AutoText entries.

To: John Aabbott

From: Maria Langer

Date:

Figure 10
Position the insertion point where you want the field to appear.

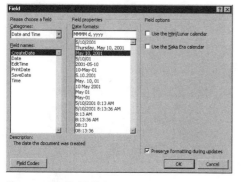

Figure 11 The Field dialog.

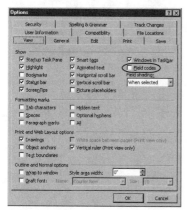

Figure 12
The Categories drop-down list.

Date: May 10, 2001|

Figure 13 In this example, the CREATEDATE field was inserted.

Date: { CREATEDATE \@ "MMMM d, yyyy" * MERGEFORMAT }

Figure 14 Here's the same field with the field codes displayed rather than the field contents.

Figure 15 Make sure Field codes is turned off in the View tab of the Options dialog.

Word Fields

Word *fields* are special codes that, when inserted in a document, display specific information. But unlike typed text, fields can change when necessary so the information they display is always up-to-date.

For example, the PrintDate field displays the date the document was last printed. If you print it again on a later date, the contents of the PrintDate field will change to reflect the new date.

✔ Tip

- Word fields is a powerful feature of Word. A thorough discussion would go far beyond the scope of this book. Instead, the following pages will provide the basic information you need to get started using Word fields.

To insert a field

1. Position the insertion point where you want the field information to appear (**Figure 10**).

2. Choose Insert > Field (**Figure 1**) to display the Field dialog (**Figure 11**).

3. Choose a code category from the Categories drop-down list (**Figure 12**).

4. In the Field names list, click to select the name of the field you want to insert.

5. In the Formats list, click to select the format for the field. The options vary for each field and are generally self-explanitory.

6. Click OK. The field is inserted in the document (**Figure 13**).

✔ Tip

- If field codes display instead of field contents (**Figure 14**), choose Tools > Options, click the View tab in the Options dialog that appears, and turn off the Field codes check box (**Figure 15**).

WORD FIELDS

139

To select a field

1. In the document window, click the field once. It turns light gray and the insertion point appears within it (**Figure 16**).

2. Drag over the field. The field turns dark gray and is selected (**Figure 17**).

✔ Tip

- Once you have selected a field, you can format it using formatting techniques discussed in **Chapter 3** or delete it by pressing Backspace.

To update a field

1. Right-click on the field to display its shortcut menu (**Figure 18**).

2. Choose Update Field. If necessary, the contents of the field changes.

✔ Tips

- To ensure that all fields are automatically updated before the document is printed, choose Tools > Options, click the Print tab in the Options dialog that appears, and turn on the Update fields check box (**Figure 19**).

- Choosing Edit Field from the field's shortcut menu (**Figure 18**) displays the Field dialog (**Figure 11**), which you can use to select a different field or different format for the field.

Figures 16 & 17
When you click a field, it turns light gray and the insertion point appears within it (top). When you drag over the field, it turns dark gray and is selected (bottom).

Figure 18
A field's shortcut menu includes the Update Field command.

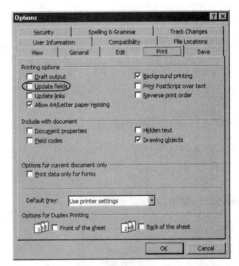

Figure 19 To ensure that all fields are updated before a document is printed, turn on the Update fields check box in the Print tab of the Options dialog.

WORD FIELDS

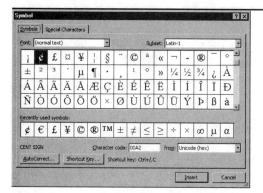

Figure 20 The Symbols tab of the Symbol window.

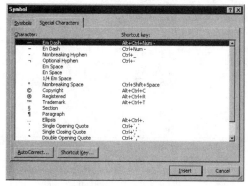

Figure 21 The Special Characters tab of the Symbol window.

Symbols & Special Characters

Symbols are special characters that don't appear on the keyboard. They include special characters within a font, such as ®, ©, ™, or é, and characters that appear only in special "dingbats" fonts, such as ■, ▲, ⇢, and ♣.

Word offers the Symbol window (**Figures 20 and 21**), which makes it easy to insert all kinds of symbols and special characters in your documents.

✔ Tips

- You don't need to use the Symbol window to insert symbols or special characters in your documents. You just need to know the keystrokes and, if necessary, the font to apply. The Symbol window takes all the guesswork out of inserting these characters.

- A *dingbats font* is a typeface that displays graphic characters rather than text characters. Monotype Sorts, Webdings, Wingdings, and Zapf Dingbats are four examples.

- In the Special Characters tab of the Symbol window (**Figure 21**), special characters appear in the current font.

To insert a symbol or special character

1. Position the insertion point where you want the character to appear (**Figure 22**).

2. Choose Insert > Symbol (**Figure 1**).

3. If necessary, click the Symbols tab in the Symbol window that appears to display its options (**Figure 20**).

4. Choose the font that you want to use to display the character from the Font drop-down list (**Figure 23**). The Characters displayed in the Symbol window change accordingly.

5. Click the character that you want to insert to select it (**Figure 24**).

6. Click Insert. The character that you clicked appears at the insertion point (**Figure 25**).

7. Repeat steps 4 though 6, if desired, to insert additional characters.

8. When you are finished inserting characters, click the close box to dismiss the Symbol window.

✔ Tips

- The (normal text) option on the Font drop-down list (**Figure 23**) uses the default font for the paragraph or character style applied to the text at the insertion point. Styles are discussed in **Chapter 4**.

- When inserting a symbol or special character in the normal font, you may prefer to use the Special Characters tab of the Symbol window (**Figure 21**). The list of special characters includes the shortcut key you can use to type the character without using the Symbol window.

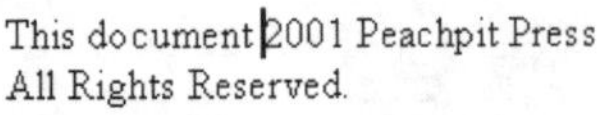

This document 2001 Peachpit Press
All Rights Reserved.

Figure 22 Position the insertion point where you want the symbol or special character to appear.

Figure 23
The Font drop-down list in the Symbol window.

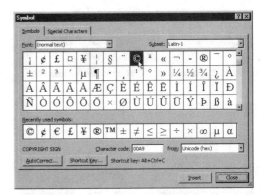

Figure 24 An example of the Symbols tab of the Symbol window being used to insert a special character in the default font.

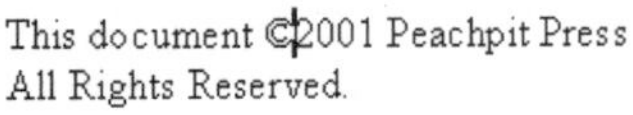

This document ©2001 Peachpit Press
All Rights Reserved.

Figure 25 The character you selected appears at the insertion point.

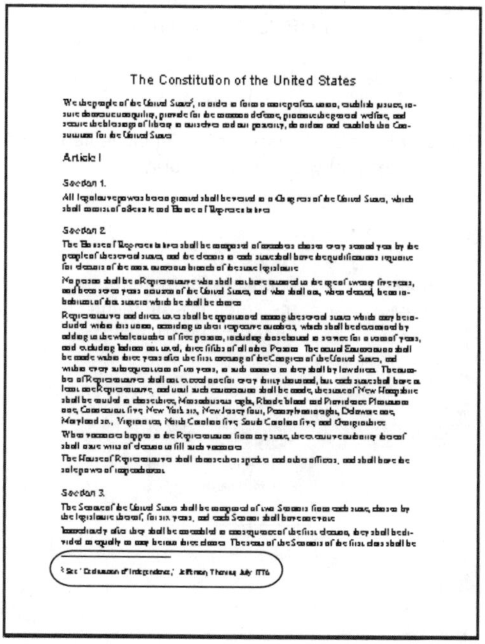

Figure 26 A page with a footnote. Word automatically inserts the footnote separator line, too.

Footnotes & Endnotes

Footnotes and endnotes are annotations for specific document text. You insert a marker—usually a number or symbol—right after the text, tell Word where you want the note to go, and enter the note. When you view the document in Print Layout view or Print Preview or print the document, the note appears where you specified.

The difference between a footnote and an endnote is its position in the document:

◆ **Footnotes** appear either after the last line of text on the page on which the annotated text appears or at the bottom of the page on which the annotated text appears (**Figure 26**).

◆ **Endnotes** appear either at the end of the section in which the annotated text appears or at the end of the document.

✔ Tips

■ Footnotes and endnotes are commonly used to show the source of a piece of information or provide additional information that may not be of interest to every reader.

■ Multiple-section documents are covered in **Chapter 4**.

■ Word automatically renumbers footnotes or endnotes when necessary when you insert or delete a note.

■ If you're old enough to remember preparing high school or college term papers on a typewriter, you'll recognize this feature as another example of how easy kids have it today. (Sheesh! I sound like my grandmother!)

To insert a footnote or endnote

1. Position the insertion point immediately after the text that you want to annotate (**Figure 27**).

2. Choose Insert > Reference > Footnote (**Figure 28**) to display the Footnote and Endnote dialog (**Figure 29**).

3. In the Location part of the dialog, select the option button for the type of note you want to insert.

4. Use the drop-down list beside the option you selected (**Figures 30** and **31**) to specify where the note should appear.

5. Choose an option from the Number format drop-down list (**Figure 32**).

   or

   Enter a character for the mark in the Custom mark box.

6. Choose an option from the Numbering drop-down list (**Figure 33**).

7. Click OK. Word inserts a marker at the insertion point, then one of two things happens:

   ▲ If you are in Normal or Online Layout view, the window splits to display a footnote or endnote pane with the insertion point blinking beside the marker (**Figure 34**).

   ▲ If you are in Print Layout view, the view shifts to the location of the footnote or endnote where a separator line is inserted. The insertion point blinks beside the marker (**Figure 35**).

8. Enter the footnote or endnote text (**Figure 36**).

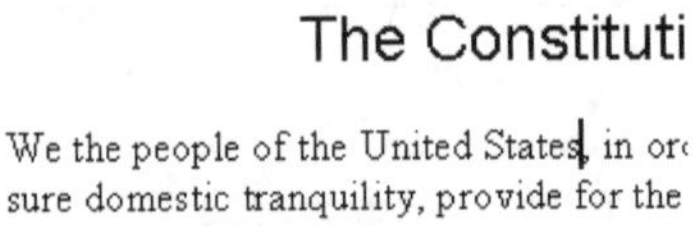

The Constituti

We the people of the United States, in ord
sure domestic tranquility, provide for the

Figure 27 Position the insertion point immediately after the text that you want to annotate.

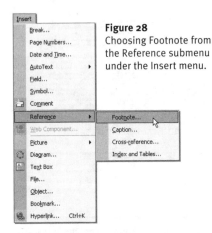

Figure 28
Choosing Footnote from the Reference submenu under the Insert menu.

Figure 29
The Footnote and Endnote dialog.

Figures 30 & 31 The Location drop-down lists for footnotes (left) and endnotes (right).

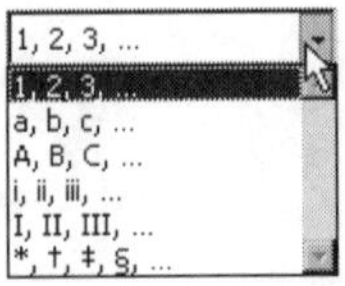

Figure 32
The Number format drop-down list.

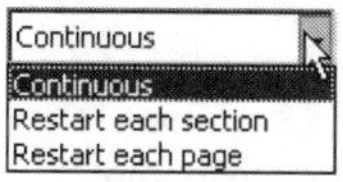

Figure 33
The Numbering drop-down list in the Footnote and Endnote dialog.

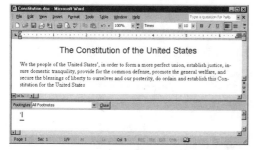

Figure 34 Entering a footnote in Normal view.

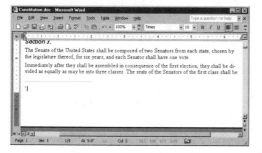

Figure 35 Entering a footnote in Print Layout view.

[1] See "Declaration of Independence," Jefferson, Thomas, July 1776|

Figure 36 Enter footnote text right after the marker.

✔ Tips

- In step 5, You can click the Symbol button to display the Symbol window (**Figure 20**), click a symbol to select it, and click OK to insert it in the Custom mark box.

- In Normal view, to close the footnote pane, click the Close button at the top of the pane.

- You can also use the Footnote and Endnote dialog (**Figure 29**) to change the options for existing footnotes and endnotes in the document. Follow the instructions on the previous page to open the dialog and set options. Click the Apply button to apply your settings and click the close button to close the dialog without inserting a note.

INSERTING FOOTNOTES & ENDNOTES

To convert notes

1. Choose Insert > Reference > Footnote (**Figure 28**) to display the Footnote and Endnote dialog (**Figure 29**).

2. Click the Convert button to display the Convert Notes dialog (**Figure 37**).

3. Select the option for the type of conversion that you want to do.

4. Click OK to dismiss the Convert Notes dialog.

5. Click the close button to dismiss the Footnote and Endnote dialog.

✔ Tip

■ The options available in the Convert Notes dialog (**Figure 37**) vary depending on the type(s) of notes in the document.

To delete a note

1. In the document window (not the note area or pane), select the note marker (**Figure 38**).

2. Press (Backspace). The note marker and corresponding note are removed from the document. If the note was numbered using the AutoNumber option, all notes after it are properly renumbered.

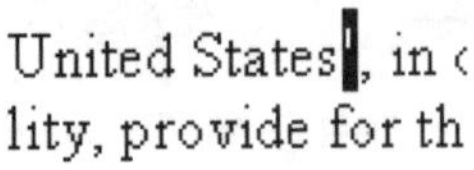

✔ Tip

■ If you have trouble selecting the tiny note marker in the document, use the Zoom drop-down list on the Standard toolbar (**Figure 39**) to increase the window's magnification so you can see it better. Zooming a window's view is covered in **Chapter 1**.

Figure 37
The Convert Notes dialog for a document that contains both footnotes and endnotes.

Figure 38 To delete a footnote or endnote, begin by selecting the note marker.

Figure 39
You can use the Zoom drop-down list on the Standard toolbar to increase the window's magnification so you can see tiny note markers.

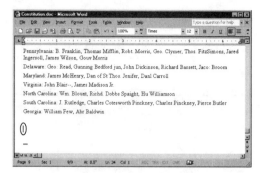

Figure 40 Position the insertion point where you want to insert the file.

Figure 41 The Insert File dialog.

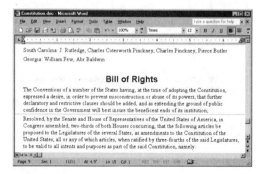

Figure 42 An inserted file.

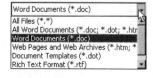

Figure 43
The Files of type drop-down list.

Files

You can use the File command under the Insert menu to insert one file (the *source* file) within another file (the *destination* file). The source file then becomes part of the destination file.

✔ Tips

- The source file can be in any format that Word recognizes.

- Copy and paste and drag and drop are two other methods for inserting the contents of one file into another. These techniques are explained in **Chapter 2**.

- A file can be inserted with or without a link. If the source file is linked, when you update the link, the destination file is updated with fresh information from the source. This means that changes in the source file are reflected in the destination file.

To insert a file

1. Position the insertion point where you want the source file to be inserted (**Figure 40**).

2. Choose Insert > File (**Figure 1**).

3. Use the Insert File dialog that appears (**Figure 41**) to locate and select the file that you want to insert.

4. Click the Insert button.

   The file is inserted (**Figure 42**).

✔ Tip

- You can use the Files of type drop-down list (**Figure 43**) to view only specific types of files in the Insert File dialog (**Figure 41**).

To insert a file as a link

Follow all of the steps on the previous page to insert a file. In step 4, choose Insert As File from the Insert button's menu (**Figure 44**).

Figure 44
The Insert button's menu.

✔ Tips

- When you click the contents of a linked file, it turns gray (**Figure 45**).

- Any changes you make in the destination file to the contents of a linked file are lost when the link is updated.

- A linked file is inserted as a field. I tell you about fields earlier in this chapter.

To update a link

1. Right-click on the linked file to display its shortcut menu (**Figure 46**).

2. Choose Update Field.

   The link's contents are updated to reflect the current contents of the source file.

✔ Tip

- If Word cannot find the source file when you attempt to update a link, it replaces the contents of the source file with an error message (**Figure 47**). There are three ways to fix this problem:

  ▲ Undo the update.

  ▲ Remove the linked file and reinsert it.

  ▲ Choose Edit > Links to fix the link with the Links dialog.

To remove an inserted file

1. Select the contents of the inserted File.

2. Press Backspace.

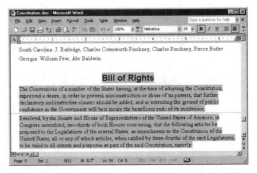

Figure 45 When you click the contents of a linked file, it turns gray.

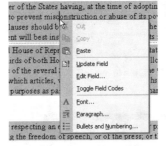

Figure 46
The shortcut menu for a linked file.

Figure 47 Word displays an error message when you attempt to update a link and it can't find the source file.

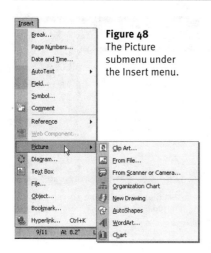

Figure 48
The Picture submenu under the Insert menu.

Pictures

Pictures are graphic objects. Word's Picture submenu (**Figure 48**) enables you to insert a variety of picture types:

◆ **Clip Art** inserts clip art, pictures, sounds, and videos from the Clip Gallery.

◆ **From File** inserts an existing picture file.

◆ **From Scanner or Camera** enables you to import images directly from a scanner or digital camera into a Word document.

◆ **Organization Chart** inserts an organization chart.

◆ **New Drawing** inserts a blank drawing.

◆ **AutoShapes** displays the AutoShapes and Drawing toolbars, which you can use to draw shapes and lines.

◆ **WordArt** inserts stylized text.

◆ **Chart** inserts a Microsoft Graph chart.

This section introduces all of these options.

✔ Tip

■ When a graphic object is inserted into a Word document, it is usually inserted in the *document layer* as an *inline image*—an image that appears on text baselines like any other text. Some graphics, however, can be drawn on or moved to the *drawing layer*. This layer is separate from the text in your Word documents and text can wrap around it.

PICTURES

To insert clip art

1. Position the insertion point where you want the clip art to appear.

2. Choose Insert > Picture > Clip Art (**Figure 48**) to display the Insert Clip Art task pane beside the document window (**Figure 49**).

3. Enter a search word in the Search text box.

4. To search only some collections, display the Search in drop-down list (**Figure 50**) and click check boxes to toggle search location options on or off.

5. To specify the type of media you want to find, display the Results should be drop-down list (**Figure 51**) and click check boxes to toggle media type options on or off.

6. Click Search.

7. Wait while Word searches for clip art that matches the criteria you specified. When it's done, it displays matches in the Insert Clip Art task pane (**Figure 52**).

8. Click the thumbnail view of a Clip Art item to insert it as an inline image in the document (**Figure 53**).

✔ Tips

- The first time you use the Clip Art command, a dialog may appear, asking whether you want to catalog all media files. Click the Now button to perform this task so you can search through the clip art files.

- You can click the plus or minus button beside an item in the Search in or Results should be drop-down list to collapse or expand its display.

Figure 49 The Insert Clip Art task pane appears beside the document window.

Figures 50 & 51 The Search in (left) and Results should be (above) drop-down lists.

Figure 52 Clip Art that matches the criteria you specified appears in the task pane.

Figure 53 Click a thumbnail to insert its image.

Figure 54 Use the Insert Picture dialog to insert a picture from a file on disk.

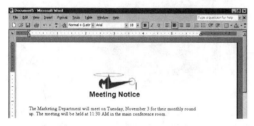

Figure 55 When you insert a picture from a file on disk, it appears at the insertion point.

To insert a picture from a file

1. Position the insertion point where you want the picture to appear.

2. Choose Insert > Picture > From File (**Figure 48**) to display the Insert Picture dialog (**Figure 54**).

3. Locate and select the file that you want to insert.

4. Click the Insert button. The file is inserted as an inline image at the insertion point (**Figure 55**).

✔ Tip

- As shown in **Figure 54**, not all images display as thumbnails in the Choose a Picture dialog.

To insert a picture from a scanner or a digital camera

1. Make sure the scanner software is properly installed and that the scanner is connected to your computer and turned on. Then place the image you wish to scan on the scanning surface.

   or

   Make sure the digital camera software is properly installed and that the camera is connected to your computer and turned on.

2. In the Word document, position the insertion point where you want the picture to appear.

3. Choose Insert > Picture > From Scanner or Camera (**Figure 48**).

4. The Insert Picture from Scanner or Camera dialog appears (**Figure 56**). If necessary, use the menu to choose the device you wish to access.

5. Click Custom Insert. A dialog with options for your device appears (**Figure 57**).

6. Follow the instructions that appear on screen to scan, select, or capture the image.

   When you are finished, the image appears in the Word document as an inline image (**Figure 58**).

✔ Tips

- If the Insert Picture from Scanner or Camera dialog (**Figure 56**) does not appear after step 3, your scanner or camera is probably not installed or connected correctly. Consult the documentation that came with the device to set it up before trying again.

- The exact procedure in step 6 varies depending on the device you are using. Word may launch your scanner or digital camera software to complete the scan or download an image. If so, consult the documentation that came with the device for complete instructions.

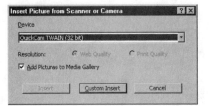

Figure 56 Use this dialog to select the scanner or camera you want to access.

Figure 57 Word displays a dialog you can use to scan, select, or capture the image. In this example, it has opened the QuickCam Twain capture window, to allow me to capture a still image from a QuickCam digital video camera. (I'm looking a bit shell-shocked here, aren't I? Deadlines!)

Figure 58 The picture appears at the insertion point in your Word document.

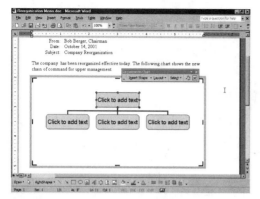

Figure 59 Word inserts a basic organization chart, all ready for customization, along with the Organization Chart toolbar.

Figure 60
Type the text you want to appear within the box.

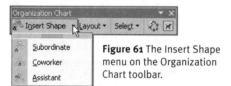

Figure 61 The Insert Shape menu on the Organization Chart toolbar.

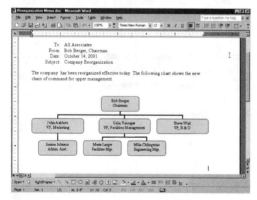

Figure 62 A completed organization chart inserted in a Word document.

To insert an organization chart

1. Position the insertion point where you want the organization chart to appear.

2. Choose Insert > Picture > Organization Chart (**Figure 48**). A box containing a basic organization chart structure appears, along with the Organization Chart toolbar (**Figure 59**).

3. Modify the basic chart to build your own custom chart:

▲ To enter information into a box, click inside the box, then type the text you want to appear (**Figure 60**).

▲ To add a box, select the box you want to attach it to and choose an option from the Insert Shape menu on the Organization Chart toolbar (**Figure 61**).

▲ To remove a box, select the box you want to remove and press Backspace.

4. When you are finished modifying the chart, click anywhere outside it. The completed chart appears as an inline image in the document and the Organization Chart toolbar disappears (**Figure 62**).

✔ Tips

■ You can format the contents of the organization chart boxes as you can any other text. Consult **Chapter 3** for details.

■ In step 2, the Drawing toolbar also appears, anchored to the bottom of the window, but it is not used to create an organization chart. The Drawing toolbar is discussed briefly on the next page.

To insert a drawing

1. Position the insertion point where you want the drawing to appear.

2. Choose Insert > Picture > New Drawing (**Figure 48**). An empty drawing canvas appears, along with the floating Drawing Canvas toolbar. The Drawing toolbar also appears anchored to the bottom of the window. You can see all this in **Figure 63**.

3. Use buttons and tools on the Drawing toolbar to create a drawing:

   ▲ To draw a line or shape, click a button or choose a menu option to select a tool and then drag in the drawing canvas.

   ▲ To move a line or shape, drag it to a new position within the drawing canvas.

   ▲ To remove a line or shape, select it and press Backspace.

4. When you are finished drawing, click anywhere outside the drawing canvas. The completed drawing appears as an inline image in the document and the Drawing Canvas toolbar disappears (**Figure 64**).

✔ Tip

■ In general, Word's drawing tools work very much like the drawing tools in other Windows application. A complete discussion of Word's drawing feature is beyond the scope of this book. Experiment with Word's tools to see how you can use them to create drawings in your documents.

Figure 63 The New Drawing command inserts an empty drawing canvas in the document and displays two toolbars.

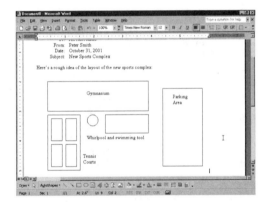

Figure 64 A completed drawing in a Word document. (Now you know why I'm a writer and not an artist.)

Figure 65 The AutoShapes and Drawing toolbars appear when you choose the AutoShapes command.

Figure 66
Click a button to display a menu of related shapes or lines.

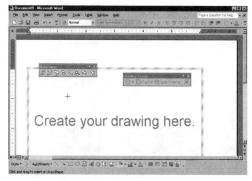

Figure 67 Selecting a drawing tool displays a drawing canvas and the Drawing Canvas toolbar.

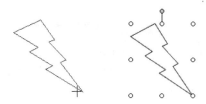

Figures 68 & 69 Drag the mouse to begin drawing the shape (left). When you release the mouse button, the shape appears with selection handles around it (right).

Figure 70
AutoShapes toolbar pop-up menus can be torn off to form their own toolbars.

To insert a shape or line

1. Choose Insert > Picture > AutoShapes (**Figure 48**). The AutoShapes and Drawing toolbars appear (**Figure 65**).

2. To draw an AutoShape, click a button on the AutoShapes toolbar to display a pop-up menu of shapes (**Figure 66**) or lines and choose the shape or line that you want to draw.

   or

   To draw a basic shape, click a button on the Drawing toolbar to select a drawing tool.

3. A drawing canvas and the Drawing Canvas toolbar appears (**Figure 67**). You have two options:

   ▲ To draw inside the drawing canvas drag to draw the shape within the drawing canvas box. When you do so, the drawing canvas remains in place so you can draw additional shapes and lines within it.

   ▲ To draw outside the drawing canvas, drag to draw the shape outside the drawing canvas box (**Figure 68**). When you do so, the drawing canvas disappears and the shape or line becomes an independent object on the document's drawing layer (**Figure 69**).

✔ Tip

■ The shape or line pop-up menu that appears when you click an AutoShapes toolbar button (**Figure 66**) can be dragged off the toolbar to create it's own toolbar (**Figure 70**).

To insert WordArt

1. Display the Word document in which you want the WordArt image to appear.

2. Choose Insert > Picture > WordArt (**Figure 48**).

3. In the WordArt Gallery dialog that appears (**Figure 71**), click to select a WordArt style.

4. Click OK.

5. In the Edit WordArt Text dialog that appears next (**Figure 72**), change the sample text to the text that you want to display. You can also select a different font and font size and turn on bold and/or italic formatting.

6. Click OK. The WordArt image is inserted as an inline image in your document (**Figure 73**).

✔ Tip

■ Once you have created a WordArt image, you can use buttons on the WordArt toolbar, which appears when the WordArt image is selected (**Figure 74**). You can click the image to select it.

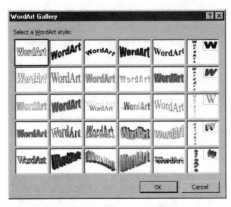

Figure 71 The WordArt Gallery dialog.

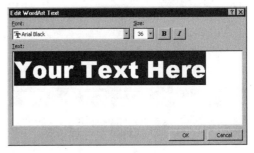

Figure 72 The default text in the Edit WordArt Text dialog.

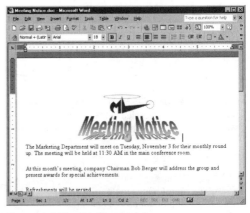

Figure 73 A WordArt image.

Figure 74 The WordArt toolbar appears when a WordArt image is selected.

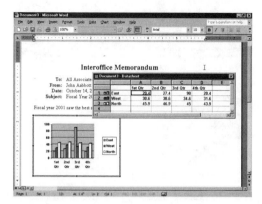

Figure 75 Word inserts a default chart and displays the corresponding Datasheet window.

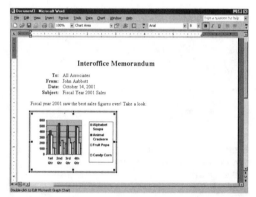

Figure 76 The completed chart appears in the document window on the drawing layer.

To insert a chart

1. Activate the Word document in which you want the chart to appear.

2. Choose Insert > Picture > Chart (**Figure 48**). Word inserts a chart in the document and displays the corresponding Datasheet window (**Figure 75**).

3. Edit the contents of the Datasheet window to reflect the data that you want to chart; the Chart window is updated automatically.

4. When you are finished, click the Datasheet window's close button. The chart is inserted as an inline image in the document (**Figure 76**).

✔ Tips

- You can edit a chart by right-clicking the chart and choosing Datasheet from the shortcut menu that appears.

- You can format a chart by double-clicking its components to display various formatting dialogs.

INSERTING CHARTS

Working with Graphic Objects

Word includes many powerful image-editing tools that you can use to work with the graphic objects in your Word documents. Although a complete discussion of all of these tools is far beyond the scope of this book, here are some instructions for performing some common image manipulation tasks.

To move a graphic object

Drag it with the mouse pointer.

◆ A graphic object in the document layer can be moved like a text character.

◆ A graphic object in the drawing layer can be moved anywhere in the document window.

To resize a graphic object

1. Click the object to select it. White or black "handles" appear around it (**Figure 77**).

2. Position the mouse pointer on a handle, press the mouse button, and drag as follows:

   ▲ Drag away from the object to make it larger.

   ▲ Drag toward the center of the object to make it smaller (**Figure 78**).

   When you release the mouse button, the object resizes (**Figure 79**).

✔ Tip

■ To resize the object proportionally, hold down [Shift] while dragging a corner handle.

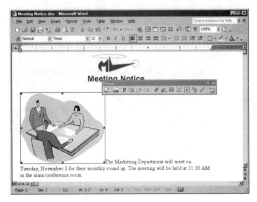

Figure 77 When you click a graphic object in the document layer, a black selection box and handles surround it and the Picture toolbar appears.

Figure 78 Drag the selection handle toward the center of the picture to make the picture smaller.

Figure 79 When you release the mouse button, the picture resizes.

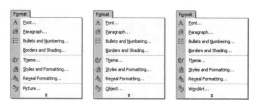

Figures 80a, 80b, & 80c The last command on the Format menu changes depending on what kind of object is selected in the document window. (These figures show the short, personalized Format menu.)

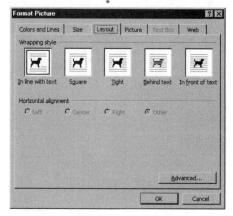

Figure 81 The Layout tab of the Format dialog enables you to set Word wrap options for a selected graphic object.

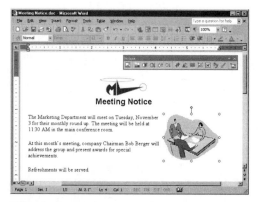

Figure 82 Once an image is set for text wrapping, you can move it anywhere in the document and text will flow around it.

To wrap text around a graphic object

1. Click the object to select it.

2. Choose the last command under the Format menu. As shown in **Figures 80a, 80b**, and **80c**, this command's name changes depending on what is selected.

3. In the Format dialog that appears, click the Layout tab to display its options (**Figure 81**).

4. Select one of the Wrapping style options:

   ▲ **In line with text** places the object in the document layer as an inline image.

   ▲ **Square** wraps text around all sides of the object with some space to spare.

   ▲ **Tight** wraps text tightly around all sides of the object.

   ▲ **Behind text** places the object behind the document layer. There is no word wrap.

   ▲ **In front of text** places the object in front of the document layer. There is no word wrap.

5. Choose one of the Horizontal alignment options to determine how the object will be aligned in the document window.

6. Click OK.

7. If you selected a Wrapping style option other than In line with text in step 4, the image is moved from the document layer to the drawing layer. Drag it into position in the document and text wraps around it (**Figure 82**).

To remove a graphic object

1. Click the object once to select it (**Figures 77** and **82**).

2. Press [Backspace]. The object disappears.

OUTLINES

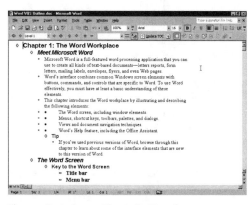

Figure 1 Part of an outline in Outline view.

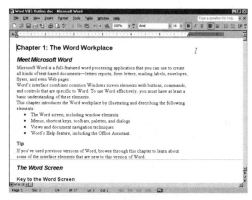

Figure 2 The outline in **Figure 1** in Normal view.

Outlines

An outline is a great tool for organizing ideas. By grouping topics and subtopics under main headings, you can set up the logical flow of a lengthy or complex document. A well-prepared outline is like a document "skeleton"—a solid framework on which the document can be built.

An outline has two components (**Figure 1**):

◆ *Headings* are topic names. Various levels of headings (1 through 9) are arranged in a hierarchy to organize and develop relationships among them.

◆ *Body text* provides information about each heading.

Microsoft Word's Outline view makes it easy to build and refine outlines. Start by adding headings that you can set to any level of importance. Then add body text. You can use drag-and-drop editing to rearrange headings and body text. You can also switch to Normal view (**Figure 2**) or another view to continue working with your document.

✔ Tips

■ Word's Outline feature automatically applies the Heading and Normal styles as you work. You can redefine these styles to meet your needs; **Chapter 4** explains how.

■ You can distinguish headings from body text in Outline view by the symbols that appear before them. Hollow dashes or plus signs appear to the left of headings while small hollow boxes appear to the left of body text (**Figure 1**).

Building an Outline

Building an outline is easy. Just create a new document, switch to Outline view, and start adding headings and body text.

✔ Tip

- You can turn an existing document into an outline by simply switching to Outline view and adding headings.

To create an outline

1. Create a new blank document.

2. Choose View > Outline (**Figure 3**).

   or

   Click the Outline View button at the bottom of the document window (**Figure 4**).

   The document switches to Outline view and the Outlining toolbar appears (**Figure 5**).

✔ Tip

- The Outlining toolbar (**Figure 6**) appears automatically any time you switch to Outline view. If it does not appear, you can display it by choosing View > Toolbars > Outline. Displaying and hiding toolbars is covered in **Chapter 1**.

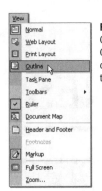

Figure 3
One way to switch to Outline view is to choose Outline from the View menu.

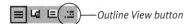—Outline View button

Figure 4 The View buttons at the bottom of the document window.

Figure 5 The document window in Outline view. The Outlining toolbar is right above the window.

Figure 6 The Outlining toolbar.

- Introduction to Word 2002

Figure 7 Enter the text that you want to use as a heading.

- Introduction to Word 2002
- |

Figure 8 When you press Enter, Word creates a new paragraph with the same heading level.

- Introduction to Word 2002
- **The Word Workplace**
- |

Figure 9 To create a new heading on the same level, simply type it in.

- Introduction to Word 2002
- **The Word Workplace**
  - *Introduction*
  - /

Figure 10 To create a heading at a lower level, click the Demote button before typing it in. When you press Enter, Word creates a new paragraph at the same (lower) heading level.

- Introduction to Word 2002
- **The Word Workplace**
  - *Introduction*
- **New & Improved Features in Word 2002**
- |

Figure 11 To create a heading at a higher level, click the Promote button while the insertion point is in the heading. When you press Enter, Word creates a new paragraph at the same (higher) heading level.

Figure 12 You can assign a specific level to a paragraph by choosing the level from the Outline Level drop-down list.

To add headings

1. Type the text that you want to use as a heading (**Figure 7**).

2. Press Enter. A new paragraph at the same heading level appears (**Figure 8**).

3. Continue using one of these techniques:

   ▲ To add a heading at the same level, repeat steps 1 and 2 (**Figure 9**).

   ▲ To add a heading at the next lower level, press Tab or click the Demote button ➡ on the Outlining toolbar. Then repeat steps 1 and 2 (**Figure 10**).

   ▲ To add a heading at the next higher level, press Shift Tab or click the Promote ⬅ button on the Outlining toolbar. Then repeat steps 1 and 2 (**Figure 11**).

   ▲ To add a heading at the Level 1 level, click the Promote to Heading 1 button ⬅ on the Outlining toolbar. Then repeat steps 1 and 2.

   ▲ To add a heading at a specific level, choose the level from the Outline Level drop-down list on the Outlining toolbar (**Figure 12**). Then repeat steps 1 and 2.

✔ Tips

■ By default, the first heading you create is Level 1—the top level. You can see the outline level in the Outline Level box `Level 1 ▾` on the Outlining toolbar when the insertion point is in the heading paragraph.

■ When you create a lower level heading beneath a heading, the marker to the left of the heading changes to a hollow plus sign to indicate that the heading has subheadings (**Figure 10**).

■ Don't worry about entering a heading at the wrong level. You can promote or demote a heading at any time—I tell you how next.

To promote or demote a heading

1. Click anywhere in the heading to position the insertion point within it (**Figure 13**).

2. To promote the heading, press ⬚Shift⬚Tab⬚ or click the Promote button ⬚ on the Outlining toolbar. The heading shifts to the left and changes into the next higher level heading (**Figure 14**).

or

To demote the heading, press ⬚Tab⬚ or click the Demote button ⬚ on the Outlining toolbar. The heading shifts to the right and changes into the next lower level heading.

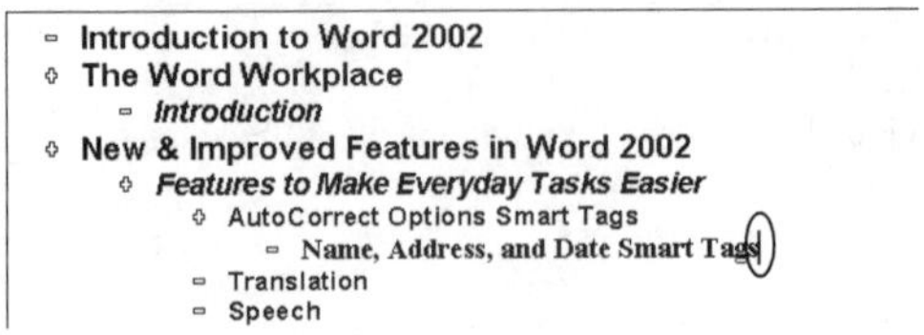

✔ Tips

■ You cannot promote a Heading 1 level heading. Heading 1 is the highest level.

■ You cannot demote a Heading 9 level heading. Heading 9 is the lowest level.

■ To promote or demote multiple headings at the same time, select the headings, then follow step 2 above.

```
▫  Introduction to Word 2002
◊  The Word Workplace
      ▫  Introduction
◊  New & Improved Features in Word 2002
      ◊  Features to Make Everyday Tasks Easier
            ◊  AutoCorrect Options Smart Tags
                  ▫  Name, Address, and Date Smart Tags
            ▫  Translation
            ▫  Speech
```

Figure 13 Position the insertion point in the heading that you want to promote or demote.

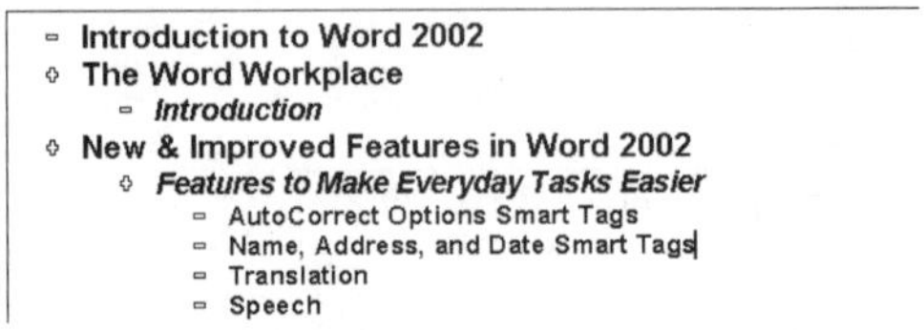

```
▫  Introduction to Word 2002
◊  The Word Workplace
      ▫  Introduction
◊  New & Improved Features in Word 2002
      ◊  Features to Make Everyday Tasks Easier
            ▫  AutoCorrect Options Smart Tags
            ▫  Name, Address, and Date Smart Tags
            ▫  Translation
            ▫  Speech
```

Figure 14 Clicking the Promote button shifts the heading to the left and changes it to the next higher heading level.

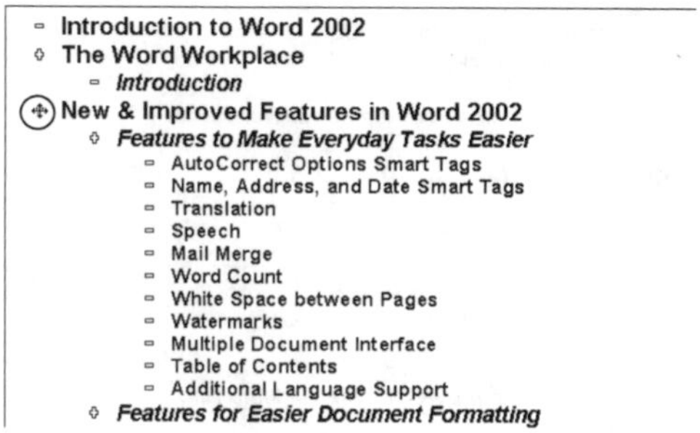

- Introduction to Word 2002
- The Word Workplace
  - *Introduction*
- ⊕ New & Improved Features in Word 2002
  - *Features to Make Everyday Tasks Easier*
    - AutoCorrect Options Smart Tags
    - Name, Address, and Date Smart Tags
    - Translation
    - Speech
    - Mail Merge
    - Word Count
    - White Space between Pages
    - Watermarks
    - Multiple Document Interface
    - Table of Contents
    - Additional Language Support
  - *Features for Easier Document Formatting*

Figure 15 Position the mouse pointer over a heading marker; it turns into a four-headed arrow.

- Introduction to Word 2002
- The Word Workplace
  - *Introduction*
- ✦ New & Improved Features in Word 2002
    - *Features to Make Everyday Tasks Easier*
    - AutoCorrect Options Smart Tags
    - Name, Address, and Date Smart Tags
    - Translation
    - Speech
    - Mail Merge
    - Word Count
    - White Space between Pages
    - Watermarks
    - Multiple Document Interface
    - Table of Contents
    - Additional Language Support
  - *Features for Easier Document Formatting*

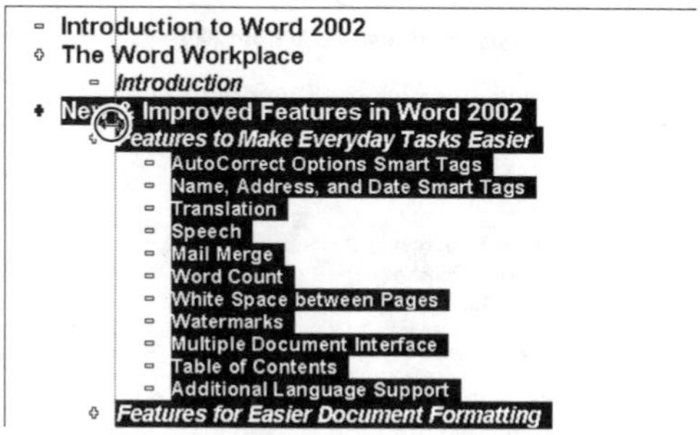

Figure 16 When you drag the heading marker, a line indicates the heading's level when you release the mouse button.

- Introduction to Word 2002
- The Word Workplace
  - *Introduction*
  - *New & Improved Features in Word 2002*
    - Features to Make Everyday Tasks Easier
      - AutoCorrect Options Smart Tags
      - Name, Address, and Date Smart Tags
      - Translation
      - Speech
      - Mail Merge
      - Word Count
      - White Space between Pages
      - Watermarks
      - Multiple Document Interface
      - Table of Contents
      - Additional Language Support
    - Features for Easier Document Formatting

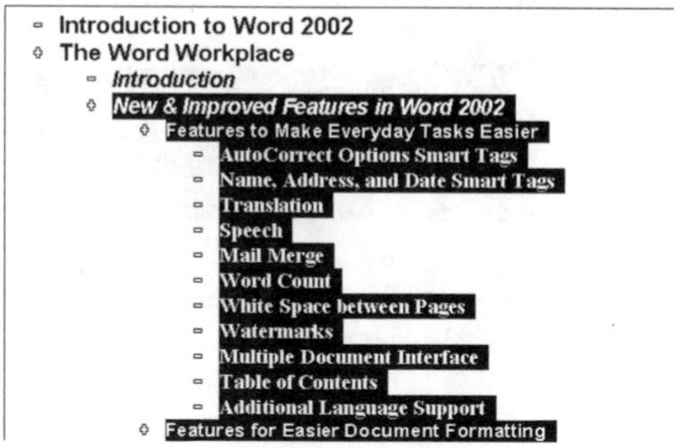

Figure 17 Release the mouse button to change the level of the heading and its subheadings.

To promote or demote a heading with its subheadings

1. Position the mouse pointer over the hollow plus sign to the left of the heading. The mouse pointer turns into a four-headed arrow (**Figure 15**).

2. To promote the headings, press the mouse button and drag to the left.

   or

   To demote the headings, press the mouse button and drag to the right (**Figure 16**).

   The heading and its subheadings are selected. As you drag, a line indicates the level to which the heading will be moved when you release the mouse button. You can see all this in **Figure 16**.

3. Release the mouse button to change the level of the heading and its subheadings (**Figure 17**).

✔ Tips

- You can also use this method to promote or demote a heading with no subheadings. Simply drag the hollow dash as instructed in step 2 to change its level.

- Another way to promote or demote a heading with its subheadings is with the Promote ⬅ or Demote ➡ button on the Outlining toolbar. Just click the hollow plus sign marker (**Figure 15**) to select the heading and its subheadings. Then click the Promote or Demote button to change the selected headings' levels.

PROMOTING & DEMOTING HEADINGS

To add body text

1. Position the insertion point at the end of the heading after which you want to add body text (**Figure 18**).

2. Press [Enter] to create a new line with the same heading level (**Figure 19**).

3. Click the Demote to Body Text button 📄 on the Outlining toolbar. The marker to the left of the insertion point changes into a small hollow square to indicate that the paragraph is body text (**Figure 20**).

4. Type the text that you want to use as body text (**Figure 21**).

✔ Tips

- Word automatically applies the Normal style to body text. You can modify the style to meet your needs; I tell you how in **Chapter 4**.

- Each time you press [Enter] while typing body text, Word creates a new paragraph of body text.

- You can convert body text to a heading by clicking the Promote ◀ or Demote ▶ button on the Outlining toolbar.

To remove outline components

1. To remove a single heading or paragraph of body text, click the hollow dash or small square marker to the left of the heading or body text. This selects the entire paragraph of the heading or body text.

   or

   To remove a heading with its subheadings and body text, click the hollow plus sign marker to the left of the heading. This selects the heading and all of its subheadings and body text (**Figure 22**).

2. Press [Backspace]. The selection is removed.

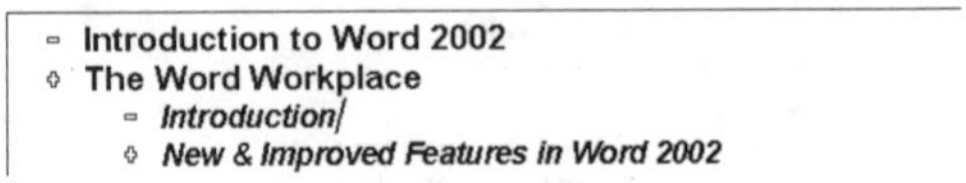

Figure 18 Position the insertion point.

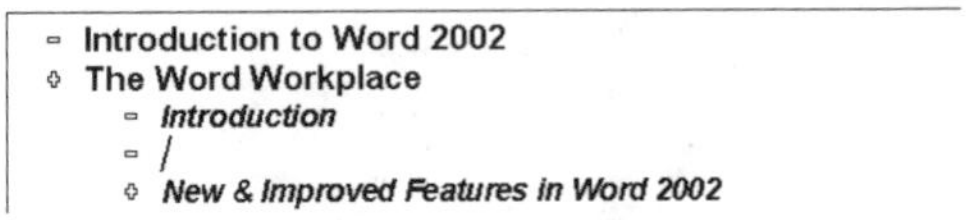

Figure 19 Press [Enter].

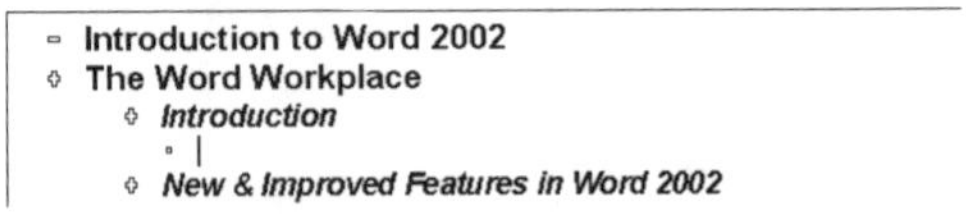

Figure 20 When you click the Demote to Body Text button, the level changes to body text.

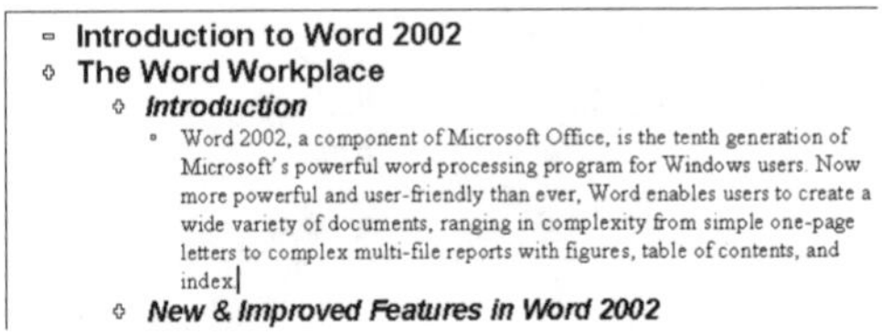

Figure 21 Type the text that you want to appear as body text.

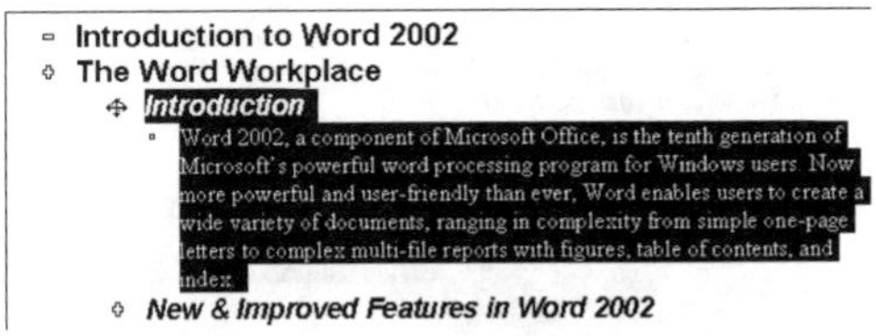

Figure 22 When you click the marker to the left of a heading, Word selects the heading and all of its subheadings and body text.

✔ Tip

- You can edit an outline in any of Word's views. Just use commands under the View menu to switch to your favorite view and edit the outline as desired.

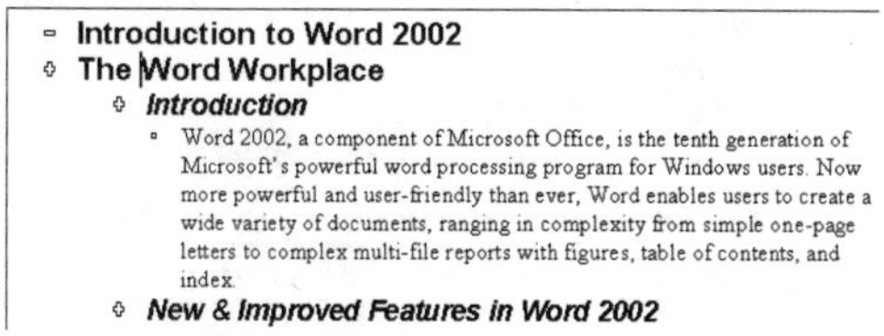

- Introduction to Word 2002
- The Word Workplace
  - *Introduction*
    - Word 2002, a component of Microsoft Office, is the tenth generation of Microsoft's powerful word processing program for Windows users. Now more powerful and user-friendly than ever, Word enables users to create a wide variety of documents, ranging in complexity from simple one-page letters to complex multi-file reports with figures, table of contents, and index.
  - *New & Improved Features in Word 2002*

Figure 23 Click to position the insertion point.

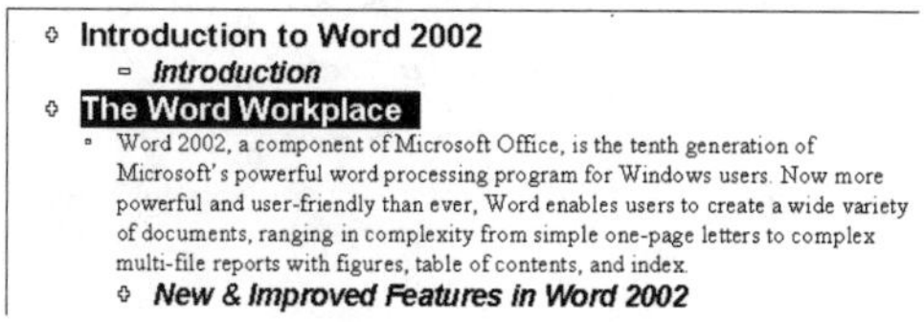

- Introduction to Word 2002
  - *Introduction*
- The Word Workplace
    - Word 2002, a component of Microsoft Office, is the tenth generation of Microsoft's powerful word processing program for Windows users. Now more powerful and user-friendly than ever, Word enables users to create a wide variety of documents, ranging in complexity from simple one-page letters to complex multi-file reports with figures, table of contents, and index.
  - *New & Improved Features in Word 2002*

Figure 24 When you click the Move Down button, the heading moves down.

Rearranging Outline Components

Word's Outline feature offers two methods to rearrange outline components:

◆ You can click the Move Up ⬆ or Move Down ⬇ button to move selected outline components up or down.

◆ You can drag heading or body text markers to move selected outline components up or down.

✔ Tips

■ Rearranging outline components using these methods changes the order in which they appear but not their level of importance.

■ Either of these methods can be used to move a single heading or paragraph of body text, multiple headings, or a heading with all of its subheadings and body text.

To move headings and/or body text with toolbar buttons

1. To move a single heading or paragraph of body text, click to position the insertion point within it (**Figure 23**).

   or

   To move a heading with its subheadings and body text, click the hollow plus sign marker to the left of the heading to select the heading, its subheadings, and its body text (**Figure 22**).

2. To move the heading up, click the Move Up ⬆ button on the Outlining toolbar. The heading moves one paragraph up.

   or

   To move the heading down, click the Move Down ⬇ button on the Outlining toolbar. The heading moves one paragraph down (**Figure 24**).

To move headings and/or body text by dragging

1. To move a single heading or paragraph of body text, position the mouse pointer over the hollow dash or small square marker to its left.

   or

   To move a heading with its subheadings and body text, position the mouse pointer on the plus sign marker to its left (**Figure 25**).

   The mouse pointer turns into a four-headed arrow (**Figure 25**).

2. To move the component(s) up, press the mouse button down and drag up (**Figure 26**).

   or

   To move the component(s) down, press the mouse button down and drag down.

   The components are selected. As you drag, a line indicates the location to which they will be moved when you release the mouse button. You can see this in **Figure 26**.

3. Release the mouse button to move the component(s) (**Figure 27**).

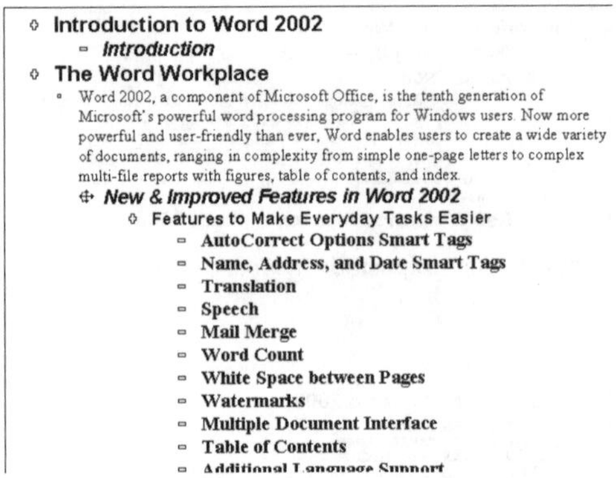

Figure 25 Position the mouse pointer over the heading marker.

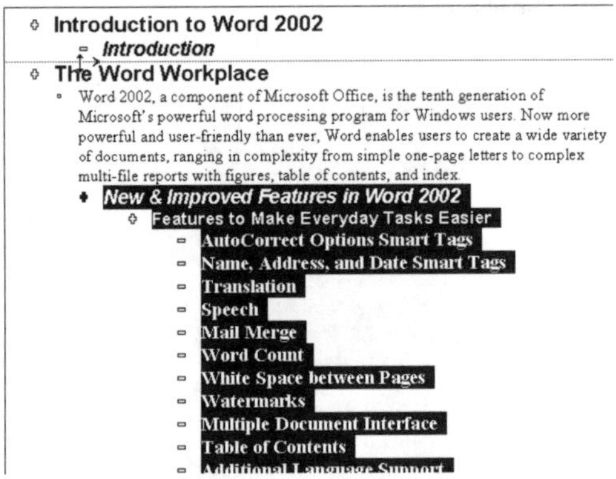

Figure 26 As you drag, a line indicates the new position when you release the mouse button.

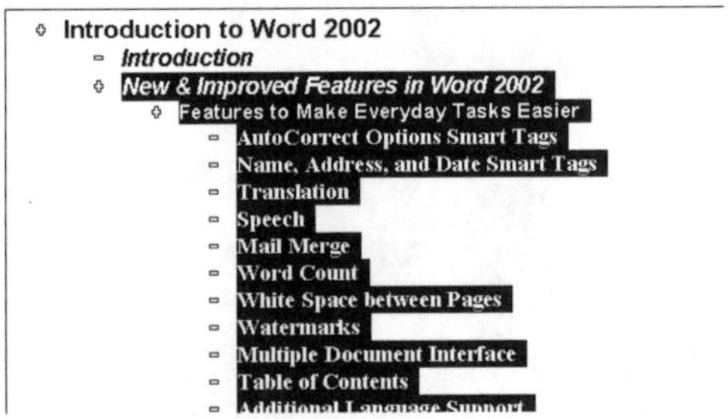

Figure 27 When you release the mouse button, the headings move.

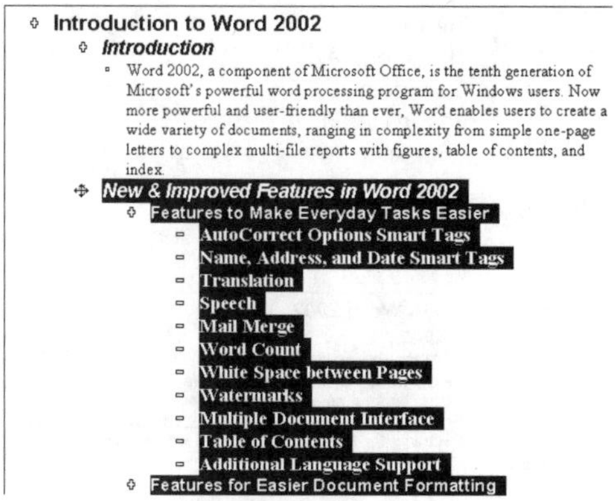

◇ Introduction to Word 2002
   ◇ *Introduction*
      ▫ Word 2002, a component of Microsoft Office, is the tenth generation of Microsoft's powerful word processing program for Windows users. Now more powerful and user-friendly than ever, Word enables users to create a wide variety of documents, ranging in complexity from simple one-page letters to complex multi-file reports with figures, table of contents, and index.
    ⇨ *New & Improved Features in Word 2002*
       ◇ Features to Make Everyday Tasks Easier
          ▫ AutoCorrect Options Smart Tags
          ▫ Name, Address, and Date Smart Tags
          ▫ Translation
          ▫ Speech
          ▫ Mail Merge
          ▫ Word Count
          ▫ White Space between Pages
          ▫ Watermarks
          ▫ Multiple Document Interface
          ▫ Table of Contents
          ▫ Additional Language Support
       ◇ Features for Easier Document Formatting

Figure 28 Click a heading's marker to select its contents.

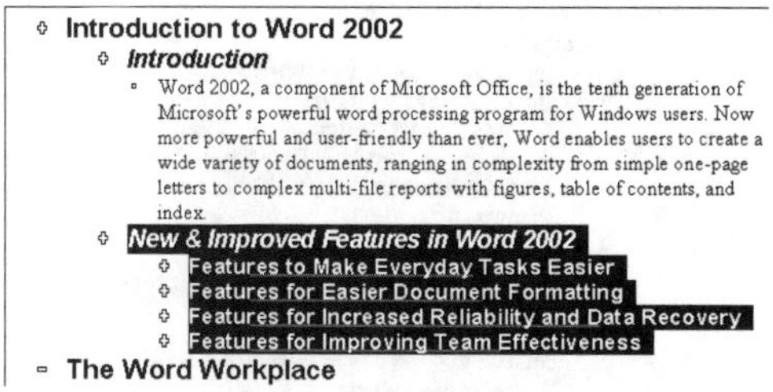

◇ Introduction to Word 2002
   ◇ *Introduction*
      ▫ Word 2002, a component of Microsoft Office, is the tenth generation of Microsoft's powerful word processing program for Windows users. Now more powerful and user-friendly than ever, Word enables users to create a wide variety of documents, ranging in complexity from simple one-page letters to complex multi-file reports with figures, table of contents, and index.
   ◇ *New & Improved Features in Word 2002*
      ◇ Features to Make Everyday Tasks Easier
      ◇ Features for Easier Document Formatting
      ◇ Features for Increased Reliability and Data Recovery
      ◇ Features for Improving Team Effectiveness
   ▫ The Word Workplace

Figure 29 When you click the Collapse button, the lowest displayed level—in this example, Level 4—is hidden.

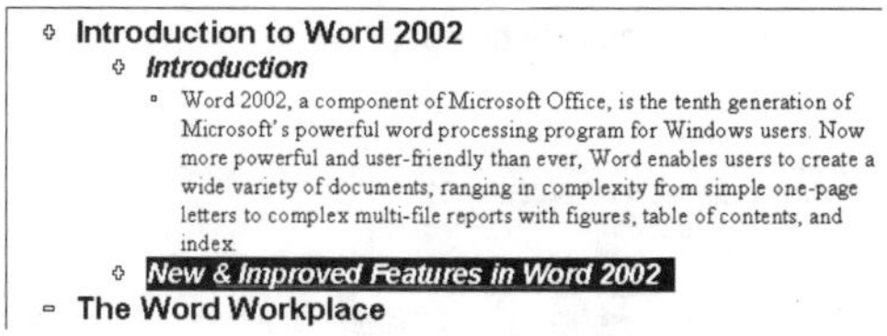

◇ Introduction to Word 2002
   ◇ *Introduction*
      ▫ Word 2002, a component of Microsoft Office, is the tenth generation of Microsoft's powerful word processing program for Windows users. Now more powerful and user-friendly than ever, Word enables users to create a wide variety of documents, ranging in complexity from simple one-page letters to complex multi-file reports with figures, table of contents, and index.
   ◇ *New & Improved Features in Word 2002*
   ▫ The Word Workplace

Figure 30 You can click the Collapse button repeatedly to hide multiple levels.

Viewing Outlines

Buttons on the Outlining toolbar (**Figure 6**) enable you to change your view of an outline:

◆ Collapse headings to hide subheadings and body text

◆ Expand headings to show subheadings and body text

◆ Show only specific heading levels

◆ Show all heading levels

◆ Show only the first line of text in each paragraph

◆ Show all lines of text in each paragraph

◆ Show or hide formatting

✔ Tip

■ These viewing options do not change the document's content—just your view of it.

To collapse a heading

1. Click the marker to the left of the heading that you want to collapse to select the heading, its subheadings, and its body text (**Figure 28**).

2. Click the Collapse button ▬ on the Outlining toolbar. The heading collapses to hide the lowest displayed level (**Figure 29**).

3. Repeat step 2 until only the levels you want to see are displayed (**Figure 30**).

or

Double-click the marker to the left of the heading that you want to collapse. The heading collapses to its level (**Figure 30**).

✔ Tip

■ When you collapse a heading with subheadings or body text, a gray line appears beneath it to indicate hidden items (**Figures 29** and **30**).

To expand a heading

1. Click the marker to the left of the heading that you want to expand to select the heading and all of its subheadings and body text.

2. Click the Expand button ⊕ on the Outlining toolbar. The heading expands to display the highest hidden level.

3. Repeat step 2 as desired to display all of the levels you want to see.

or

Double-click the marker to the left of the heading that you want to expand. The heading expands to show all levels.

To view only certain heading levels

On the Show Level drop-down list on the Outlining toolbar (**Figure 31**), choose the option that corresponds to the lowest level of heading that you want to display.

The outline collapses or expands to show just that level (**Figures 32** and **33**).

To view all heading levels

Choose Show All Levels from the Show Level drop-down list on the Outlining toolbar (**Figure 31**).

The outline expands to show all headings and body text (**Figure 34**).

Figure 31
The Show Level drop-down list on the Outlining toolbar.

◊ Introduction to Word 2002
 ◊ *Introduction*
 ◊ *New & Improved Features in Word 2002*
  ◊ Features to Make Everyday Tasks Easier
  ◊ Features for Easier Document Formatting
  ◊ Features for Increased Reliability and Data Recovery
  ◊ Features for Improving Team Effectiveness
 ▭ **The Word Workplace**

Figure 32 In this example, the Show Level 3 option was chosen to display heading levels 1, 2, and 3.

◊ Introduction to Word 2002
 ◊ *Introduction*
 ◊ *New & Improved Features in Word 2002*
  ◊ Features to Make Everyday Tasks Easier
   ◊ **AutoCorrect Options Smart Tags**
   ◊ **Name, Address, and Date Smart Tags**
   ◊ **Translation**
   ◊ **Speech**
   ◊ **Mail Merge**
   ◊ **Word Count**
   ◊ **White Space between Pages**
   ▭ **Watermarks**
   ▭ **Multiple Document Interface**
   ▭ **Table of Contents**
   ▭ **Additional Language Support**
  ◊ Features for Easier Document Formatting
   ▭ **Reveal Formatting**
   ▭ **Styles and Formatting**
   ▭ **Bulleted / Numbered Lists**
   ▭ **List Styles**
   ▭ **Table Styles**

Figure 33 In this example, the Show Level 4 Option was chosen to display heading levels 1, 2, 3, and 4.

◊ Introduction to Word 2002
 ◊ *Introduction*
  ▫ Word 2002, a component of Microsoft Office, is the tenth generation of Microsoft's powerful word processing program for Windows users. Now more powerful and user-friendly than ever, Word enables users to create a wide variety of documents, ranging in complexity from simple one-page letters to complex multi-file reports with figures, table of contents, and index.
  ▫ This Visual QuickStart Guide will help you learn Word 2002 by providing step-by-step instructions, plenty of illustration, and a generous helping of tips. On these pages, you'll find everything you need to know to get up and running quickly with Word 2002—and more!
 ◊ *New & Improved Features in Word 2002*
  ▫ Word 2002 includes many brand new features, as well as major improvements to existing features. Here's a list.
  ◊ **Features to Make Everyday Tasks Easier**
   ▫ One of Microsoft's objectives when developing Word 2002 was to make the tasks most users perform every day easier and more intuitive to perform. Here's an overview of some of the changes Microsoft made to achieve this goal.
   ◊ **AutoCorrect Options Smart Tags**
    ▫ Now, when Word's AutoCorrect feature changes your text, you can use a Smart Tag to reverse the correction or

Figure 34 Choosing Show All Levels displays all levels of headings and the body text.

◊ **Introduction to Word 2002**
  ◊ *Introduction*
    ▫ Word 2002, a component of Microsoft Office, is the tenth generation of ...
    ▫ This Visual QuickStart Guide will help you learn Word 2002 by ...
  ◊ *New & Improved Features in Word 2002*
    ▫ Word 2002 includes many brand new features, as well as major ...
    ◊ **Features to Make Everyday Tasks Easier**
      ▫ One of Microsoft's objectives when developing Word 2002 was ...
      ◊ **AutoCorrect Options Smart Tags**
        ▫ Now, when Word's AutoCorrect feature changes your ...
      ◊ **Name, Address, and Date Smart Tags**
        ▫ Name, address, and date Smart Tags make it easy to add ...
      ◊ **Translation**
        ▫ You can now tap into a variety of language translation ...
      ◊ **Speech**
        ▫ New speech features make it possible for Word to read ...
      ◊ **Mail Merge**
        ▫ Mail Merge is now easier to use, with an intuitive task ...
      ◊ **Word Count**
        ▫ The Word Count toolbar enables you to keep track of ...
      ◊ **White Space between Pages**
        ▫ You can now remove white space between pages in Print ...

Figure 35 Turning on the Show First Line Only button displays only the first line of each heading or paragraph of body text.

◊ Introduction to Word 2002
  ◊ Introduction
    ▫ Word 2002, a component of Microsoft Office, is the tenth generation of Microsoft's powerful word processing program for Windows users. Now more powerful and user-friendly than ever, Word enables users to create a wide variety of documents, ranging in complexity from simple one-page letters to complex multi-file reports with figures, table of contents, and index.
    ▫ This Visual QuickStart Guide will help you learn Word 2002 by providing step-by-step instructions, plenty of illustration, and a generous helping of tips. On these pages, you'll find everything you need to know to get up and running quickly with Word 2002—and more!
  ◊ New & Improved Features in Word 2002
    ▫ Word 2002 includes many brand new features, as well as major improvements to existing features. Here's a list.
    ◊ Features to Make Everyday Tasks Easier
      ▫ One of Microsoft's objectives when developing Word 2002 was to make the tasks most users perform every day easier and more intuitive to perform. Here's an overview of some of the changes Microsoft made to achieve this goal.
      ◊ AutoCorrect Options Smart Tags
        ▫ Now, when Word's AutoCorrect feature changes your text, you can use a Smart Tag to reverse the correction or instruct Word to stop making the correction.

Figure 36 Turning off the Show Formatting button displays all text in the default paragraph font for the Normal style—in this case, 12-point New Times Roman.

To display only the first line of every paragraph

Click the Show First Line Only button ▤ on the Outlining toolbar.

The Outline view changes to display only the first line of each heading and paragraph of body text (**Figure 35**).

✔ Tip

■ The Show First Line Only button works like a toggle switch. When turned on, only the first line of every paragraph is displayed. When turned off, all lines of every paragraph are displayed. This button is turned off by default.

To hide formatting

Click the Show Formatting button ▨ on the Outlining toolbar.

The Outline view changes to display all headings and body text in the default paragraph font for the Normal style (**Figure 36**).

✔ Tip

■ The Show Formatting button works like a toggle switch. When turned on, paragraph formatting is displayed. When turned off, all text appears in the default paragraph font for the Normal style. This button is turned on by default.

VIEWING OUTLINE TEXT

Working with an Outline in Another View

You can switch to Normal (**Figure 37**), Print Layout (**Figure 38**), or Web Layout (**Figure 37**) view while working with an outline. There's nothing special about an outline except the additional outlining features available in Outline view. It's the same document when you switch to another view.

✔ Tips

- You can switch between any of Word's views at any time.

- I explain how to switch from one view to another in **Chapter 1**.

- Once the structure of a lengthy or complex document has been established in Outline view, you may find it easier to complete the document in Normal or Print Layout view.

- In Normal, Print Layout, and Web Layout views, you can apply the Heading and Normal styles using the Style menu on the Formatting toolbar. Styles are covered in **Chapter 4**.

- The Document Map lists all of the outline's headings (**Figure 39**). Double-click a heading to move quickly to that part of the document. You can show the Document Map in Normal or Web Layout view. The Document Map is discussed in **Chapter 1**.

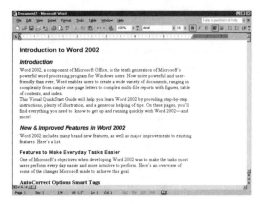

Figure 37 An outline in Normal view,...

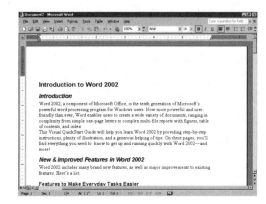

Figure 38 ...Print Layout view,...

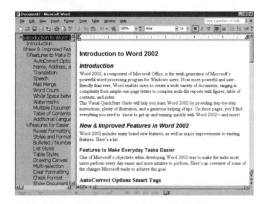

Figure 39 ...and Web Layout view with the Document Map showing.

Figure 40
Choose Index and
Tables from the
Insert menu.

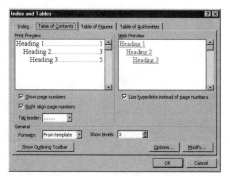

Figure 41 The Table of Contents tab of the Index
and Tables dialog.

Figure 42
The Formats
drop-down list.

Figure 43 A table of contents for three heading levels,
generated using the Formal format.

✔ Tips

- The Use hyperlinks instead of page numbers
  option in step 5 is for Word documents
  saved as Web pages. **Chapter 14** discusses
  hyperlinks and Web pages.

Creating a Table of Contents

One of the benefits of using Word's Outline
feature is that headings are easily gathered
together to create a table of contents.

✔ Tip

- Although there are other ways to generate
  a table of contents in Word, basing a table
  of contents on an outline is the easiest way.

To create a table of contents based on an outline

1. Position the insertion point where you
   want the table of contents to appear.

2. Choose Insert > Reference > Index and
   Tables (**Figure 40**).

3. In the Index and Tables dialog that appears,
   click the Table of Contents tab to display
   its options (**Figure 41**).

4. Choose one of the options in the Formats
   drop-down list (**Figure 42**). Samples appear
   in the two Preview areas.

5. Set other options throughout the dialog:

   ▲ **Show page numbers** tells Word to
     include page references for each entry.

   ▲ **Right align page numbers** aligns page
     numbers along the right side of the page.

   ▲ **Use Hyperlinks instead of page num-
     bers** turns each entry into a clickable
     link to the heading.

   ▲ **Tab leader** enables you to select the
     characters that appear between the entry
     and its page number.

   ▲ **Show levels** enables you to specify the
     number of heading levels that should
     be included in the table of contents.

6. Click OK. Word generates the table of
   contents and inserts it as a field at the
   insertion point (**Figure 43**).

TABLES

Item Name	Description	Item Number	Price
Envelopes, #10	#10 envelopes, 20 lb. white, all-purpose. 500 per box.	ENV10	$15.99/box
Envelopes, #9	#9 envelopes, 20 lb. white, all-purpose. 500 per box.	ENV09	$12.99/box
Permanent Marker, Blue	Mark of Zorro brand permanent marker. 0.5 mm felt tip. Airtight cap. Blue.	MRK01	$2.99 each
Permanent Marker, Red	Mark of Zorro brand permanent marker. 0.5 mm felt tip. Airtight cap. Red.	MRK03	$2.99 each
Laser Paper, White	White, 20 lb. paper, designed for use in laser printers. 8-1/2 x 11 inches. 500 sheets per ream.	PAP05	$5.99/ream
InkJet Paper, White	White, 20 lb. paper, designed for use in inkjet printers. 8-1/2 x 11 inches. 500 sheets per ream.	PAP11	$7.99/ream
Copier Paper, White	White, 20 lb. paper, designed for use in copy machines. 8-1/2 x 11 inches. 500 sheets per ream.	PAP01	$4.99/ream
Shipping Boxes, 9 x 12	9 x 12 inches, corrugated cardboard shipping boxes. White.	BOX05	$10.99/pkg

Figure 1 A four-column, nine-row table with borders. Each box is an individual cell.

Tables

Microsoft Word's table feature enables you to create tables of information.

A table consists of table cells arranged in columns and rows (**Figure 1**). You enter information into each cell, which is like a tiny document of its own. You can put multiple paragraphs of text into a cell and format characters or paragraphs as discussed in **Chapters 3** and **4**.

Table structure and format are extremely flexible and can be modified to meet your needs. A cell can expand vertically to accommodate long blocks of text or graphics; you can also resize it manually as desired. You can format cells, merge cells, and split cells. You can even put a table within a table cell. These capabilities make the table feature a good choice for organizing a wide variety of data.

✔ Tip

- You can also use tab stops and tab characters to create simple tables without cells. **Chapter 3** explains how to do this. This method, however, is not nearly as flexible as using cell tables.

Creating a Table

Word offers four ways to create a table:

◆ Use the **Insert Table** command and dialog to create a table at the insertion point.

◆ Use the **Insert Table** toolbar button to create a table at the insertion point.

◆ Use the **Draw Table** command and toolbar button to draw a table anywhere on a page.

Figure 2 Use commands at the top of the Table menu to create a table.

◆ Use the **Convert Text to Table** command to convert existing text to a table.

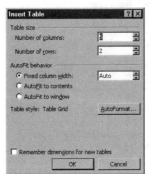

Figure 3
The Insert Table dialog.

To insert a table with the Insert Table dialog

1. Position the insertion point where you want the table to appear.

2. Choose Table > Insert > Table (**Figure 2**) to display the Insert Table dialog (**Figure 3**).

3. Enter the number of columns and rows for the table in the Number of columns and Number of rows boxes.

4. Choose an AutoFit behavior option:

   ▲ **Fixed column width** sets the width of each column regardless of its contents or the window width. If you select this option, enter Auto in the text box to set the table as wide as the print area and divide the table into columns of equal width or enter a value in the text box to specify the width of each column.

   ▲ **AutoFit to contents** sets each column to fit the contents of the widest cell in the column and makes the table as wide as all of the columns combined.

   ▲ **AutoFit to window** sets the table's width based on the width of the window and divides the table into columns of equal width.

5. Click OK. The table appears, with the insertion point in the top left cell (**Figure 5**).

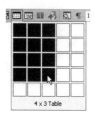

Figure 4
The Insert Table button's menu of columns and rows.

Here are some of the products we offer:

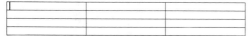

Figure 5 An empty three-column, four-row table inserted after some text.

✔ Tips

- You can click the AutoFormat button in the Insert Table dialog (**Figure 3**) to format the table as you create it. AutoFormatting tables is covered later in this chapter.

- To set the options in the Insert Table dialog (**Figure 3**) as the default options for all new tables you create, turn on the Remember dimensions for new tables check box.

- You can use this technique to insert a table into a table cell. Just make sure the insertion point is within a table cell before you choose Table > Insert > Table (**Figure 2**).

To insert a table with the Insert Table button

1. Position the insertion point where you want the table to appear.

2. Click the Insert Table button 🔲 on the Standard toolbar to display a menu of columns and rows.

3. Select the number of columns and rows you want in the table (**Figure 4**).

   The table appears, with the insertion point in the top left cell (**Figure 5**).

✔ Tips

- This is probably the fastest way to insert an empty table into a document.

- You can use this technique to insert a table into a table cell. Just make sure the insertion point is within a table cell before you use the Insert Table button's menu.

To draw a table

1. Choose Table > Draw Table (**Figure 2**) or click the Tables and Borders button on the Standard toolbar.

2. If you are not in Print Layout view, Word switches to that view. The Tables and Borders toolbar appears (**Figure 6**). If necessary, click the Draw Table button to select it.

3. Position the Draw Table tool where you want the upper-left corner of the table.

4. Press the mouse button down and drag diagonally to draw a box the size and shape of the table you want (**Figure 7**). When you release the mouse button, the outside border of the table appears (**Figure 8**).

5. Drag the Draw Table tool from the top border of the table to the bottom to draw each column boundary (**Figure 9**).

6. Drag the Draw Table tool from the left border of the table to the right to draw each row boundary (**Figure 10**).

   When you're finished, the table might look something like the one in **Figure 11**.

✔ Tip

■ Don't worry if you can't draw column and row boundaries exactly where you want them. Changing column widths and row heights is discussed later in this chapter.

Figure 6 The Tables and Borders toolbar appears when you draw a table.

Figure 7 Drag diagonally to draw a box the size and shape of the table you want.

Figure 8 The outside border for a single-cell table appears.

Figure 9 Draw vertical lines for column boundaries...

Figure 10 ...and horizontal lines for row boundaries.

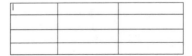

Figure 11 A drawn table.

Figure 12 Tab-separated text selected for conversion to a table.

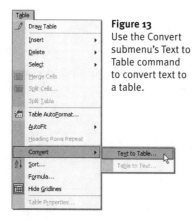

Figure 13
Use the Convert submenu's Text to Table command to convert text to a table.

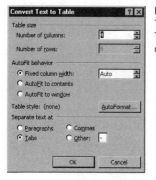

Figure 14
The Convert Text to Table dialog.

To convert text to a table

1. Select the text that you want to convert to a table (**Figure 12**).

2. Choose Table > Convert > Text to Table (**Figure 13**).

3. In the Convert Text to Table dialog that appears (**Figure 14**), confirm that the correct separator has been selected and the correct values appear in the text boxes. Make any required changes.

4. Click OK.

   The text turns into a table (**Figure 15**).

✔ Tips

- This method works best with tab- or comma-separated text.

- The AutoFit behavior options in the Convert Text to Table dialog (**Figure 14**) are the same as in the Insert Table dialog. I explain them earlier in this chapter.

- In most instances, Word will correctly "guess" the settings for the Convert Text to Table dialog (**Figure 14**) and no changes will be required in step 3 above.

Substance	Date Tested	Tested By	Results
MSG	5/18/02	Maria Langer	452.3516
Magnesium	6/4/02	John Aabbott	51.84
Sulfur	6/15/02	Mary Johannesburg	145236.145872
Aspirin	10/17/02	Tim Jones	1.1

Figure 15 The text in Figure 12 converted to a table.

Anatomy of a Table

A table includes a variety of different elements (**Figure 16**):

- **Column boundaries** appear on either side of a column.

- **Row boundaries** appear on the top and bottom of a row.

- **Cell boundaries** are the portions of column and row boundaries that appear around an individual cell.

- **End-of-cell markers** appear within each table cell. They indicate the end of the cell's contents—just like the end-of document marker marks the end of a Word document.

- **Borders** are lines that can appear on any column, row, or cell boundary. These lines print when the table is printed.

- **Gridlines** (**Figure 17**) are lines that appear on any column, row, or cell boundary. Unlike borders, however, gridlines don't print.

✔ Tips

- To see the end-of-cell marker, display nonprinting characters by turning on the Show/Hide ¶ button ▮ on the Standard toolbar. I tell you more about nonprinting characters and the Show/Hide ¶ button in **Chapter 1**.

- By default, Word creates tables with borders on all column and row boundaries. You can change or remove them using techniques discussed in **Chapter 4**.

- You can only see gridlines on boundaries that do not have borders (**Figure 17**). In addition, the Gridlines option on the Table menu (**Figure 18**) must be turned on for gridlines to appear.

End-of-cell marker

Figure 16 Table elements include column, row, and cell boundaries, end-of-cell markers, and, in this example, borders.

Figure 17 When a table has no borders, gridlines can identify the boundaries.

Figure 18
The Table menu.

Figure 19 Position the mouse pointer in the cell's selection bar.

Figure 20 Click to select the cell.

Permanent Marker, Red	Mark of Zorro brand permanent marker. 0.5 mm felt tip. Airtight cap. Red.	MRK03
Laser Paper, White	White, 20 lb. paper, designed for use in laser printers. 8-1/2 x 11 inches. 500 sheets per ream.	PAP05
Inkjet Paper, White	White, 20 lb. paper, designed for use in inkjet printers. 8-1/2 x 11 inches. 500 sheets per ream.	PAP11

Figure 21 Position the I-beam pointer at the beginning of the cell's contents.

Permanent Marker, Red	Mark of Zorro brand permanent marker. 0.5 mm felt tip. Airtight cap. Red.	MRK03
Laser Paper, White	White, 20 lb. paper, designed for use in laser printers. 8-1/2 x 11 inches. 500 sheets per ream.	PAP05
Inkjet Paper, White	White, 20 lb. paper, designed for use in inkjet printers. 8-1/2 x 11 inches. 500 sheets per ream.	PAP11

Figure 22 Drag through the cell's contents to select it.

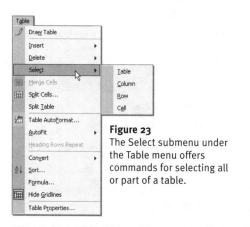

Figure 23
The Select submenu under the Table menu offers commands for selecting all or part of a table.

Selecting Table Cells

In many cases, to format the contents of table cells or restructure a table, you must begin by selecting the cells you want to change. Selecting table cells is very similar to selecting other document text, but there are some tricks to make it easier.

To select a cell

1. Position the mouse pointer in the far left side of the cell so it points to the right (**Figure 19**). This is the cell's selection bar.

2. Click once. The cell becomes selected (**Figure 20**).

or

1. Position the mouse pointer at the beginning of a cell's contents. The mouse pointer must look like an I-beam pointer (**Figure 21**).

2. Press the mouse button down and drag through the contents of the cell. When you release the mouse button, the cell is selected (**Figure 22**).

or

1. Position the insertion point anywhere within the cell you want to select.

2. Choose Table > Select > Cell (**Figure 23**).

To select a row

1. Position the mouse pointer in the selection bar of any cell in the row (**Figure 19**) in the selection bar at the far left side of the window.

2. Double-click. The entire row becomes selected (**Figure 24**).

or

1. Click to position the blinking insertion point in any cell in the row (**Figure 25**) or select any cell in the row (**Figure 22**).

2. Choose Table > Select > Row (**Figure 23**). The entire row is selected (**Figure 26**).

To select a column

1. Position the mouse pointer over the top boundary of the column that you want to select. It turns into an arrow pointing down (**Figure 27**).

2. Click once. The column is selected (**Figure 28**).

or

Hold down Alt while clicking anywhere in the column that you want to select.

or

1. Click to position the blinking insertion point in any cell in the column (**Figure 25**) or select any cell in the column (**Figure 22**).

2. Choose Table > Select > Column (**Figure 23**). The entire column is selected (**Figure 29**).

To select the entire table

Hold down Alt while double-clicking anywhere in the table. The table is selected (**Figure 30**).

or

1. Click to position the blinking insertion point in any cell in the table (**Figure 25**) or select any cell in the table (**Figure 22**).

2. Choose Table > Select > Table (**Figure 23**). The entire table is selected (**Figure 31**).

Figure 24 Double-click in a cell's selection bar to select the entire row.

Permanent Marker, Red	Mark of Zorro brand permanent marker. 0.5 mm felt tip. Airtight cap. Red.	MRK03
Laser Paper, White	White, 20 lb. paper, designed for use in laser printers. 8-1/2 x 11 inches. 500 sheets per ream.	PAP05
Inkjet Paper, White	White, 20 lb. paper, designed for use in inkjet printers. 8-1/2 x 11 inches. 500 sheets per ream.	PAP11

Figure 25 Position the insertion point in any cell in the row.

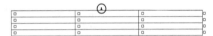

Permanent Marker, Red	Mark of Zorro brand permanent marker. 0.5 mm felt tip. Airtight cap. Red.	MRK03
Laser Paper, White	White, 20 lb. paper, designed for use in laser printers. 8-1/2 x 11 inches. 500 sheets per ream.	PAP05
Inkjet Paper, White	White, 20 lb. paper, designed for use in inkjet printers. 8-1/2 x 11 inches. 500 sheets per ream.	PAP11

Figure 26 When you choose Table > Select > Row, the entire row is selected.

Figure 27 Position the mouse pointer over the top boundary of the column.

Figure 28 Click once to select the column.

Permanent Marker, Red	Mark of Zorro brand permanent marker. 0.5 mm felt tip. Airtight cap. Red.	MRK03
Laser Paper, White	White, 20 lb. paper, designed for use in laser printers. 8-1/2 x 11 inches. 500 sheets per ream.	PAP05
Inkjet Paper, White	White, 20 lb. paper, designed for use in inkjet printers. 8-1/2 x 11 inches. 500 sheets per ream.	PAP11

Figure 29 When you choose Table > Select > Column, the entire column is selected.

Figure 30 A selected table.

Permanent Marker, Red	Mark of Zorro brand permanent marker. 0.5 mm felt tip. Airtight cap. Red.	MRK03
Laser Paper, White	White, 20 lb. paper, designed for use in laser printers. 8-1/2 x 11 inches. 500 sheets per ream.	PAP05
Inkjet Paper, White	White, 20 lb. paper, designed for use in inkjet printers. 8-1/2 x 11 inches. 500 sheets per ream.	PAP11

Figure 31 Another selected table.

Figure 32 Position the insertion point in the cell in which you want to enter text.

Figure 33 Type to enter the text.

Figure 34 Select the text that you want to move into a cell.

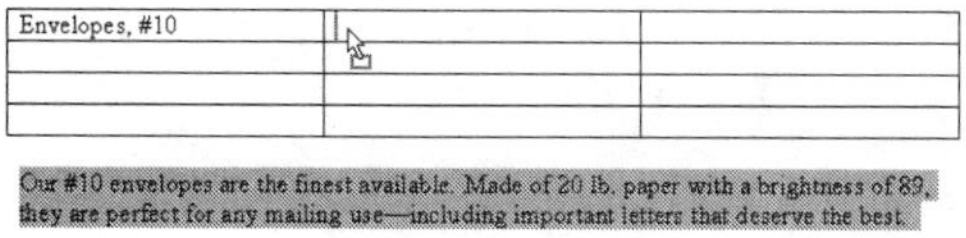

Figure 35 Drag the selection into the cell.

Figure 36 When you release the mouse button, the selection moves into the cell.

Entering & Formatting Table Information

You enter text and other information into a table the same way you enter it into any document: type, paste, or drag it in. Then format it as desired using techniques in **Chapters 3** and **4**.

✔ Tips

- Think of each cell as a tiny document window. The cell boundaries are like document margins. You can enter as much information as you like and apply any kind of formatting.

- As you enter information into a cell, the cell expands vertically as necessary to accommodate the text.

- I tell you about copying and moving text with the Cut, Copy, and Paste commands and drag-and-drop text editing in **Chapter 2**.

To enter text into a cell

1. Position the insertion point in the cell (**Figure 32**).

2. Type the text that you want to appear in the cell (**Figure 33**).

   or

   Use the Edit menu's Paste command to paste the Clipboard contents (a previously copied or cut selection) into the cell.

or

1. Select text in another part of the document (**Figure 34**) or another document.

2. Drag the selected text into the cell in which you want it to appear (**Figure 35**). When you release the mouse button, the text appears in the cell (**Figure 36**).

✔ Tip

- To enter a tab character in a cell, press Control Tab.

To enter special text or objects into a cell

1. Position the insertion point in the cell.

2. Choose the appropriate command from the Insert menu (**Figure 37**) to insert special text or objects.

   or

   Use the Edit menu's Paste command to paste the Clipboard contents (a previously copied or cut selection) into the cell.

or

1. Select special text or objects in another part of the document (**Figure 38**) or another document.

2. Drag the selection into the cell in which you want it to appear. When you release the mouse button (**Figure 39**), it appears in the cell (**Figure 40**).

✔ Tip

■ I tell you about options under the Insert menu in **Chapter 7**.

To advance from one cell to another

To advance to the next cell in the table, press [Tab].

or

To advance to the previous cell in the table, press [Shift][Tab].

✔ Tip

■ If you use either of these techniques to advance to a cell that is not empty, the cell's contents become selected. Otherwise, the insertion point appears in the cell.

Figure 37
You can use the Insert menu to insert special text or objects into a table cell.

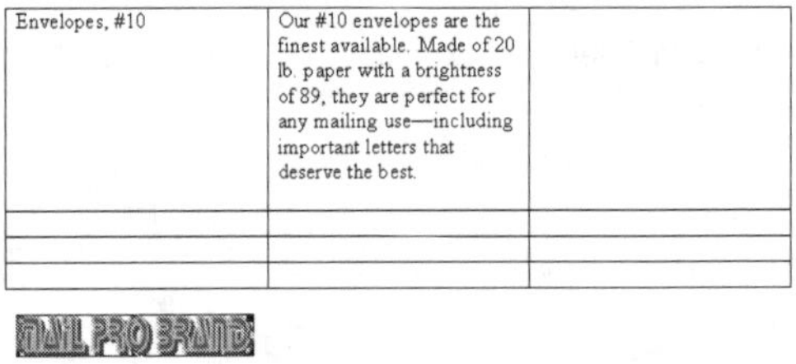

Figure 38 Select the object that you want to move into a cell.

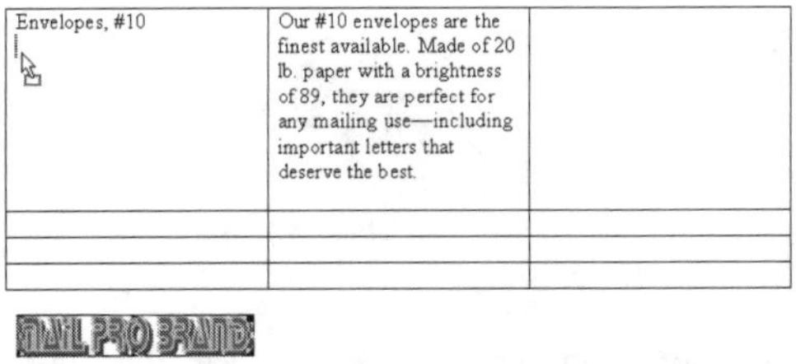

Figure 39 Drag the object into the cell.

Figure 40 When you release the mouse button, the object moves.

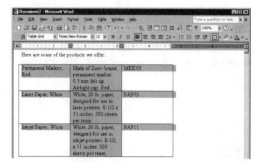

Figure 41 Select the table that you want to align.

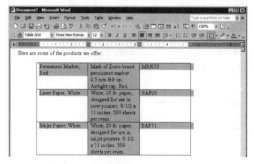

Figure 42 When you click the Center button on the Formatting toolbar, the table centers between the left and right document margins.

To format characters or paragraphs in a cell

1. Select the characters that you want to format.

2. Apply font formatting (such as font, font size, and font style) and/or paragraph formatting (such as alignment, indentation, and line spacing) as discussed in **Chapters 3** and **4**.

✔ Tips

- Almost every kind of font or paragraph formatting can be applied to the contents of individual cells.

- I tell you more about formatting tables when I discuss the Table AutoFormat feature later in this chapter.

To align a table

1. Select the entire table (**Figure 41**).

2. Click one of the alignment buttons on the Formatting toolbar:

   ▲ **Align Left** ▤ shifts the table against the left margin. This is the default setting.

   ▲ **Center** ▤ shifts the table to center it between the left and right margins (**Figure 42**).

   ▲ **Align Right** ▤ shifts the table against the right margin.

✔ Tips

- The Justify button ▤ does not move the table. Instead it applies full justification to all paragraphs within the table.

- You will only notice a change in a table's alignment if the table is narrower than the printable area between the document's left and right margins.

Inserting & Deleting Cells

You can insert or remove columns, rows, or individual cells at any time to change the structure of a table.

To insert a column

1. Select a column adjacent to where you want to insert a column (**Figure 43**).

2. To insert a column to the left of the selected column, choose Table > Insert > Columns to the Left (**Figure 44**) or click the Insert Columns button ![button] on the Standard toolbar.

   or

   To insert a column to the right of the selected column, choose Table > Insert > Columns to the Right (**Figure 44**).

   An empty column is inserted (**Figure 45**).

✔ Tip

■ To insert multiple columns, select the same number of columns that you want to insert (if possible) in step 1 or repeat step 2 until the number of columns that you want to insert have been inserted.

To insert a row

1. Select a row adjacent to where you want to insert a row (**Figure 46**).

2. To insert a row above the selected row, choose Table > Insert > Rows Above (**Figure 44**) or click the Insert Rows button ![button] on the Standard toolbar.

   or

   To insert a row below the selected row, choose Table > Insert > Rows Below (**Figure 44**).

   An empty row is inserted (**Figure 47**).

Substance	Date Tested	Tested By	Results
MSG	5/18/02	Maria Langer	452.3516
Magnesium	6/4/02	John Aabbott	51.84
Sulfur	6/15/02	Mary Johannesburg	145236.145872
Aspirin	10/17/02	Tim Jones	1.1

Figure 43 Select the column adjacent to where you want to insert a column.

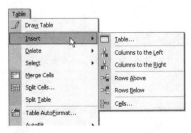

Figure 44 The Insert submenu offers options for inserting tables, columns, rows, or cells.

Substance		Date Tested	Tested By	Results
MSG		5/18/02	Maria Langer	452.3516
Magnesium		6/4/02	John Aabbott	51.84
Sulfur		6/15/02	Mary Johannesburg	145236.145872
Aspirin		10/17/02	Tim Jones	1.1

Figure 45 When you choose Columns to the Left from the Insert submenu, a column is inserted to the left of the selected column.

Substance	Date Tested	Tested By	Results
MSG	5/18/02	Maria Langer	452.3516
Magnesium	6/4/02	John Aabbott	51.84
Sulfur	6/15/02	Mary Johannesburg	145236.145872
Aspirin	10/17/02	Tim Jones	1.1

Figure 46 Select a row adjacent to where you want to insert the row.

Substance	Date Tested	Tested By	Results
MSG	5/18/02	Maria Langer	452.3516
Magnesium	6/4/02	John Aabbott	51.84
Sulfur	6/15/02	Mary Johannesburg	145236.145872
Aspirin	10/17/02	Tim Jones	1.1

Figure 47 When you choose Rows Above from the Insert submenu, a row is inserted above the selected row.

Substance	Date Tested	Tested By	Results
MSG	5/18/02	Maria Langer	452.3516
Magnesium	6/4/02	John Aabbott	51.84
Sulfur	6/15/02	Mary Johannesburg	145236.145872
Aspirin	10/17/02	Tim Jones	1.1

Figure 48 Pressing [Tab] while the insertion point is in the last cell of the table adds a row at the bottom of the table.

Substance	Date Tested	Tested By	Results
MSG	5/18/02	Maria Langer	452.3516
Magnesium	6/4/02	John Aabbott	51.84
Sulfur	6/15/02	Mary Johannesburg	145236.145872
Aspirin	10/17/02	Tim Jones	1.1

Figure 49 Select the cell where you want to insert a cell.

Figure 50
The Insert Cells dialog.

Substance	Date Tested	Tested By	Results	
MSG	5/18/02	Maria Langer		452.3516
Magnesium	6/4/02	John Aabbott	51.84	
Sulfur	6/15/02	Mary Johannesburg	145236.145872	
Aspirin	10/17/02	Tim Jones	1.1	

Substance	Date Tested	Tested By	Results
MSG	5/18/02	Maria Langer	
Magnesium	6/4/02	John Aabbott	452.3516
Sulfur	6/15/02	Mary Johannesburg	51.84
Aspirin	10/17/02	Tim Jones	145236.145872
			1.1

Figures 51a & 51b You can shift cells to the right (top) or down (bottom) when you insert a cell.

✔ Tips

- Another way to insert a row at the bottom of the table is to position the insertion point in the last cell of the table and press [Tab]. An empty row is inserted (**Figure 48**).

- To insert multiple rows, select the same number of rows that you want to insert (if possible) in step 1 or repeat step 2 until the number of rows that you want to insert have been inserted.

To insert a cell

1. Select the cell at the location where you want to insert a cell (**Figure 49**).

2. Choose Table > Insert > Cells (**Figure 44**) or click the Insert Cells button on the Standard toolbar.

3. In the Insert Cells dialog that appears (**Figure 50**), select an option:

   ▲ **Shift cells right** inserts a cell in the same row and moves the cells to its right to the right (**Figure 51a**).

   ▲ **Shift cells down** inserts a cell in the same column and moves the cells below it down (**Figure 51b**).

   ▲ **Insert entire row** inserts a row above the selected cell.

   ▲ **Insert entire column** inserts a column to the left of the selected cell.

4. Click OK.

✔ Tip

- To insert multiple cells, select the same number of cells that you want to insert (if possible) in step 1 or repeat steps 2 and 3 until the number of cells that you want to insert have been inserted.

To delete a column, row, or cell

1. Select the column (**Figure 52**), row (**Figure 55**), or cell (**Figure 57**) that you want to remove.

2. Choose the appropriate command from the Table menu's Delete submenu (**Figure 53**) to delete the selected column, row, or cell.

   or

   Press Backspace.

3. If you delete a column, it disappears and the columns to its right shift to the left (**Figure 54**).

   or

   If you delete a row, it disappears and the rows below it shift up (**Figure 56**).

   or

   If you delete a cell, choose an option in the Delete Cells dialog that appears (**Figure 58**):

   ▲ **Shift cells left** deletes the cell and moves the cells to its right to the left (**Figure 59a**).

   ▲ **Shift cells up** deletes the cell and moves the cells below it up (**Figure 59b**).

   ▲ **Delete entire row** deletes the row.

   ▲ **Delete entire column** deletes the column.

   Then click OK.

✔ Tips

■ The contents of a column, row, or cell are deleted with it.

■ You can select multiple contiguous columns, rows, or cells in step 1 above to delete them all at once.

Substance	Date Tested	Tested By	Results
MSG	5/18/02	Maria Langer	452.3516
Magnesium	6/4/02	John Aabbott	51.84
Sulfur	6/15/02	Mary Johannesburg	145236.145872
Aspirin	10/17/02	Tim Jones	1.1

Figure 52 Select the column that you want to delete.

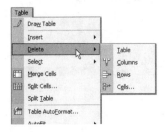

Figure 53 Use commands on the Delete submenu to delete a selected table, column, row, or cell.

Substance	Date Tested	Results
MSG	5/18/02	452.3516
Magnesium	6/4/02	51.84
Sulfur	6/15/02	145236.145872
Aspirin	10/17/02	1.1

Figure 54 The column is deleted.

Substance	Date Tested	Tested By	Results
MSG	5/18/02	Maria Langer	452.3516
Magnesium	6/4/02	John Aabbott	51.84
Sulfur	6/15/02	Mary Johannesburg	145236.145872
Aspirin	10/17/02	Tim Jones	1.1

Figure 55 Select the row that you want to delete.

Substance	Date Tested	Tested By	Results
MSG	5/18/02	Maria Langer	452.3516
Sulfur	6/15/02	Mary Johannesburg	145236.145872
Aspirin	10/17/02	Tim Jones	1.1

Figure 56 The row is deleted.

Substance	Date Tested	Tested By	Results
MSG	5/18/02	Maria Langer	452.3516
Magnesium	6/4/02	John Aabbott	51.84
Sulfur	6/15/02	Mary Johannesburg	145236.145872
Aspirin	10/17/02	Tim Jones	1.1

Figure 57 Select the cell that you want to delete.

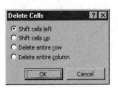

Figure 58 The Delete Cells dialog.

Substance	Date Tested	Tested By	Results
MSG	5/18/02	Maria Langer	
Magnesium	6/4/02	John Aabbott	51.84
Sulfur	6/15/02	Mary Johannesburg	145236.145872
Aspirin	10/17/02	Tim Jones	1.1

Substance	Date Tested	Tested By	Results
MSG	5/18/02	Maria Langer	51.84
Magnesium	6/4/02	John Aabbott	145236.145872
Sulfur	6/15/02	Mary Johannesburg	1.1
Aspirin	10/17/02	Tim Jones	

Figures 59a & 59b You can shift cells to the left (left) or up (right) when you delete a cell.

Item Name	Description	Number	Price
Permanent Marker, Red	Mark of Zorro brand permanent marker. 0.5 mm felt tip. Airtight cap. Red.	MRK03	$2.99 each
Laser Paper, White	White, 20 lb. paper, designed for use in laser printers. 8-1/2 x 11 inches. 500 sheets per ream.	PAP05	$12.99/ream

Figure 60 Select the cells that you want to merge.

Item Name	Description	Number	Price
Permanent Marker, Red	Mark of Zorro brand permanent marker. 0.5 mm felt tip. Airtight cap. Red.	MRK03	$2.99 each
Laser Paper, White	White, 20 lb. paper, designed for use in laser printers. 8-1/2 x 11 inches. 500 sheets per ream.	PAP05	$12.99/ream

Figure 61 The cells are merged into one cell.

Item Name	Description	Number	Price
Permanent Marker, Red	Mark of Zorro brand permanent marker. 0.5 mm felt tip. Airtight cap. Red.	MRK03	$2.99 each
Laser Paper, White	White, 20 lb. paper, designed for use in laser printers. 8-1/2 x 11 inches. 500 sheets per ream.	PAP05	$12.99/ream

Figure 62 Select the cell that you want to split.

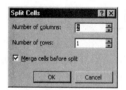

Figure 63
The Split
Cells dialog.

Item Name	Description	Number	Price
Permanent Marker, Red	Mark of Zorro brand permanent marker. 0.5 mm felt tip. Airtight cap. Red.	MRK03	$2.99 each
Laser Paper, White	White, 20 lb. paper, designed for use in laser printers. 8-1/2 x 11 inches. 500 sheets per ream.	PAP05	$12.99/ream

Figure 64 A cell split into one column and two rows.

Merging & Splitting Cells & Tables

You can modify the structure of a table by merging and splitting cells or splitting the table:

◆ Merging cells turns multiple cells into one cell that spans multiple columns or rows.

◆ Splitting a cell turns a single cell into multiple cells in the same column or row.

◆ Splitting a table turns a single table into two separate tables.

To merge cells

1. Select the cells that you want to merge (**Figure 60**).

2. Choose Table > Merge Cells (**Figure 18**). The cells become a single cell (**Figure 61**).

✔ Tip

■ When you merge cells containing text, each cell's contents appear in a separate paragraph of the merged cell (**Figure 61**).

To split cells

1. Select the cell(s) that you want to split (**Figure 62**).

2. Choose Table > Split Cells (**Figure 18**) to display the Split Cells dialog (**Figure 63**).

3. Enter the number of columns and rows for the cell split in the Number of columns and Number of rows text boxes.

4. Click OK. The cell splits as specified (**Figure 64**).

Continued on next page...

MERGING & SPLITTING CELLS

Continued from previous page.

✔ Tips

- To split a cell in the middle of its contents, in step 1 above position the insertion point where you want the split to occur.

- To merge and split multiple cells at the same time, in step 1, select all the cells (**Figure 60**). Then, in step 3, make sure the Merge cells before split check box is turned on (**Figure 63**). When you click OK, the cells are merged and split (**Figure 65**).

To split a table

1. Position the insertion point anywhere in the row below where you want the split to occur (**Figure 66**).

2. Choose Table > Split Table (**Figure 18**).

   The table splits above the row you indicated (**Figure 67**).

Item Name	Description	Number	Price
Permanent Marker, Red	Mark of Zorro brand permanent marker. 0.5 mm felt tip. Airtight cap. Red.	MRK03	$2.99 each
Laser Paper, White	White, 20 lb. paper, designed for use in laser printers. 8-1/2 x 11 inches. 500 sheets per ream.	PAP05	$12.99/ream

Figure 65 The cells selected in **Figure 60** after merging and splitting them into one column and three rows.

Item Name	Description	Number	Price
Permanent Marker, Red	Mark of Zorro brand permanent marker. 0.5 mm felt tip. Airtight cap. Red.	MRK03	$2.99 each
Laser Paper, White	White, 20 lb. paper, designed for use in laser printers. 8-1/2 x 11 inches. 500 sheets per ream.	PAP05	$12.99/ream
Inkjet Paper, White	White, 20 lb. paper, designed for use in inkjet printers. 8-1/2 x 11 inches. 500 sheets per ream.	PAP11	$12.99/ream
Paper Clips, Small	Standard small paperclips. Silver in color. 100 per box.	FAS04	$2.95/box

Figure 66 Position the insertion point in the row below where you want the split to occur.

Item Name	Description	Number	Price
Permanent Marker, Red	Mark of Zorro brand permanent marker. 0.5 mm felt tip. Airtight cap. Red.	MRK03	$2.99 each
Laser Paper, White	White, 20 lb. paper, designed for use in laser printers. 8-1/2 x 11 inches. 500 sheets per ream.	PAP05	$12.99/ream
Inkjet Paper, White	White, 20 lb. paper, designed for use in inkjet printers. 8-1/2 x 11 inches. 500 sheets per ream.	PAP11	$12.99/ream
Paper Clips, Small	Standard small paperclips. Silver in color. 100 per box.	FAS04	$2.95/box

Figure 67 The table splits above the insertion point.

Item Name	Description	Number	Price
Permanent Marker, Red	Mark of Zorro brand permanent marker. 0.5 mm felt tip. Airtight cap. Red.	MRK03	$2.99 each
Laser Paper, White	White, 20 lb. paper, designed for use in laser printers. 8-1/2 x 11 inches. 500 sheets per ream.	PAP05	$12.99/ream

Figure 68 Position the mouse pointer on the column's right boundary.

Item Name	Description	Number	Price
Permanent Marker, Red	Mark of Zorro brand permanent marker. 0.5 mm felt tip. Airtight cap. Red.	MRK03	$2.99 each
Laser Paper, White	White, 20 lb. paper, designed for use in laser printers. 8-1/2 x 11 inches. 500 sheets per ream.	PAP05	$12.99/ream

Figure 69 Drag the column boundary.

Item Name	Description	Number	Price
Permanent Marker, Red	Mark of Zorro brand permanent marker. 0.5 mm felt tip. Airtight cap. Red.	MRK03	$2.99 each
Laser Paper, White	White, 20 lb. paper, designed for use in laser printers. 8-1/2 x 11 inches. 500 sheets per ream.	PAP05	$12.99/ream

Figure 70 When you release the mouse button, the column and the column to its right resize.

Item Name	Description	Number	Price
Permanent Marker, Red	Mark of Zorro brand permanent marker. 0.5 mm felt tip. Airtight cap. Red.	MRK03	$2.99 each
Laser Paper, White	White, 20 lb. paper, designed for use in laser printers. 8-1/2 x 11 inches. 500 sheets per ream.	PAP05	$12.99/ream

Figure 71 You can also resize a column by dragging the Move Table Column area for the column's right boundary.

Resizing Columns & Rows

Word offers two ways to manually change the width of columns or height of rows:

◆ Drag to change column widths and row heights.

◆ Use the Table Properties dialog to change column widths and row heights.

To change a column's width by dragging

1. Position the mouse pointer on the boundary between the column that you want to change and the one to its right. The mouse pointer turns into a double line with arrows (**Figure 68**).

2. Press the mouse button down and drag:

   ▲ Drag to the right to make the column wider.

   ▲ Drag to the left to make the column narrower.

   As you drag, a dotted line indicating the new boundary moves with the mouse pointer (**Figure 69**).

3. Release the mouse button. The column boundary moves to the new position, resizing both columns (**Figure 70**).

✔ Tips

■ To resize a column without changing the width of other columns, in step 1, position the mouse pointer on the Move Table Column area for the column's right boundary (**Figure 71**). Because this method changes only one column's width, it also changes the width of the table.

■ If a cell is selected when you drag to resize a column, only the selected cell's width changes.

To change a row's height by dragging

1. If necessary, switch to Print Layout view.

2. Position the mouse pointer on the boundary between the row that you want to change and the one below it. The mouse pointer turns into a double-line with arrows (**Figure 72**).

3. Press the mouse button down and drag:

   ▲ Drag up to make the row shorter.

   ▲ Drag down to make the row taller.

   As you drag, a dotted line indicating the new boundary moves with the mouse pointer (**Figure 73**).

4. Release the mouse button. The row boundary moves to the new position. The rows beneath it shift accordingly (**Figure 74**).

✔ Tips

■ Another way to resize a row by dragging is to position the mouse pointer on the Adjust Table Row area of the row's bottom boundary (**Figure 75**). Then follow steps 3 and 4 above.

■ Changing a row's height changes the total height of the table.

■ You can't make a row's height shorter than the height of the text within the row.

Item Name	Description	Number	Price
Permanent Marker, Red	Mark of Zorro brand permanent marker. 0.5 mm felt tip. Airtight cap. Red.	MRK03	$2.99 each
Laser Paper, White	White, 20 lb. paper, designed for use in laser printers. 8-1/2 x 11 inches. 500 sheets per ream.	PAP05	$12.99/ream

Figure 72 Position the mouse pointer on the bottom boundary.

Item Name	Description	Number	Price
Permanent Marker, Red	Mark of Zorro brand permanent marker. 0.5 mm felt tip. Airtight cap. Red.	MRK03	$2.99 each
Laser Paper, White	White, 20 lb. paper, designed for use in laser printers. 8-1/2 x 11 inches. 500 sheets per ream.	PAP05	$12.99/ream

Figure 73 Drag the row boundary.

Item Name	Description	Number	Price
Permanent Marker, Red	Mark of Zorro brand permanent marker. 0.5 mm felt tip. Airtight cap. Red.	MRK03	$2.99 each
Laser Paper, White	White, 20 lb. paper, designed for use in laser printers. 8-1/2 x 11 inches. 500 sheets per ream.	PAP05	$12.99/ream

Figure 74 When you release the mouse button, the boundary moves, changing the row's height.

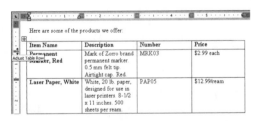

Figure 75 You can also resize a row by dragging the Adjust Table Row area for the row's bottom boundary.

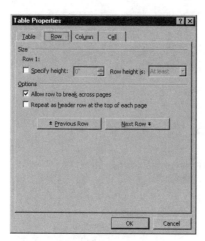

Figure 76 The Row tab of the Table Properties dialog.

Figure 77 Use this drop-down list to specify how the row height measurement you enter should be used.

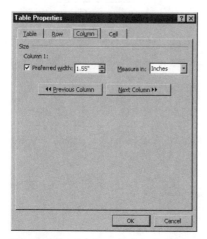

Figure 78 The Column tab of the Table Properties dialog.

Figure 79 Use this drop-down list to specify how the column width measurement you enter should be used.

To set row height or column width

1. Select a cell in the row or column for which you want to set height or width.

2. Choose Table > Table Properties (**Figure 18**) to display the Table Properties dialog.

3. To set row height, click the Row tab to display its options (**Figure 76**). Turn on the Specify height check box, enter a value in the box beside it, and choose an option from the Row height is drop-down list (**Figure 77**).

   or

   To set column width, click the Column tab to display its options (**Figure 78**). Turn on the Preferred width check box, enter a value in the box beside it, and choose an option from the Measure in drop-down list (**Figure 79**).

4. Click OK.

✔ Tips

- To set column width and row height at the same time, in step 1, select a cell that is in both the column and row that you want to change. Then follow the remaining steps, including both parts of step 3.

- You can click the Previous Row and Next Row buttons in the Row tab (**Figure 76**) and the Previous Column and Next Column buttons in the Column tab (**Figure 78**) of the Table Properties dialog to cycle through and set values for all the rows and columns in the table.

- The Table Properties dialog also offers a number of advanced features for formatting tables, rows, columns, and cells that are beyond the scope of this book.

Using AutoFit

Table AutoFit options (**Figure 81**) instruct Word to automatically set the column width or row height depending on the table or window width or cell contents. The options are:

◆ **AutoFit to Contents** automatically sizes a column's width based on its contents.

◆ **AutoFit to Window** automatically sizes a table's width to fill the space between the margins.

◆ **Fixed Column Width** locks a column's width so it does not automatically change.

◆ **Distribute Rows Evenly** equalizes the height of rows.

◆ **Distribute Columns Evenly** equalizes the width of columns.

To adjust columns to best fit contents

1. To adjust all table columns, click anywhere in the table (**Figure 80**).

    or

    To adjust just one or more columns, select the column(s).

2. Choose Table > AutoFit > AutoFit to Contents (**Figure 81**).

    The column(s) adjust to minimize word wrap (**Figure 82**).

To adjust a table's width to fill the window

1. Click anywhere in the table (**Figure 80**).

2. Choose Table > AutoFit > AutoFit to Window (**Figure 81**).

    The table's width adjusts to fill the space between the margins (**Figure 83**). Columns are resized proportionally.

Figure 80 Position the insertion point anywhere in the table.

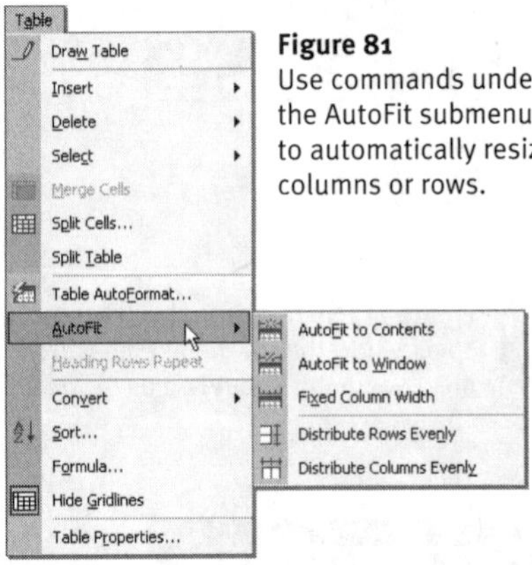

Figure 81 Use commands under the AutoFit submenu to automatically resize columns or rows.

Figure 82 The AutoFit to Contents command minimizes word wrap within cells.

Figure 83 The AutoFit to Window command resizes columns proportionally so the table fits in the space between the margins

Item Name	Description	Number	Price
Permanent Marker, Red	Mark of Zorro brand permanent marker. 0.5 mm felt tip. Airtight cap. Red.	MRK03	$2.99 each
Laser Paper, White	White, 20 lb. paper, designed for use in laser printers. 8-1/2 x 11 inches. 500 sheets per ream.	PAP05	$12.99/ream
Inkjet Paper, White	White, 20 lb. paper, designed for use in inkjet printers. 8-1/2 x 11 inches. 500 sheets per ream.	PAP11	$12.99/ream
Paper Clips, Small	Standard small paperclips. Silver in color. 100 per box.	FAS04	$2.95/box

Figure 84 Select the columns for which you want to equalize width.

Item Name	Description	Number	Price
Permanent Marker, Red	Mark of Zorro brand permanent marker. 0.5 mm felt tip. Airtight cap. Red.	MRK03	$2.99 each
Laser Paper, White	White, 20 lb. paper, designed for use in laser printers. 8-1/2 x 11 inches. 500 sheets per ream.	PAP05	$12.99/ream
Inkjet Paper, White	White, 20 lb. paper, designed for use in inkjet printers. 8-1/2 x 11 inches. 500 sheets per ream.	PAP11	$12.99/ream
Paper Clips, Small	Standard small paperclips. Silver in color. 100 per box.	FAS04	$2.95/box

Figure 85 The space used by the columns is distributed evenly between them.

Item Name	Description	Number	Price
Permanent Marker, Red	Mark of Zorro brand permanent marker. 0.5 mm felt tip. Airtight cap. Red.	MRK03	$2.99 each
Laser Paper, White	White, 20 lb. paper, designed for use in laser printers. 8-1/2 x 11 inches. 500 sheets per ream.	PAP05	$12.99/ream
Inkjet Paper, White	White, 20 lb. paper, designed for use in inkjet printers. 8-1/2 x 11 inches. 500 sheets per ream.	PAP11	$12.99/ream
Paper Clips, Small	Standard small paperclips. Silver in color. 100 per box.	FAS04	$2.95/box

Figure 86 Select the rows for which you want to equalize height.

Item Name	Description	Number	Price
Permanent Marker, Red	Mark of Zorro brand permanent marker. 0.5 mm felt tip. Airtight cap. Red.	MRK03	$2.99 each
Laser Paper, White	White, 20 lb. paper, designed for use in laser printers. 8-1/2 x 11 inches. 500 sheets per ream.	PAP05	$12.99/ream
Inkjet Paper, White	White, 20 lb. paper, designed for use in inkjet printers. 8-1/2 x 11 inches. 500 sheets per ream.	PAP11	$12.99/ream
Paper Clips, Small	Standard small paperclips. Silver in color. 100 per box.	FAS04	$2.95/box

Figure 87 The row heights change as necessary so each selected row is the same height.

To equalize the width of columns

1. Select the columns for which you want to equalize width (**Figure 84**).

2. Choose Table > AutoFit > Distribute Columns Evenly (**Figure 81**). The column widths change to evenly distribute space within the same area (**Figure 85**).

To equalize the height of rows

1. Select the rows for which you want to equalize height (**Figure 86**).

2. Choose Table > AutoFit > Distribute Rows Evenly (**Figure 81**). The row heights change so that all selected rows are the same height (**Figure 87**).

✔ Tip

- Using the Distribute Rows Evenly command usually increases the height of the table, since all selected rows become the same height as the tallest row.

Table Headings

A table heading consists of one or more rows that appear at the top of the table. If page breaks occur within a table, the table heading appears at the top of each page of the table (**Figure 88**).

✔ Tip

- Setting a row as a table heading does not change its appearance. You must manually apply formatting or use the Table AutoFormat command to make headings look different from other data in the table. I tell you about formatting text in **Chapters 3** and **4** and about the Table AutoFormat command on the next page.

To set a table heading

1. Select the row(s) that you want to use as a table heading (**Figure 89**).

2. Choose Table > Heading Rows Repeat (**Figure 90**).

   The selected rows are set as headings.

To remove a table heading

1. Select the row(s) that comprise the heading (**Figure 89**).

2. Choose Table > Heading Rows Repeat (**Figure 90**).

   The headings setting is removed from the selected rows.

✔ Tip

- Removing the heading feature from selected row(s) does not delete the row(s) from the table.

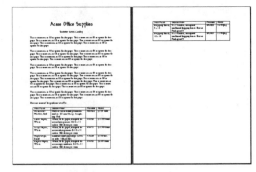

Figure 88 If a page break splits a table into multiple pages, the headings appear at the top of each page of the table.

ITEM NAME	DESCRIPTION	NUMBER	PRICE
Permanent Marker, Red	Mark of Zorro brand permanent marker. 0.5 mm felt tip. Airtight cap. Red.	MRK03	$2.99 each
Laser Paper, White	White, 20 lb. paper, designed for use in laser printers. 8-1/2 x 11 inches. 500 sheets per ream.	PAP05	$12.99/ream
Inkjet Paper, White	White, 20 lb. paper, designed for use in inkjet printers. 8-1/2 x 11 inches. 500 sheets per ream.	PAP11	$12.99/ream
Paper Clips, Small	Standard small paperclips. Silver in color. 100 per box.	FAS04	$2.95/box
Copier Paper, White	White, 20 lb. paper, designed for use in copy machines. 8-1/2 x 11 inches. 500 sheets per ream.	PAP01	$8.99/ream
Shipping Boxes, 9 x 12	9 x 12 inches, corrugated cardboard shipping boxes. Brown. Package of 5.	BOX05	10.99/pkg
Shipping Boxes, 10 x 14	9 x 14 inches, corrugated cardboard shipping boxes. Brown. Package of 5.	BOX07	11.99/pkg

Figure 89 Select the row(s) that you want to use as a heading.

Figure 90 Choose Heading Rows Repeat from the Table menu a second time to remove the heading feature from selected row(s).

Item Name	Description	Number	Price
Permanent Marker, Red	Mark of Zorro brand permanent marker. 0.5 mm felt tip. Airtight cap. Red.	MRK03	$2.99 each
Laser Paper, White	White, 20 lb. paper, designed for use in laser printers. 8-1/2 x 11 inches. 500 sheets per ream.	PAP05	$12.99/ream
Inkjet Paper, White	White, 20 lb. paper, designed for use in inkjet printers. 8-1/2 x 11 inches. 500 sheets per ream.	PAP11	$12.99/ream
Paper Clips, Small	Standard small paperclips. Silver in color. 100 per box.	FAS04	$2.95/box
Copier Paper, White	White, 20 lb. paper, designed for use in copy machines. 8-1/2 x 11 inches. 500 sheets per ream.	PAP01	$8.99/ream
Shipping Boxes, 9 x 12	9 x 12 inches, corrugated cardboard shipping boxes. Brown. Package of 5.	BOX05	10.99/pkg
Shipping Boxes, 10 x 14	9 x 14 inches, corrugated cardboard shipping boxes. Brown. Package of 5.	BOX07	11.99/pkg

Figure 91 Select the table that you want to format.

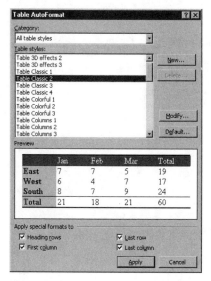

Figure 92 The Table AutoFormat dialog.

Item Name	Description	Number	Price
Permanent Marker, Red	Mark of Zorro brand permanent marker. 0.5 mm felt tip. Airtight cap. Red.	MRK03	$2.99 each
Laser Paper, White	White, 20 lb. paper, designed for use in laser printers. 8-1/2 x 11 inches. 500 sheets per ream.	PAP05	$12.99/ream
Inkjet Paper, White	White, 20 lb. paper, designed for use in inkjet printers. 8-1/2 x 11 inches. 500 sheets per ream.	PAP11	$12.99/ream
Paper Clips, Small	Standard small paperclips. Silver in color. 100 per box.	FAS04	$2.95/box
Copier Paper, White	White, 20 lb. paper, designed for use in copy machines. 8-1/2 x 11 inches. 500 sheets per ream.	PAP01	$8.99/ream
Shipping Boxes, 9 x 12	9 x 12 inches, corrugated cardboard shipping boxes. Brown. Package of 5.	BOX05	10.99/pkg
Shipping Boxes, 10 x 14	9 x 14 inches, corrugated cardboard shipping boxes. Brown. Package of 5.	BOX07	11.99/pkg

Figure 93 The table from **Figure 91** with the Table Classic 2 format applied.

Table AutoFormat

Word's Table AutoFormat feature offers a quick and easy way to combine many formatting options for an entire table.

To use Table AutoFormat

1. Select the table that you want to format (**Figure 91**).

2. Choose Table > Table AutoFormat (**Figure 18**) to display the Table Auto-Format dialog (**Figure 92**).

3. Click to select one of the formats in the scrolling list.

4. Toggle check boxes in the Apply special formats to area to specify which part(s) of the table should get the special formatting.

5. When you're finished setting options, click OK. The formatting for the AutoFormat is applied to the table (**Figure 93**).

✔ Tips

- Each time you make a change in the Table AutoFormat dialog (**Figure 92**), the Preview area changes to show the effect of your changes.

- The Table AutoFormat dialog (**Figure 92**) applies table styles to the selected cells. You can also use this dialog to create new table styles or modify existing ones. Styles are discussed in **Chapter 4**.

- If you don't like the formatting applied by the Table AutoFormat feature, use the Undo command to reverse them. Then try again or format the table manually.

To remove AutoFormatting

Follow steps 1 and 2 above, but select Table Grid in the scrolling list (**Figure 92**) in step 3, and then click OK.

Removing a Table

You can remove a table two ways:

◆ Delete the table, thus removing it and its contents from the document.

◆ Convert the table to text, thus removing the structure of the table from the document but not the table's contents.

To delete a table

1. Select the table that you want to delete.

2. Choose Table > Delete > Table (**Figure 53**).

   or

   Press [Backspace].

   The table, and all of its data, is removed from the document.

To convert a table to text

1. Select the table that you want to convert to text.

2. Choose Table > Convert > Table to Text (**Figure 94**).

3. In the Convert Table to Text dialog that appears (**Figure 95**), select the radio button for the type of delimiter that you want to use to separate the contents of table cells when the cell boundaries are removed.

4. Click OK.

   The table is converted to text.

Figure 94
Use the Table to Text command to remove a table without removing its contents.

Figure 95
The Convert Table to Text dialog.

ENVELOPES & LABELS

Envelopes & Labels

Microsoft Word's Envelopes and Labels feature can create and print addressed envelopes and mailing labels based on document contents or other information you provide. This feature makes it easy to print professional-looking envelopes and labels for all of your mailing needs.

✔ Tips

■ Word supports a wide variety of standard envelope and label sizes and formats. Settings can also be changed for printing on nonstandard envelopes or labels.

■ You can use the Mail Merge Wizard to create envelopes and labels based on database information. **Chapter 11** explains how.

■ Word 2002 is able to print postage on envelopes and labels—if you have installed and subscribed to the electronic postage feature. Although instructions for using electronic postage is beyond the scope of this book, you can learn more about it by visiting the Microsoft Office eServices page, http://office.microsoft.com/Services/.

■ If you use Microsoft Outlook, you can use the Insert Address button ▣ ▾ that appears in the Envelopes and Labels dialog to automatically insert an Outlook address for an envelope or label. A detailed discussion of this feature is beyond the scope of this book; experiment with it on your own if it sounds like something you might find useful.

Creating an Envelope

In Word, you create an envelope with the Envelopes tab of the Envelopes and Labels dialog (**Figure 2**). This tab enables you to provide several pieces of information:

◆ **Delivery address** is the address the envelope will be mailed to.

◆ **Return address** is the address that appears in the upper-left corner of the envelope. You can use your own address, specify another address, or omit the address entirely.

From the Envelopes tab of the Envelopes and Labels dialog, you can also access the Envelope Options dialog (**Figure 3**), which enables you to set envelope and printing options.

Once you have set options for an envelope, you can either print it immediately or add it to the currently active document so it can be printed later.

The following pages cover all aspects of setting up, printing, and saving an envelope.

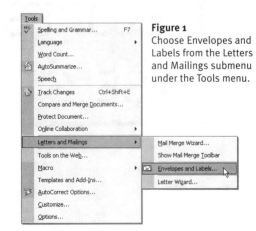

Figure 1
Choose Envelopes and Labels from the Letters and Mailings submenu under the Tools menu.

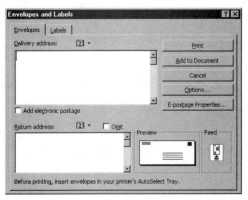

Figure 2 The Envelopes tab of the Envelopes and Labels dialog.

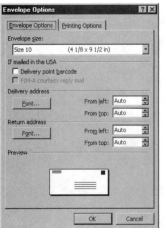

Figure 3
The Envelope Options tab of the Envelope Options dialog.

CREATING ENVELOPES

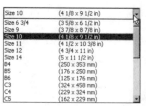

Figure 4
The Envelope size drop-down list includes many standard envelope sizes.

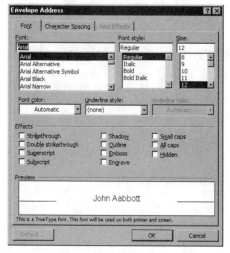

Figure 5 Use this dialog—which looks and works like the Font dialog discussed in **Chapters 3** and **4**—to set font options for the delivery and return addresses.

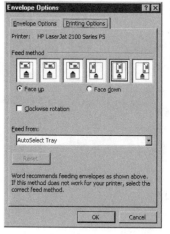

Figure 6
The Printing Options tab of the Envelope Options dialog.

To set up an envelope

1. Choose Tools > Letters and Mailings > Envelopes and Labels (**Figure 1**).

2. In the Envelopes and Labels dialog that appears, click the Envelopes tab to display its options (**Figure 2**).

3. Enter the name and address of the person to whom the envelope should be addressed in the Delivery address box.

4. If desired, enter a return address in the Return address box.

   or

   To create an envelope without a return address, turn on the Omit check box. This omits the return address from the envelope, even if one appears in the Return address box.

5. Click the Options button.

6. In the Envelope Options dialog that appears, click the Envelope Options tab (**Figure 3**).

7. Choose a size from the Envelope size drop-down list (**Figure 4**).

8. To set the font options for either address, click the Font button in its area. Then use the dialog that appears (**Figure 5**) to set formatting options and click OK.

9. In the Envelope Options dialog click the Printing Options tab (**Figure 6**).

10. Check the Feed method options to make sure that they are properly set for your printer. If they are not, make changes as necessary.

11. Select an option from the Feed from drop-down list.

12. Click OK to save your settings and dismiss the Envelope Options dialog.

Continued on next page...

SETTING UP ENVELOPES

Continued from previous page.

✔ Tips

- In step 1, you cannot choose the Envelopes and Labels command unless a document window is open.

- If you are creating an envelope for a letter in the active document window, the Delivery address may already be filled in based on the inside address of the letter (**Figure 7**). You can "help" Word enter the correct address in this box by selecting the recipient's address before opening the Envelopes and Labels dialog.

- To override Word's automatic positioning of addresses, enter measurements in the From left and From top text boxes in the Envelope Options tab of the Envelope Options dialog (**Figure 3**) for the address you want to move.

- To include a postal barcode on the envelope, turn on the Delivery point barcode check box in the Envelope Options tab of the Envelope Options dialog (**Figure 3**). You can then also turn on the FIM-A check box if desired to add additional postal coding to the face of the envelope.

- In step 8, you can save font formatting changes as default settings by clicking the Default button in the dialog (**Figure 5**). Font formatting is covered in detail in **Chapters 3** and **4**.

- In step 10, Word can usually set options correctly for printers capable of printing envelopes (**Figure 6**). Make changes to these options only if you know that the settings are incorrect.

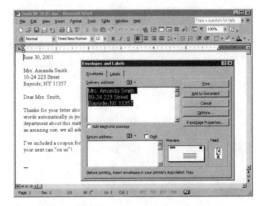

Figure 7 When you create an envelope for a letter, Word is usually "smart" enough to fill in the Delivery address for you.

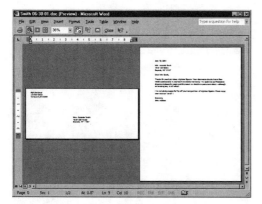

Figure 8 An envelope added as a separate document section when viewed in Print Preview.

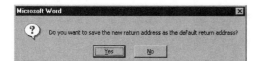

Figure 9 When you enter a new return address in the Envelopes and Labels dialog, Word offers to save it as the default.

To print an envelope

Click the Print button in the Envelopes tab of the Envelopes and Labels dialog (**Figure 2**).

Word prints the envelope.

✔ Tip

■ Printing is covered in greater detail in **Chapter 6**.

To save the envelope as part of the active document

In the Envelopes tab of the Envelopes and Labels dialog (**Figure 2**), click the Add to Document button.

Word adds a new section to the document with the proper settings to print that section as an envelope (**Figure 8**).

✔ Tip

■ I tell you about document sections in **Chapter 4**.

To create a default return address

1. Follow the instructions earlier in this chapter to set up an envelope with a new return address.

2. In the Envelopes tab of the Envelopes and Labels dialog (**Figure 2**) click either the Print button to print the envelope or the Add to Document button to add the envelope to the active document.

3. A dialog like the one in **Figure 9** appears. Click Yes.

✔ Tip

■ When you save a default return address, that address automatically appears in the Envelopes tab of the Envelopes and Labels dialog each time you create an envelope.

PRINTING & SAVING ENVELOPES

Creating Labels

In Word, you create labels with the Labels tab of the Envelopes and Labels dialog (**Figure 10**). This dialog enables you to set up labels by entering the address that should appear on the label and the number of labels that should be printed. You can also access the Label Options dialog, which offers additional options for the type of label on which you want to print.

Once you have set options for a label, you can either print it immediately or save it as a new document so it can be printed later.

The following pages cover all aspects of setting up, printing, and saving a label.

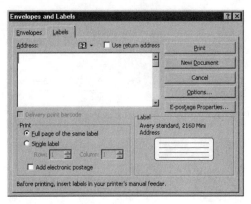

Figure 10 The Labels tab of the Envelopes and Labels dialog.

To set label options

1. Choose Tools > Letters and Mailings > Envelopes and Labels (**Figure 1**).

2. In the Envelopes and Labels dialog that appears, click the Labels tab to display its options (**Figure 10**).

3. Enter the name and address of the person to whom the label should be addressed in the Address box.

4. Select an option in the Print area:

   ▲ **Full page of the same label** prints the entire page of labels with the name and address that appears in the Address box.

   ▲ **Single label** prints only one label. If you select this option, be sure to enter the row and column number (if applicable) for the label you want to print.

5. To select the type of label you want to print on, click the Options button in the Label area to display the Label Options dialog (**Figure 11**). Select the appropriate Printer information option, then choose an option from the Label products drop-down list (**Figure 12**) and select the Product number for the label you want to use. Then click OK.

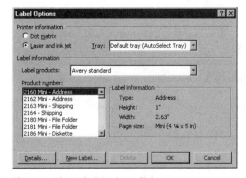

Figure 11 The Label Options dialog.

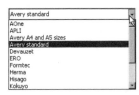

Figure 12
The Label products drop-down list includes all the major label manufacturers.

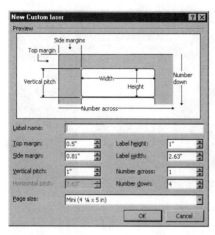

Figure 13 Use a dialog like this one to create your own custom label sizes.

✔ Tips

- In step 1, you cannot choose the Envelopes and Labels command unless a document window is open.

- If you are creating a label for a letter in the active document window, the Address may already be filled in based on the inside address of the letter. You can "help" Word enter the correct address in this box by selecting the recipient's address before opening the Envelopes and Labels dialog.

- If you saved a default return address as instructed earlier in this chapter, you can automatically enter the return address by turning on the Use return address check box in the Labels tab of the Envelopes and Labels dialog (**Figure 10**). This is a handy way to create a sheet of return address labels.

- If you're not sure which Product number to select in step 5, consult the information on the box of labels.

- You can create your own custom label settings. In step 5, click the New Label button to display the New Custom dialog (**Figure 13**). Enter a name and measurements for the label, and click OK. The name of your new labels will appear in the Product number list in the Label Options dialog (**Figure 11**) when Other is selected from the Label products drop-down list (**Figure 12**).

- In step 5, you can customize the selected label by clicking the Details button. The dialog that appears looks and works very much like the one in **Figure 13**. Make changes as desired and click OK.

To print labels

Click the Print button in the Labels tab of the Envelopes and Labels dialog (**Figure 10**).

Word prints the labels.

✔ Tips

■ When printing single labels on a laser or inkjet printer, print on the labels at the bottom of the sheet first. This helps prevent printer jamming when labels at the top of the sheet have been removed.

■ Printing is covered in greater detail in **Chapter 6**.

To save the labels as a new document

In the Labels tab of the Envelopes and Labels dialog (**Figure 10**), click the Add to Document button.

Word creates a new document containing the labels (**Figure 14**).

✔ Tips

■ This option is only available when creating a full page of the same label.

■ Word uses its table feature to create labels. Tables are covered in **Chapter 9**.

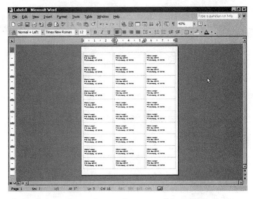

Figure 14 Here's a sheet of return address labels in Print Layout view. You can see the table gridlines separating each label.

Mail Merge

Mail Merge

Microsoft Word's Mail Merge feature enables you to create mailing labels, form letters, and other documents based on database information. This feature merges fields or categories of information with static text to produce merged documents.

The mail merge process uses two special kinds of documents:

♦ A *main document* contains the information that remains the same for each version of the merged document. In a form letter, for example, the main document would consist of the letter text that appears in every letter.

♦ A *data source* contains the information that changes for each version of a merged document. In a form letter, the data source would consist of the names and addresses of the individuals who will receive the letter.

The results of a mail merge can be sent directly to the printer, sent as e-mail or saved as a file on disk.

✔ Tips

■ You can use a single main document with any number of data sources. Similarly, you can use a data source with any number of main documents.

■ You can create a data source with Word as discussed in this chapter or with another application such as Microsoft Excel or Microsoft Outlook.

■ Word's mail merge feature also includes powerful query and conditional functions. These are advanced features that are beyond the scope of this book.

The Mail Merge Wizard

Word's Mail Merge Wizard (**Figure 1**) is a task pane that leads you, step-by-step, through the process of performing a mail merge. Each step offers options based on selections you made in previous steps. At any point in the process, you can go back and change options.

To use the Mail Merge Wizard: an overview

1. Open the Mail Merge Wizard (**Figure 1**).

2. Select the type of document you want to create.

3. Open or create a main document.

4. Open or create a data source document and select the records to include in the merge.

5. If necessary, edit the main document to include static text and merge fields.

6. Preview the merge documents.

7. Perform the merge.

✔ Tip

■ This chapter provides details for all of these steps.

To open the Mail Merge Wizard

Choose Tools > Letters and Mailings > Mail Merge Wizard (**Figure 2**).

✔ Tips

■ You cannot open the Mail Merge Wizard unless a document window is open.

■ The Mail Merge Wizard is a reworked version of the Mail Merge Helper that was in previous versions of Word.

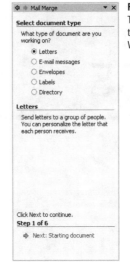

Figure 1
The first step of the Mail Merge Wizard.

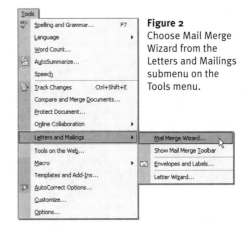

Figure 2
Choose Mail Merge Wizard from the Letters and Mailings submenu on the Tools menu.

Figure 3 An example of a main document for a form letter. The merge fields are circled.

Creating or Opening a Main Document

A main document (**Figure 3**) has two components:

♦ **Static text** that does not change. In a form letter, for example, static text would be the information that remains the same for each individual who will get the letter.

♦ **Merge fields** that indicate what data source information should be merged into the document and where it should go. In a form letter, the static text *Dear* might be followed by the field *«FirstName»*. When merged, the contents of the FirstName field are merged into the document after the word *Dear* to result in *Dear Joe*, *Dear Sally*, etc.

Normally, a main document can be created with one or two steps:

♦ Enter the static text first, then insert the fields when the data source is complete. This method is useful when you use an existing document as a main document.

♦ Enter the static text and insert the fields at the same time when the data source document is complete. This method may save time and prevent confusion when creating a main document from scratch.

✔ Tips

■ You cannot insert fields into a main document until after the data source has been created and associated with the main document.

■ You enter, edit, and format static text in a main document the same way you do in any other Word document.

■ As shown in **Figure 3**, Word 2002 includes predefined blocks of merge fields that make it easy to insert addresses and salutations into main documents.

To select a type of main document

1. Open a document on which you want to base the main document (**Figure 4**).

   or

   Create a new document.

2. Open the Mail Merge Wizard.

3. Select one of the options in the Select document type area of the Mail Merge Wizard (**Figure 1**):

   ▲ **Letters** are form letters customized for multiple recipients.

   ▲ **E-mail messages** are like letters, but they are sent via e-mail.

   ▲ **Envelopes** are envelopes addressed to multiple recipients.

   ▲ **Labels** are labels addressed to multiple recipients.

   ▲ **Directory** is a collection of information about multiple items, such as a phone directory or a catalog.

4. Click the Next: Starting document link at the bottom of the Mail Merge Wizard.

5. Continue following the appropriate instructions on one of the next two pages.

✔ Tips

■ You cannot open the Mail Merge Wizard unless a document window is open.

■ You can find more information about working with envelopes and labels in **Chapter 10**.

Figure 4 A form letter without merge fields.

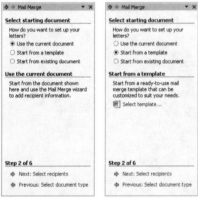

Figures 5, 6, & 7
The second step of the Mail Merge Wizard prompts you for more information about your main document. You can use the current document (top left), start from a template (top right), or start from an existing document (bottom).

Figure 8 If you indicate that you want to start from a template, use the Select Template dialog to select the template you want to use.

Figure 9 If you indicate that you want to start from an existing document, use the Open dialog to select and open the document you want to use.

✔ Tip

■ Templates are discussed in **Chapter 2**.

To start a main document for letters, e-mail messages, or a directory

1. Follow the instructions in the section titled "To select a type of main document." Be sure to select Letters, E-mail messages, or Directory in step 3.

2. In the Mail Merge Wizard (step 2), select an option in the Select starting document area:

▲ **Use the current document** (**Figure 5**) sets the active document as the main document for the merge. If you select this option, skip ahead to step 4.

▲ **Start from a template** (**Figure 6**) enables you to base the main document for the merge on a template.

▲ **Start from existing document** (**Figure 7**) enables you to open an existing document to use as the main document for the merge.

3. Select the main document for the merge:

▲ If you selected Start from template in step 2 above, click the Select template link (**Figure 6**) to display the Mail Merge tab of the Select Template dialog (**Figure 8**). Select the template you want to use and click OK.

▲ If you selected Start from existing document in step 2 above, select one of the documents listed in the Mail Merge Wizard (**Figure 7**). If the file you want is not listed, select the (More files...) option, click Open, use the Open dialog that appears (**Figure 9**) to locate and select the document you want, and click Open. The document opens.

4. Click the Next: Select recipients link at the bottom of the Mail Merge Wizard.

5. Continue following the appropriate instructions in the "Creating or Opening a Data Source" section.

To start a main document for envelopes or labels

1. Follow the instructions in the section titled "To select a type of main document." Be sure to select Envelopes or Labels in step 3.

2. In the Mail Merge Wizard (step 2), select an option in the Select starting document area:

   ▲ **Change document layout** (**Figures 10** and **11**) lets you modify the active document for envelopes or labels. If you select this option, skip ahead to step 4.

   ▲ **Start from existing document** (**Figure 12**) lets you open an existing document as a main document for your envelopes or labels.

3. Select one of the main documents listed in the Mail Merge Wizard (**Figure 12**). If the file you want is not listed, select the (More files...) option, click Open, and use the Open dialog that appears (**Figure 9**) to locate, select, and open the document you want to use.

4. Set options for your envelopes or labels:

   ▲ For envelopes, click the Envelope options link (**Figure 10**). Then use the two tabs of the Envelope Options dialog that appears (**Figures 13** and **14**) to set options for your envelopes and click OK.

   ▲ For labels, click the Label options link (**Figure 11**). Then use the Label Options dialog that appears (**Figure 15**) to set options for your labels and click OK.

5. Click the Next: Select recipients link at the bottom of the Mail Merge Wizard.

6. Continue following the appropriate instructions in the "Creating or Opening a Data Source" section.

✔ Tip

■ Envelope and label options are covered in **Chapter 10**.

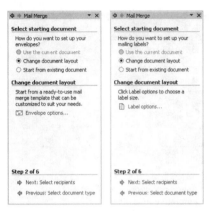

Figures 10, 11, & 12
The second step of the Mail Merge Wizard prompts you for more information about your main document. You can change the current document layout for envelopes (top left) or labels (top right), or start from an existing document (bottom).

Figures 13, 14, & 15 Use the Envelope Options dialog tabs (top) or Label Options dialog (bottom) to set options for your envelopes or labels.

STARTING A MAIN DOCUMENT

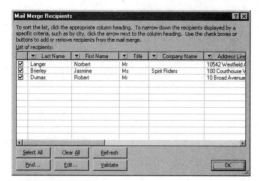

Figure 16 A data source with three records, created within Microsoft Word.

Creating or Opening a Data Source

A data source (**Figure 16**) has two components:

◆ **Fields** are categories of information. In a form letter, for example, *Last Name* and *City* might be two fields. Each field has a unique name which identifies it in both the main document and data source document.

◆ **Records** are collections of information for individual items. In a form letter, the John Smith record would include all fields for John Smith—his name, address, city, state, and postal code.

When you perform a mail merge, Word inserts the data from a data source record into a main document, replacing field names with field contents. It repeats the main document for each record in the data source (**Figure 17**).

✔ Tip

■ This chapter explains how to create or open a Word-based data source. You can also use Microsoft Outlook data or an Excel list as a data source; **Chapter 13** explains how.

Figure 17 The data source in **Figure 16** merged into the main document in **Figure 3**.

To create a data source

1. Follow the instructions earlier in this chapter to select a main document type and start a main document.

2. In the Mail Merge Wizard (step 3), select the Type a new list option (**Figure 18**).

3. Click the Create link to display the New Address List dialog (**Figure 19**). It lists commonly used field names for form letters, mailing labels, and envelopes.

4. Enter information for a specific record into each of the text boxes. You can press Tab to move to the next box or Shift Tab to move to the previous box.

5. To add another record, click the Add New button and repeat step 4.

6. When you are finished adding records, click Close.

7. A Save Address List dialog appears (**Figure 20**). Use it to name and save the data source file.

8. Word displays the Mail Merge Recipients dialog (**Figure 16**). Continue following instructions in the section titled "To select recipients."

Figure 18
When you indicate that you want to type a new list, the Mail Merge Wizard includes a link for creating the data source.

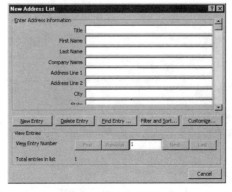

Figure 19 Use the New Address List form to enter information for each person you want to include in the data source.

Figure 20 Once you have created a data source, save it in the My Data Sources folder.

Figure 21 The Customize Address List dialog lists all the fields in the data source and offers buttons for modifying them.

Figure 22
Use the Add Field dialog to enter the name for a new field.

Figure 23
Use the Rename Field dialog to enter a new name for a field.

✔ Tips

- You can use other buttons in the New Address List dialog (**Figure 19**) to scroll through, delete, search for, and sort records. A detailed discussion of these tasks is beyond the scope of this book; experiment with these buttons on your own.

- You can customize the fields in the New Address List dialog (**Figure 19**) to include only the fields you need. Click the Customize button to display the Customize Address List dialog (**Figure 21**), then use its buttons to modify the Field Names list:

  ▲ To add a field name, click Add, enter the name in Add Field dialog that appears (**Figure 22**), and click OK.

  ▲ To remove a field name from the list, click to select it, then click Delete.

  ▲ To rename a field, click Rename, enter a new name in Rename Field dialog that appears (**Figure 23**), and click OK.

  ▲ To move a field name up in the list, click to select it, then click Move Up.

  ▲ To move a field name down in the list, click to select it, then click Move Down.

  When you are finished editing the list, click OK.

- In step 7, Word automatically displays the contents of the My Data Sources folder that it creates in the My Documents folder. Saving your data source documents in this folder makes it easy to find them for future merges.

- To edit a completed data source, click the Edit button in the Mail Merge Recipients dialog (**Figure 16**). This displays a dialog similar to the one in **Figure 19**, which you can use to add, modify, or delete records.

CREATING A DATA SOURCE

To open an existing data source

1. Follow the instructions earlier in this chapter to select a main document type and start a main document.

2. In the Mail Merge Wizard (step 3), select the Use an existing list option (**Figure 24**).

3. Click the Browse link to display the Select Data Source dialog (**Figure 25**). Select the data source you want to use and click Open.

4. Word displays the Mail Merge Recipients dialog (**Figure 16**). Continue following instructions in the section titled "To select recipients."

✔ Tips

- Use this technique to associate an existing data source with a main document.

- To edit a data source, click the Edit button in the Mail Merge Recipients dialog (**Figure 16**). This displays a dialog similar to the one in **Figure 19**, which you can use to add, modify, or delete records.

To change the data source document associated with a main document

1. Follow the instructions earlier in this chapter to select a main document type and start a main document.

2. In the Mail Merge Wizard (step 3), select the Use an existing list option (**Figure 26**).

3. Click the Select a different list link to display the Select Data Source dialog (**Figure 25**). Select the data source you want to use and click Open.

4. Word displays the Mail Merge Recipients dialog (**Figure 16**). Continue following instructions in the section titled "To select recipients."

Figure 24
When you indicate that you want to use an existing list, the Mail Merge Wizard includes a link for selecting a data source.

Figure 25 Use the Select Data Source dialog to select a data source document to associate with a main document.

Figure 26
When a data source is already associated with a main document, the Mail Merge Wizard offers a link to select a different list.

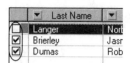

Figure 27 A check beside a recipient name indicates that the recipient will be included in the merge.

To select recipients

1. In the Mail Merge Recipients dialog (**Figure 16**), click to toggle the check boxes beside the records for recipients you want to include in the list (**Figure 27**). A check indicates that the record will be included; no check indicates that the record will be excluded.

2. Click OK to save your selections and dismiss the Mail Merge Recipients window.

3. Continue following the appropriate instructions in the "Completing a Main Document" section.

✔ Tip

- If the Mail Merge Recipients dialog (**Figure 16**) is not showing, click the Edit recipient list link in the Mail Merge Wizard (step 3; **Figure 26**).

SELECTING RECIPIENTS

Completing a Main Document

Before you can perform a mail merge, you must complete the main document by entering static text (if necessary) and inserting merge fields. How you do this depends on the type of main document you have created.

To complete letters, e-mail messages, or a directory

1. Click the Next link near the bottom of the Mail Merge Wizard (step 3):

   ▲ For letters, click Next: Write your letter (**Figures 18**, **24**, and **26**).

   ▲ For e-mail messages, click Next: Write your e-mail message.

   ▲ For a directory, click Next: Arrange your directory.

2. If you haven't already done so, enter static text into the document window by typing or pasting it in (**Figure 28**).

3. Position the insertion point where you want to insert a merge field (**Figure 28**). Then:

   ▲ To insert a predefined block of merge fields, click one of the first four options in the Mail Merge Wizard (**Figure 29**). Then use the dialog box that appears to set options for the block. **Figures 30** and **31** show two examples.

   ▲ To insert an individual merge field, click the More items link in the Mail Merge Wizard (**Figure 29**). In the Insert Merge Field dialog that appears (**Figure 32**), make sure Database Fields is selected, then select the field you want to insert and click the Insert button. Click Close to dismiss the dialog.

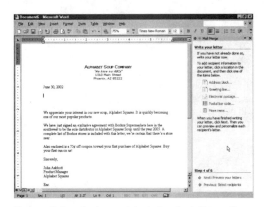

Figure 28 A main document window for letters, all ready for merge fields to be inserted.

Figure 29
The fourth step of the Mail Merge Wizard enables you to insert merge fields into your main document.

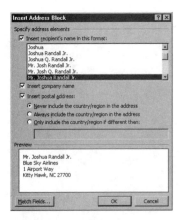

Figure 30 Use this dialog to set up an address block for a main document.

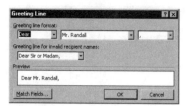

Figure 31 Use this dialog to set options for inserting a greeting line in a main document.

Figure 32
To insert an individual merge field, select the name of the field and click Insert.

4. Repeat step 3 for each merge field that you want to insert.

Figure 3 shows an example of a main document with merge fields inserted.

5. Click the Next link near the bottom of the Mail Merge Wizard (step 4):

▲ For letters, click Next: Preview your letters (**Figure 29**).

▲ For e-mail messages, click Next: Preview your e-mail messages.

▲ For a directory, click Next: Preview your directory.

6. Continue following instructions in the section titled "Previewing the merge."

✔ Tips

■ When inserting predefined merge field blocks, consult the Preview area of the dialog box you use to set options (**Figures 30** and **31**) to see how your settings will appear in the merged document.

■ Be sure to include proper spacing and punctuation as necessary between merge fields. To do this, position the insertion point where you want the space or punctuation to appear and press the appropriate keyboard key to insert it.

■ If you insert a field in the wrong place, simply select it and drag it to the correct position within the document window.

■ To remove a field, select it and press Backspace.

To complete envelopes

1. Click the Next: Arrange your envelope link at the bottom of the Mail Merge Wizard (step 3).

2. If you haven't already done so, enter static text into the document window by typing or pasting it in (**Figure 33**).

3. Position the insertion point in the address frame of the document window (**Figure 33**). Then:

   ▲ To insert a predefined block of merge fields, click one of the first four options in the Mail Merge Wizard (**Figure 34**). Then use the dialog box that appears to set options for the block. **Figures 30** and **31** show two examples.

   ▲ To insert an individual merge field, click the More items link in the Mail Merge Wizard (**Figure 34**). In the Insert Merge Field dialog that appears (**Figure 32**), make sure Database Fields is selected, then select the field you want to insert and click the Insert button. Click Close to dismiss the dialog.

4. Repeat step 3 for each merge field that you want to insert.

   Figure 35 shows an example of a main document for an envelope with the Address-Block merge field inserted.

5. Click the Next: Preview your envelopes link at the bottom of the Mail Merge Wizard (step 4, **Figure 34**).

6. Continue following instructions in the section titled "Previewing the merge."

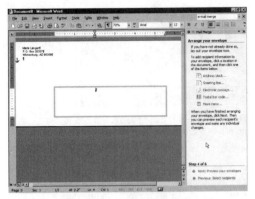

Figure 33 A main document window for envelopes, all ready for merge fields to be inserted.

Figure 34
The fourth step of the Mail Merge Wizard enables you to insert merge fields into your main document.

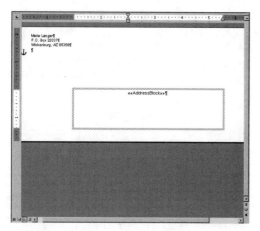

Figure 35 A main document for envelopes with the AddressBlock field inserted.

✔ Tips

- Word automatically inserts your default return address (if it has been saved) in the return address area of the envelope (**Figure 33**). You can edit or delete this text if desired. Saving a return address is discussed in **Chapter 10**.

- In step 3, if you cannot see the address frame, click the Show/Hide ¶ button ¶ on the Standard toolbar to display formatting marks. Then click beside the paragraph mark (¶) that appears in the middle of the document. The address frame appears around it. Formatting marks are covered in **Chapter 2**; frames is an advanced feature that is beyond the scope of this book.

- When inserting predefined merge field blocks, consult the Preview area of the dialog box you use to set options (**Figures 30** and **31**) to see how your settings will appear in the merged document.

- Be sure to include proper spacing and punctuation as necessary between merge fields. To do this, position the insertion point where you want the space or punctuation to appear and press the appropriate keyboard key to insert it.

- If you insert a field in the wrong place, simply select it and drag it to the correct position within the document window.

- To remove a field, select it and press Backspace.

To complete mailing labels

1. Click the Next: Arrange your labels link at the bottom of the Mail Merge Wizard (step 3).

2. If necessary, enter static text into the first cell of the table by typing or pasting it in.

3. Position the insertion point in the first cell of the table (**Figure 36**). Then:

   ▲ To insert a predefined block of merge fields, click one of the first four options in the Mail Merge Wizard (**Figure 37**). Then use the dialog box that appears to set options for the block. **Figures 30** and **31** show two examples.

   ▲ To insert an individual merge field, click the More items link in the Mail Merge Wizard (**Figure 37**). In the Insert Merge Field dialog that appears (**Figure 32**), make sure Database Fields is selected, then select the field you want to insert and click the Insert button. Click Close to dismiss the dialog.

4. Repeat step 3 for each merge field that you want to insert.

5. When you are finished inserting fields in the first cell of the table, click the Update all labels button in the Mail Merge Wizard (**Figure 37**) to copy the label layout to all of the labels in the table (**Figure 38**).

6. Click the Next: Preview your labels link at the bottom of the Mail Merge Wizard (step 4, **Figure 37**).

7. Continue following instructions in the section titled "Previewing the merge."

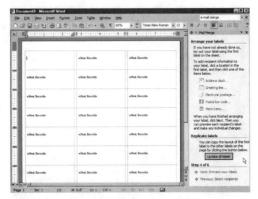

Figure 36 A main document for mailing labels, all ready for merge fields to be inserted.

Figure 37
When creating labels, the fourth step of the Mail Merge Wizard enables you to insert merge fields and copy the first label's layout to all labels in the document.

Word field

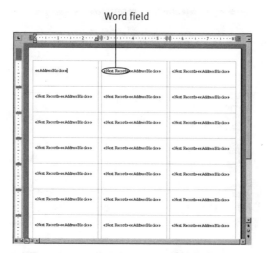

Figure 38 A completed main document for labels.

✔ Tips

- When inserting predefined merge field blocks, consult the Preview area of the dialog box you use to set options (**Figures 30** and **31**) to see how your settings will appear in the merged document.

- Be sure to include proper spacing and punctuation as necessary between merge fields. To do this, position the insertion point where you want the space or punctuation to appear and press the appropriate keyboard key to insert it.

- If you insert a field in the wrong place, simply select it and drag it to the correct position within the document window.

- To remove a field, select it and press [Backspace].

- Do not change the Word fields included in the mailing labels main document (**Figure 38**). Altering or removing a field can prevent the mailing labels from merging or printing properly.

Previewing the Merge

Before you perform the merge, the Mail Merge Wizard gives you an opportunity to see what the merged documents will look like. If you like what you see, you can perform the merge. If you don't like what you see, you can go back and make changes to fine-tune the merge setup.

To preview the merge

Use the arrow buttons in the Mail Merge Wizard (step 5) to scroll through the recipients that appear in the document window (**Figures 39**, **40**, and **41**).

✔ Tips

■ You can exclude a recipient from the merge by clicking the Exclude this Recipient button in the Mail Merge Wizard (step 5) while the recipient's record is displayed (**Figures 39** and **40**).

■ To edit the data source, click the Edit recipient list link in the Mail Merge Wizard (step 5, **Figures 39**, **40**, and **41**). This displays the Mail Merge Recipients dialog (**Figure 16**), which you can use to select recipients and modify the data source file.

Figure 39 Previewing a mail merge for a letter, ...

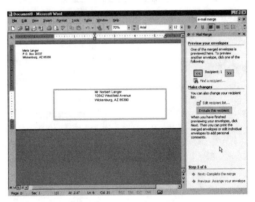

Figure 40 ... envelopes, ...

Figure 41 ... and labels.

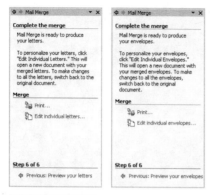

Figures 42, 43, & 44
The last step of the Mail Merge Wizard for letters (top left), envelopes (top right), and labels (bottom).

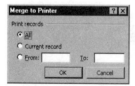

Figure 45
The Merge to Printer dialog.

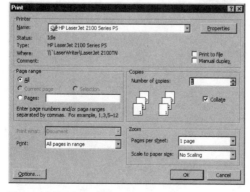

Figure 46 The Print dialog.

Completing the Merge

The last step in performing a mail merge is to merge the main document and data source. Word offers three options for merging documents:

◆ **Print** merges the documents directly to a printer. This option is available for letters, envelopes, and labels.

◆ **Electronic mail** merges the documents directly to e-mail. This option is available for e-mail messages only.

◆ **Edit individual** *document type* or **To New Document** creates a file with all of the merged data. This option is available for letters, envelopes, labels, and directories.

To merge to a printer

1. Click the Complete the merge link near the bottom of the Mail Merge Wizard (step 5, **Figures 39**, **40**, and **41**).

2. In the Mail Merge Wizard (step 6), click the Print link (**Figures 42, 43**, and **44**).

3. The Merge to Printer dialog appears (**Figure 45**). Select an option to indicate which records should print:

   ▲ **All** prints all records in the data source that have been included in the merge.

   ▲ **Current record** prints the record that is displayed in the document window.

   ▲ **From / To** enables you to enter a range of records. Enter starting and ending record numbers in each text box.

4. Click OK.

5. Use the Print dialog that appears (**Figure 46**) to set options for printing the merged documents and click OK to print.

✔ Tip

■ Printing and the Print dialog (**Figure 46**) are covered in detail in **Chapter 6**.

MERGING TO A PRINTER

To merge to electronic mail

1. Click the Complete the merge link near the bottom of the Mail Merge Wizard (step 5).

2. In the Mail Merge Wizard (step 6), click the Electronic mail link (**Figure 47**) to display the Merge to E-mail dialog (**Figure 48**).

3. Choose the field containing the e-mail addresses for the recipients from the To drop-down list (**Figure 49**).

4. Enter a subject for the messages in the Subject line text box.

5. Choose a format from the Mail format drop-down list (**Figure 50**):

   ▲ **Attachment** sends the merged document as a Word document attached to an e-mail message. The recipient must have Word (or a program capable of opening Word documents) to view the merged document.

   ▲ **Plain text** sends the merged document as plain text inside an e-mail message. This format removes all document formatting.

   ▲ **HTML** sends the merged document with HTML encoding inside an e-mail message. This format preserves most document formatting, but the recipient must have an e-mail program capable of displaying HTML.

6. Select a Send records option to indicate which records should be sent via e-mail:

   ▲ **All** sends all records in the data source that have been included in the merge.

   ▲ **Current record** sends the record that is displayed in the document window.

   ▲ **From / To** enables you to enter a range of records. Enter starting and ending record numbers in each text box.

7. Click OK. The document is merged and sent via e-mail to the recipients.

Figure 47
The sixth step of the Mail Merge Wizard for e-mail messages.

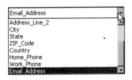

Figure 48
Use the Merge to E-Mail dialog to set options for merging records directly to electronic mail.

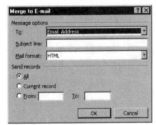

Figure 49
Use the To drop-down list to choose the field containing the e-mail address. (This is usually the Email_Address field.)

Figure 50
Choose an e-mail message format.

Figure 51 If this dialog appears, choose an option from the Profile Name drop-down list and click OK.

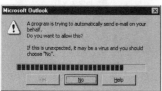

Figures 52 & 53 These two dialogs may appear when you send e-mail messages as attachments or plain text. You must click Yes to send the messages.

✔ Tips

■ For an e-mail merge to work properly, you must have MAPI-compatible e-mail software installed (such as Microsoft Outlook) and set up as your default e-mail program. Consult the documentation that came with Windows or your e-mail program to learn how to configure your computer for e-mail.

■ After step 7, a series of dialogs like the ones in **Figures 51**, **52**, and **53** may appear if you selected Attachment or Plain text in step 5. This is a security feature of Microsoft Word. In the Choose Profile dialog (**Figure 51**), choose an e-mail profile from the drop-down list and click OK. In the two warning dialogs (**Figures 52** and **53**), you must click Yes to send the messages.

To merge to a new document

1. Click the Complete the merge link near the bottom of the Mail Merge Wizard (step 5, **Figures 39**, **40**, and **41**).

2. In the Mail Merge Wizard (step 6), click the link for Edit individual letters (**Figure 42**), Edit individual envelopes (**Figure 43**), Edit individual labels (**Figure 44**), or To New Document (**Figure 54**).

3. The Merge to New Document dialog appears (**Figure 55**). Select an option to indicate which records should be included in the document:

   ▲ **All** includes all records in the data source that have been included in the merge.

   ▲ **Current record** includes only the record that is displayed in the document window.

   ▲ **From / To** enables you to enter a range of records. Enter starting and ending record numbers in each text box.

4. Click OK. Word creates a new document with the records you specified.

✔ Tip

■ Once Word has created a new document containing all the merged information, you can edit, save, or print it as desired.

Figure 54
The sixth step of the Mail Merge Wizard for a directory.

Figure 55
Use this dialog to indicate which records should be merged.

Working with Others

Collaboration Features

In office environments, a document is often the product of multiple people. In the old days, a draft document would be printed and circulated among reviewers. Along the way, it would be marked up with colored ink and covered with sticky notes full of comments. Some poor soul would have to make sense of all the markups and notes to create a clean document. The process was time consuming and was sometimes repeated through several drafts to fine-tune the document for publication.

Microsoft Word, which is widely used in office environments, includes many features that make the collaboration process quicker and easier:

◆ **Properties** stores information about the document's creator and contents.

◆ **Comments** enables reviewers to enter notes about the document. The notes don't print—unless you want them to.

◆ **Versions** enables reviewers to save multiple versions of the same document. At any time, you can revert to a previous version.

◆ **Change Tracking** enables reviewers to edit the document while keeping the original document intact. Changes can be accepted or rejected to finalize the document.

◆ **Document Protection** limits how a document can be changed.

Document Properties

The Properties dialog (**Figures 2** and **4**) enables you to store information about a document. This information can be viewed by anyone who opens the document.

✔ Tip

- The Properties dialog is organized into tabs for storing information. The Summary and Statistics tabs are covered here; explore the other tabs on your own.

To open the Properties dialog

1. Open the document for which you want to view or edit properties.

2. Choose File > Properties (**Figure 1**).

To enter summary information

1. Open the Properties dialog.

2. If necessary, click the Summary tab to display its options (**Figure 2**).

3. Enter or edit information in each field as desired:

   ▲ **Title** is the title of the document. This does not have to be the same as the file name. This field may already be filled in based on the first line of the document.

   ▲ **Subject** is the subject of the document.

   ▲ **Author** is the person who created the document. This field may already be filled in based on information stored in the User Information tab of the Options dialog.

   ▲ **Manager** is the person responsible for the document content.

   ▲ **Company** is the organization for which the author or manager works.

Figure 1
The File menu.

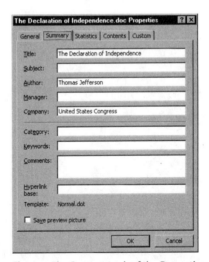

Figure 2 The Summary tab of the Properties dialog offers text boxes for recording information about the document.

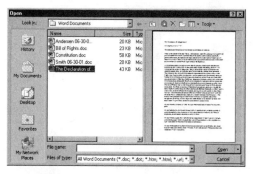

Figure 3 When you create a preview picture, it appears in the Open dialog.

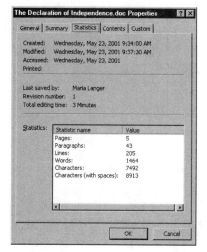

Figure 4 The Statistics tab of the Properties dialog provides additional information about the document.

▲ **Category** is a category name assigned to the document. It can be anything you like.

▲ **Keywords** are important words related to the document.

▲ **Comments** are notes about the document.

▲ **Hyperlink base** is an Internet address or path to a folder on a hard disk or network volume. This option works in conjunction with hyperlinks inserted in the document.

4. To create a document preview image that will appear in the Preview area of the Open dialog (**Figure 3**), turn on the Save preview picture check box.

5. Click OK to save your entries.

✔ Tips

■ It is not necessary to enter information in any Summary tab boxes (**Figure 2**).

■ I tell you more about the User Information tab of the Options dialog in **Chapter 15**.

To view document statistics

1. Open the Properties dialog.

2. If necessary, click the Statistics tab to display its information (**Figure 4**).

3. When you are finished viewing statistics, click OK to dismiss the dialog.

✔ Tip

■ Information in the Statistics tab (**Figure 4**) cannot be changed.

DOCUMENT PROPERTIES

Comments

Comments are annotations that you and other document reviewers can add to a document. These notes can be viewed on screen but don't print unless you want them to.

To insert a comment

1. Select the text for which you want to insert a comment (**Figure 5**).

2. Choose Insert > Comment (**Figure 6**).

   A few things happen: A comment marker (colored parentheses) appears around the selected text, the Reviewing toolbar appears, the window splits, and the insertion point moves to the Reviewing pane at the bottom of the window under a color-coded heading with your name (**Figure 7**).

3. Type in your comment. It can be as long or as short as you like (**Figure 8**).

✔ Tips

- Word gets your initials from the User Information tab of the Options dialog. I tell you more about that in **Chapter 15**.

- The colored parentheses that appear in the document window (**Figure 7**) do not print.

To close the Reviewing pane

Click the Reviewing Pane button  on the Reviewing toolbar.

✔ Tip

- If the Reviewing toolbar is not displayed, choose View > Toolbars > Reviewing to display it.

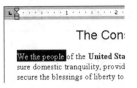

Figure 5 Start by selecting the text you want to enter a comment about.

Figure 6 Choose Comment from the Insert menu.

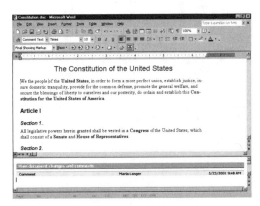

Figure 7 Word prepares to accept your comment.

Figure 8 Enter your comment in the Reviewing pane at the bottom of the window.

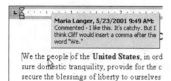

Figure 9 When you position the mouse pointer over commented text, the comment appears in a colored box.

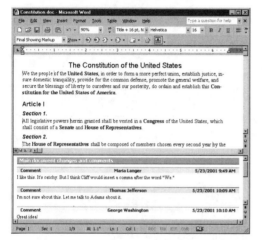

Figure 10 When the Reviewing pane appears, it shows all comments entered in the document.

Figure 11 Choose Final Showing Markup to show all comments and markups in a document.

Figure 12 Choose List of markup from the Print what drop-down list in the Print dialog to print document comments.

To view comments

Position the mouse pointer over text enclosed by colored parentheses. A colored box appears. It contains the name of the person who wrote the comment, the date and time the comment was written, and the comment text (**Figure 9**).

or

Click the Reviewing Pane button ▣ on the Reviewing toolbar to display the Reviewing pane and the comments it contains (**Figure 10**).

✔ Tips

- If the colored parentheses do not appear in the document, choose Final Showing Markup from the Display for Review drop-down list on the Reviewing toolbar (**Figure 11**).

- If the Reviewing toolbar is not displayed, choose View > Toolbars > Reviewing to display it.

- You can change the size of the Reviewing pane by dragging the border between it and the main document window.

To delete a comment

1. If necessary, choose View > Toolbars > Reviewing to display the Reviewing toolbar.

2. In the document window, position the insertion point anywhere within the parentheses surrounding commented text.

3. Click the Reject Change/Delete Comment button ▨ ▾ on the Reviewing toolbar. All traces of the comment disappear.

To print comments

1. Follow the instructions in **Chapter 6** to prepare the document for printing and open the Print dialog.

2. Choose List of markup from the Print what drop-down list (**Figure 12**).

3. Click OK.

Versions

Word's Versions feature enables you to save multiple versions of a document. You can then revert to any version to undo editing changes made over time.

To save a version

1. Choose File > Versions (**Figure 1**).

2. In the Versions dialog that appears (**Figure 13**), click Save Now.

3. The Save Version dialog appears (**Figure 14**). If desired, enter comments about the version, then click OK.

   The current state of the document is saved as a version within the document file.

To automatically save a version of the file when you close it

1. Choose File > Versions (**Figure 1**).

2. In the Versions dialog that appears (**Figure 13**), turn on the Automatically save a version on close check box.

3. Click Close.

   From that point forward, every time you close the document, it will be saved as a version.

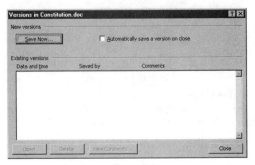

Figure 13 The Versions dialog before any versions have been saved.

Figure 14 Use this dialog to enter comments about the version you are saving.

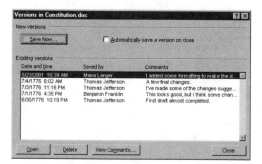

Figure 15 The versions that have been saved are listed in reverse chronological order.

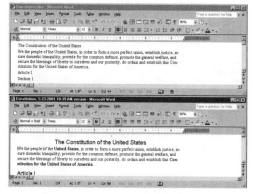

Figure 16 When you open another version of a document, it appears in its own window. Word automatically arranges the windows so you can see them both.

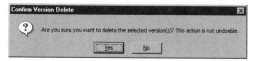

Figure 17 A dialog like this one appears when you delete a version.

To open a version

1. With a document that includes multiple versions open and active, choose File > Versions (**Figure 1**).

2. In the Versions dialog that appears (**Figure 15**), select the version you want to open.

3. Click Open.

   The version of the document that you selected opens. Word arranges both document windows—the one that was open in step 1 and the one that you opened in step 3—so you can see them at the same time (**Figure 16**).

✔ Tips

- You can click the View Comments button in the Versions dialog (**Figure 15**) to see the entire text of a comment. It appears in a dialog like the one in **Figure 14**.

- If you save an opened version of a document, it is saved as a separate document.

To delete a version

1. Choose File > Versions (**Figure 1**).

2. In the Versions dialog that appears (**Figure 15**), select the version you want to delete.

3. Click Delete.

4. A confirmation dialog like the one in **Figure 17** appears. Click Yes.

   The version you deleted is removed from the list in the Versions dialog.

✔ Tip

- Each time you save a file version, you increase the size of the file. If your file becomes too large, you can delete early versions to reduce its size.

OPENING & DELETING VERSIONS

Change Tracking

Word's Change Tracking feature makes it possible for multiple reviewers to edit a document without actually changing the document. Instead, each reviewer's markups are displayed in color in the document window. At the conclusion of the reviewing process, someone with final say over document contents reviews all of the edits and either accepts or rejects each of them. The end result is a final document that incorporates the accepted changes.

To turn change tracking on or off

Choose Tools > Track Changes (**Figure 18**) or press Ctrl Shift E.

◆ If change tracking was turned off, it is enabled and the Reviewing toolbar appears (**Figure 19**).

◆ If change tracking was turned on, it is disabled.

✔ Tip

■ You can tell whether change tracking is enabled by looking at the Track Changes button on the Reviewing toolbar (**Figure 19**). If the button appears with a border around it, change tracking is enabled.

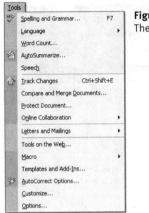

Figure 18
The Tools menu.

Figure 19 The Reviewing toolbar with change tracking enabled.

Figure 20 When you edit a document with change tracking enabled, your changes appear as revision marks.

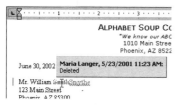

Figure 21 When you point to a revision mark, a box appears with information about it.

To track changes

1. Turn on change tracking as instructed on the previous page.

2. Make changes to the document.

   Your changes appear as colored markups and a vertical line appears in the left margin beside each edit (**Figure 20**).

✔ Tip

- If the document is edited by more than one person, each person's revision marks appear in a different color. This makes it easy to distinguish one editor's changes from another's.

To view revision information

Point to a revision mark. A colored box with information about the change appears (**Figure 21**).

✔ Tip

- This is a handy way to see who made a change and when it was made.

To accept or reject changes

1. If necessary, choose View > Toolbars > Reviewing to display the Reviewing toolbar (**Figure 19**).

Then:

2. Click the Next  or Previous  button on the Reviewing toolbar to select the next or previous change (**Figure 22**).

3. Accept or reject the selected change:

   ▲ To accept the change, click the Accept Change button on the Reviewing toolbar. The change is incorporated into the document and its revision mark disappears (**Figure 23a**).

   ▲ To reject the change, click the Reject Change/Delete Comment button on the Reviewing toolbar. The revision mark disappears (**Figure 23b**).

4. Repeat steps 2 and 3 until all changes have been reviewed and either accepted or rejected.

Or then:

2. Accept or reject all changes:

   ▲ To accept all changes, choose Accept All Changes in Document from the Accept Change button's menu on the Reviewing toolbar (**Figure 24**). All revisions are incorporated into the document and the revision marks disappear.

   ▲ To reject all changes, choose Reject All Changes in Document from the Reject Change/Delete Comment button's menu on the Reviewing toolbar (**Figure 25**). The revision marks disappear and the document is returned to the way it was before change tracking was enabled.

Figure 22 Word selects the change.

Figures 23a & 23b The change selected in **Figure 22** after it has been accepted (left) or rejected (right). As shown here, accepting the change (the deletion of the word *Smith*) removes the selected text from the document and rejecting the change retains the selected text and removes revision marks from it.

Figure 24 Use this pop-up menu to accept all changes in a document.

Figure 25 Use this pop-up menu to reject all changes in a document.

Figure 26
Use the Protect Document dialog to set document protection options.

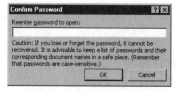

Figure 27 Re-enter the protection password in the Confirm Password dialog.

Document Protection

Word's Document Protection feature enables you to limit the types of changes others can make to a document. Specifically, you can limit changes to:

◆ **Tracked changes** enables users to change the document only with the change tracking feature turned on.

◆ **Comments** only enables users to add comments to the document.

◆ **Forms** enables users to enter information only into form fields. (This is an advanced feature of Word that is beyond the scope of this book.)

To protect a document

1. Choose Tools > Protect Document (**Figure 18**).

2. In the Protect Document dialog that appears (**Figure 26**), select the type of protection you want.

3. If desired, enter a password in the Password box.

4. Click OK.

5. If you entered a password, the Confirm Password dialog appears (**Figure 27**). Enter the password again and click OK.

✔ Tips

■ Entering a password in the Protect Document dialog (**Figure 26**) is optional. However, if you do not use a password with this feature, the document can be unprotected by anyone.

■ If you enter a password in the Protect Document dialog (**Figure 26**), don't forget it! If you can't remember the password, you can't unprotect the document!

To work with a protected document

What you can do with a protected document depends on how you protected it:

◆ If you protected the document for change tracking, the change tracking feature is enabled. Any change you make to the document appears as revision marks.

◆ If you protected the document for comments, you can only insert comments in the document. If you attempt to edit text, a message telling you that the document is locked for editing appears in the document window's status bar (**Figure 28**).

To unprotect a document

1. Choose Tools > Unprotect Document (**Figure 29**).

2. If protection is enforced with a password, a dialog like the one in **Figure 30** appears. Enter the password and click OK.

This command is not available because the document is locked for edit.

Figure 28 When a document is protected for comments, a message like this appears in the status bar when you try to edit the document.

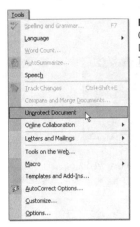

Figure 29 Choose Unprotect Document from the Tools menu.

Unprotect Document

Password:

OK   Cancel

Figure 30 Enter the protection password in this dialog to unprotect the document.

UNPROTECTING A DOCUMENT

USING OTHER PROGRAMS

Using Word with Other Programs

Microsoft Word works well with a number of other programs. These programs can expand Word's capabilities:

- ◆ OLE objects created with other Microsoft Office and Windows programs can be inserted into Word documents.

- ◆ Word documents can be inserted into documents created with other Microsoft Office programs.

- ◆ Word documents can be e-mailed to others using Microsoft Outlook.

- ◆ Outlook address book information can be used as a data source for a Word mail merge.

This chapter explains how you can use Word with some of these other programs.

✔ Tip

- ■ This chapter provides information about programs other than Microsoft Word. To follow instructions for a specific program, that program must be installed on your computer.

OLE Objects

An *object* is all or part of a file created with an OLE-aware program. *OLE* or *Object Linking and Embedding* is a Microsoft technology that enables you to insert a file as an object within a document (**Figure 1**)—even if the file was created with a different program. Clicking or double-clicking the inserted object runs the program that created it so you can modify its contents.

Word's Object command enables you to insert OLE objects in two different ways:

◆ **Create and insert a new OLE object.** This method runs a specific OLE-aware program so you can create an object.

◆ **Insert an existing OLE object.** This method enables you to locate, select, and insert an existing file as an object.

✔ Tips

■ All Microsoft programs are OLE-aware. Many software programs created by other developers are also OLE-aware; check the documentation that came with a specific software package for details.

■ Microsoft Word comes with a number of OLE-aware programs that can be used to insert objects. The full Microsoft Office package includes even more of these programs.

■ You can learn more about inserting text and multimedia elements in **Chapter 7**.

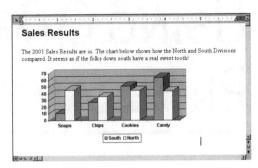

Figure 1 A Microsoft Graph Chart object inserted in a Microsoft Word document.

Figure 2
Choose Object from
the Insert menu.

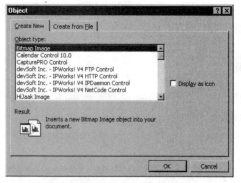

Figure 3 The Object dialog. The options in the
Object type list vary depending on the software
installed on your computer.

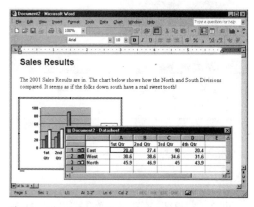

Figure 4 The default Microsoft Graph window.

To insert a new object

1. Position the insertion point where you
   want the object to appear.

2. Choose Insert > Object (**Figure 2**) to
   display the Object dialog.

3. If necessary, click the Create New tab to
   display its options (**Figure 3**).

4. In the Object type list, click to select the
   type of object that you want to insert.

5. Click OK. Word runs the program that
   you selected. It may take a moment for it
   to appear. **Figure 4** shows the default
   Microsoft Graph window and toolbar.

6. Use the program to create the object that
   you want.

7. When you are finished creating the object,
   click outside of the object. The program's
   toolbars and menus disappear and you can
   continue working with Word (**Figure 1**).

✔ Tips

- Some of the programs that come with
  Word and appear in the Object dialog may
  not be fully installed. If that is the case,
  Word will prompt you to insert the program CD to install the software.

- For more information about using one of
  the OLE-aware programs that comes with
  Word or Office, use the program's Help
  menu or Office Assistant.

- Some OLE-aware programs may display a
  dialog or similar interface. Use the controls
  within the dialog to create and insert the
  object.

To insert an existing object

1. Position the insertion point where you want the object to appear.

2. Choose Insert > Object from the Insert menu (**Figure 2**) to display the Object dialog.

3. Click the Create from File tab to display its options (**Figure 5**).

4. Click the Browse button.

5. Use the Browse dialog that appears (**Figure 6**) to locate and select the file that you want to insert. Then click Insert.

6. The pathname for the file appears in the Object dialog. Click OK. The file is inserted as an object in the document (**Figure 7**).

✔ Tip

- To insert a file as an object, the program that created the file must be properly installed on your computer or accessible through a network connection. Word informs you if the program is missing.

To customize an inserted object

Follow the instructions in the previous two sections to create and insert a new object or insert an existing object. In the Object dialog (**Figures 3** and **5**), turn on check boxes as desired:

- **Link to File** creates a link to the object's file so that when it changes, the object inserted within the Word document can change. This is similar to inserting a link, which is explained in **Chapter 7**. This option is only available when inserting an existing file as an object.

- **Display as icon** displays an icon that represents the object rather than the object itself (**Figure 8**).

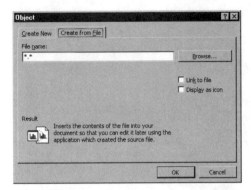

Figure 5 The Create from File tab of the Object dialog.

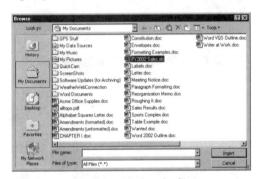

Figure 6 Use this dialog to select the file you want to insert.

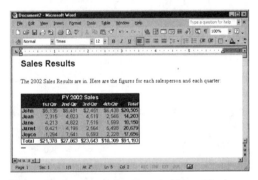

Figure 7 An Excel worksheet inserted into a Word document.

Figure 8 A Microsoft Excel 2002 worksheet displayed as an icon.

FY2002 Sales.xls

	A	B	C	D	E	F
1	FY 2002 Sales					
2		1st Qtr	2nd Qtr	3rd Qtr	4th Qtr	Total
3	John	$5,135	$6,481	$2,451	$6,438	$20,505
4	Jean	2,315	4,823	4,519	2,546	14,203
5	Jane	4,213	4,822	7,516	1,599	18,150
6	Janet	8,421	4,196	2,564	5,498	20,679
7	Joyce	1,294	7,541	6,593	2,228	17,656
8	Total	$21,378	$27,863	$23,643	$18,309	$91,193

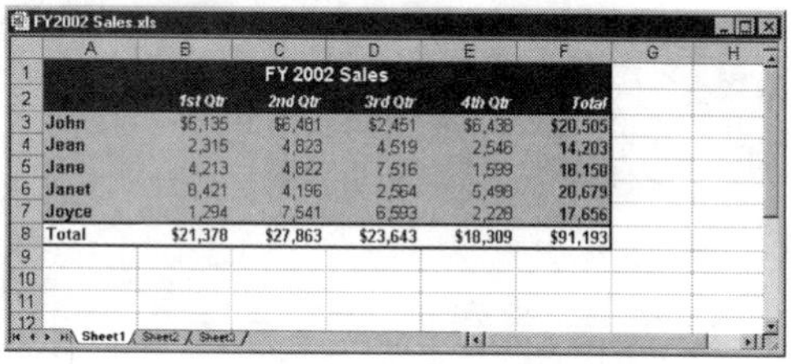

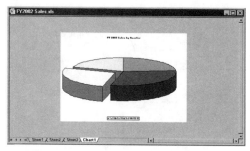

Figure 9 Spreadsheet software like Excel is most often used to create worksheets full of financial information.

Inventory.xls

	A	B	C	D	E	F	G	H
1	Product Code	Department	Cost	Sale Price	Reorder Point	Qty on Hand	Time to Order?	Resale Value
2	DBF166U	Girls Clothes	23.75	24.99	140	467		11,670
3	BZX72F	Women's Clothes	22.95	24.99	150	396		9,896
4	DCI222G	Girls Clothes	19.15	20.99	30	110		2,309
5	ZXF14K	Pets	18.83	20.99	140	234		4,912
6	MTD1725J	Toys	9.89	10.99	10	205		2,253
7	BDZ1023T	Women's Clothes	16.84	18.99	80	365		6,931
8	TJX198C	Housewares	9.30	10.99	30	351		3,857
9	PJY157Z	Garden	13.18	15.99	140	129	Reorder Now!	2,063
10	IFP244D	Lingerie	22.31	26.99	70	36	Reorder Now!	972
11	FEU2113N	Misses Clothes	11.60	13.99	100	286		4,001
12	NGD1623E	Hardware	8.92	10.99	170	95	Reorder Now!	1,044
13	HHL92K	Big & Tall Men's Clothes	23.31	28.99	140	240		6,958
14	WER1314B	Computers	12.68	15.99	120	225		3,598
15	NST19N	Hardware	7.09	8.99	190	318		2,859
16	TLE15Y	Housewares	20.54	25.99	160	320		8,317
17	ZET21W	Pets	7.85	9.99	60	467		4,665
18	TVQ811R	Housewares	10.17	12.99	20	371		4,819
19	GUA1619W	Junior Clothes	10.17	12.99	0	266		3,455

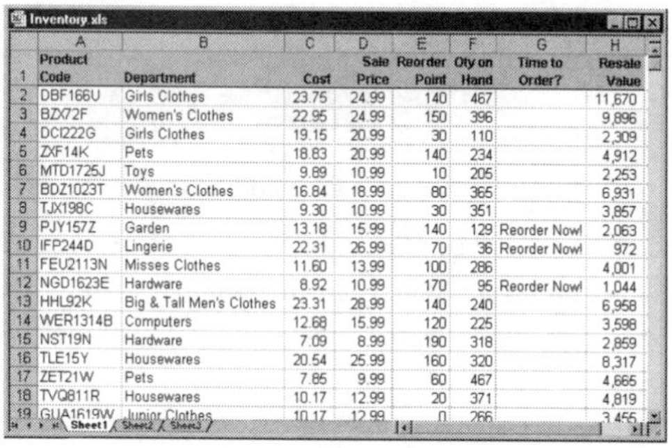

Figure 10 Excel has built-in features for managing lists of information.

Figure 11 Excel also includes powerful charting capabilities.

Using Excel with Word

Excel is the spreadsheet component of Microsoft Office. A *spreadsheet* is like a computerized accountant's worksheet—you enter information and formulas and the software automatically calculates results (**Figure 9**). Best of all, if you change one of the numbers in the worksheet, the results of calculations automatically change as necessary.

You can use Excel with Word to:

- Include information from an Excel document in a Word document (**Figure 7**).
- Perform a Word data merge with an Excel list as a data source.

✔ Tips

- Spreadsheet software is especially handy for financial calculations, but it is often used to maintain lists of data (**Figure 10**).
- Excel also includes powerful charting capabilities so you can create charts based on spreadsheet information (**Figure 11**).
- To learn more about using Excel 2002, pick up a copy of *Excel 2002 for Windows: Visual QuickStart Guide*, a Peachpit Press book by Maria Langer.

To include Excel document content in a Word document

To insert an Excel document as an object in a Word document, consult the section about OLE objects earlier in this chapter.

or

1. In the Excel document, select the cells (**Figure 12**) or chart (**Figure 13**) that you want to include in the Word document.

2. Choose Edit > Copy or press Ctrl C (**Figure 14**).

3. Switch to Word and position the insertion point in the Word document where you want the Excel content to appear.

4. Choose Edit > Paste or press Ctrl V (**Figure 15**). The selection appears in the Word document at the insertion point (**Figures 16** and **17**).

✔ Tips

- You can also use drag-and-drop editing techniques to drag an Excel document selection into a Word document. Drag-and-drop is discussed in **Chapter 2**.

- Worksheet cells are pasted into Word as a Word table (**Figure 16**). Tables are covered in **Chapter 9**.

- An Excel chart is pasted into Word as a picture (**Figure 17**). Working with pictures is discussed in **Chapter 7**.

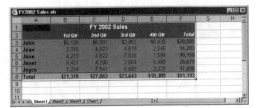

Figure 12 Select the cells...

Figure 13 ...or the chart that you want to include.

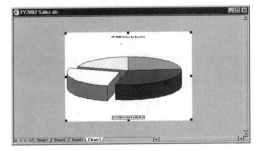

Figure 14 Choosing Copy from Excel's Edit menu.

Figure 15 Choosing Paste from Word's Edit menu.

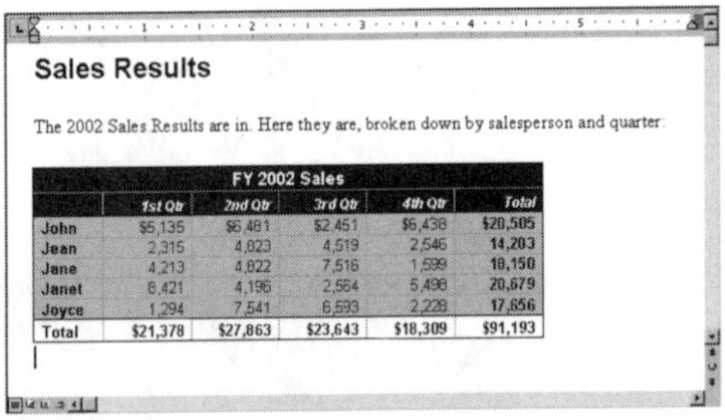

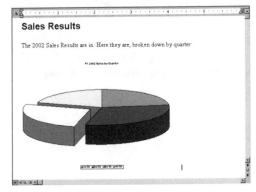

Figure 16 Worksheet cells are pasted into a Word document as a Word table.

Figure 17 A chart is pasted into a Word document as a picture.

Figure 18
Step 3 of the Mail Merge Wizard enables you to specify a data source.

To use an Excel list as a data source for a mail merge

1. Follow the instructions in **Chapter 11** to display the Mail Merge Wizard and create a main document.

2. In step 3 of the Mail Merge Wizard (**Figure 18**), select the Use an existing list option.

3. Click the Browse link and then use the Select Data Source dialog that appears (**Figure 19**) to locate, select, and open the Excel file containing the list you want to use for the merge.

4. If the Select Table dialog appears (**Figure 20**), select the worksheet containing the data you want to use. If the first row of the Excel worksheet contains column headings, make sure the check box for First row of data contains column headers is turned on. Then click OK.

5. The Mail Merge Recipients dialog appears (**Figure 21**). It contains all of the data from the Excel list. Follow the steps in **Chapter 11** to complete the main document and merge the data.

✔ Tip

- Word's mail merge feature is covered in detail in **Chapter 11**.

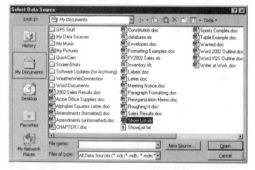

Figure 19 Select the Excel file containing the data.

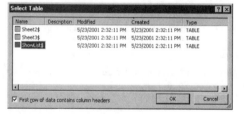

Figure 20 If the file contains more than one worksheet, select the worksheet containing the data.

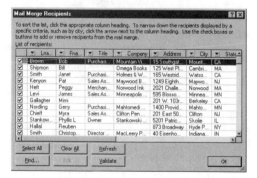

Figure 21 The Excel data appears in the Mail Merge Recipients dialog.

USING EXCEL WITH WORD

Using PowerPoint with Word

PowerPoint is the presentation software component of Microsoft Office. *Presentation software* enables you to create slides for use at meetings and seminars (**Figure 22**). The slides can be printed on paper, output as 35mm slides, saved Web pages or graphic files, or shown directly from the computer.

You can use PowerPoint with Word to:

◆ Create a PowerPoint presentation from a Word outline.

◆ Include PowerPoint slides in a Word document.

✔ Tip

■ To learn more about using PowerPoint, consult the documentation that came with the program or its onscreen help feature.

To use a Word outline in a PowerPoint presentation

1. Display the Word outline document you want to use in PowerPoint (**Figure 23**).

2. Choose File > Send To > Microsoft PowerPoint (**Figure 24**).

   The outline is imported into PowerPoint. A new slide is created for each top-level heading. **Figure 22** shows what the outline in **Figure 23** looks like after being sent to PowerPoint and formatted using one of PowerPoint's built-in templates.

✔ Tip

■ Word's Outline feature is discussed in detail in **Chapter 8**.

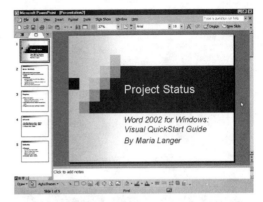

Figure 22 PowerPoint enables you to create slides for presenting information.

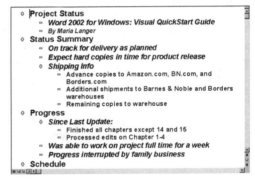

Figure 23 Start with the Word outline that you want to use in PowerPoint.

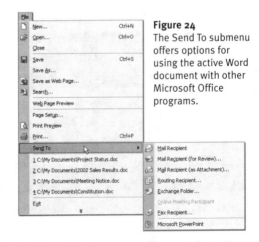

Figure 24 The Send To submenu offers options for using the active Word document with other Microsoft Office programs.

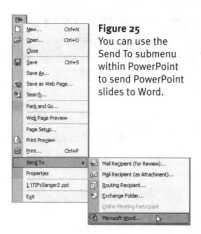

Figure 25
You can use the Send To submenu within PowerPoint to send PowerPoint slides to Word.

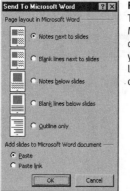

Figure 26
The Send To Microsoft Word dialog enables you to select layout and paste options for slides.

To insert PowerPoint slides into a Word document

1. Display the PowerPoint presentation that you want to use in a Word document.

2. Choose File > Send To > Microsoft Word (**Figure 25**). The Send To Microsoft Word dialog appears (**Figure 26**).

3. Select one of the page layout options in the top part of the dialog to determine how slides will be laid out on Word pages.

4. Select one of the options at the bottom of the dialog to specify whether the slides will be pasted in or pasted in as a link.

5. Click OK.

6. A new Word document is created. Slides are pasted into the document using the layout you specified in step 3. **Figure 27** shows an example of the slides from **Figure 22** pasted into Word with blank lines beside each slide.

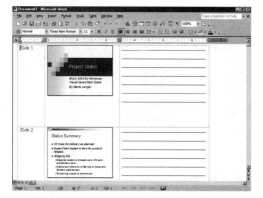

Figure 27 Slides are pasted into a new Word document using the layout you specified.

USING POWERPOINT WITH WORD

249

Using Outlook with Word

Outlook is the e-mail and personal information management software component of Microsoft Office. *E-mail software* enables you to send and receive electronic mail messages (**Figure 28**). *Personal information management software* enables you to store and organize calendar (**Figure 29**) and address book (**Figure 30**) data.

You can use Outlook with Word to:

◆ E-mail a Word document to a friend, family member, or co-worker.

◆ Perform a Word data merge with an Outlook address book as the data source.

✔ Tips

■ To learn more about using Outlook, consult the documentation that came with the program or its onscreen help feature.

■ As discussed in **Chapter 11**, performing a mail merge to e-mail messages uses Outlook (or another e-mail program) to send merged data as e-mail messages.

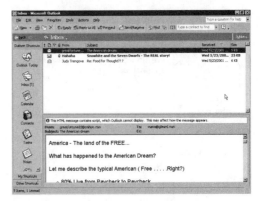

Figure 28 Entourage can handle e-mail (like this junk mail message—I get plenty of them!), ...

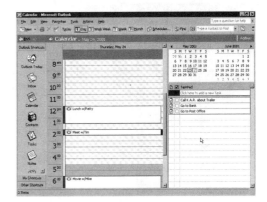

Figure 29 ...calendar events, ...

Figure 30 ...and address book information.

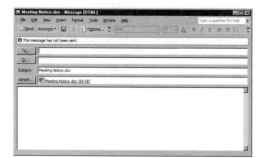

Figure 31 Entourage displays an e-mail form.

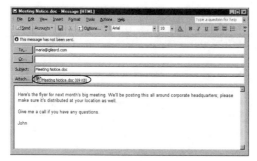

Figure 32 Here's what a finished message might look like. Note that the name of the Word document being sent appears in the Attachments area.

To send a Word document via e-mail

1. Display the Word document you want to send via e-mail.

2. Choose File > Send To > Mail Recipient (as Attachment) (**Figure 24**).

3. Word runs Outlook and displays an empty e-mail window with the To field selected (**Figure 31**). Enter the e-mail address for the person you want to send the document to.

4. If desired, edit the contents of the Subject field.

5. In the message body, enter a message to accompany the file. **Figure 32** shows an example.

6. To send the message, click the Send button. Outlook connects to the Internet and sends the message.

7. Switch back to Word to continue working with the document.

✔ Tips

- These instructions assume that Outlook is the default e-mail program as set in the Internet control panel. If a different program has been set as the default e-mail program, ignore steps 3 through 6 and send the message as you normally would with your e-mail program.

- Outlook (or your default e-mail program) must be properly configured to send and receive e-mail messages. Check the program's documentation or onscreen help if you need assistance with setup.

USING OUTLOOK WITH WORD

To use an Outlook address book as a data source for a data merge

1. Follow the instructions in **Chapter 11** to display the Mail Merge Wizard and create a main document.

2. In step 3 of the Mail Merge Wizard (**Figure 33**), select the Select from Outlook contacts option.

3. Click the Choose Contacts folder link and then use the Select Contact List folder dialog that appears (**Figure 34**) to locate and select the folder containing the data you want to use for the merge. Click OK.

4. The Mail Merge Recipients dialog appears (**Figure 35**). It contains all of the data from the Outlook folder. Follow the steps in **Chapter 11** to complete the main document and merge the data.

✔ Tip

■ Word's mail merge feature is covered in detail in **Chapter 11**.

Figure 33
Step 3 of the Mail Merge Wizard enables you to specify a data source.

Figure 34 Select the Outlook contact folder containing the data.

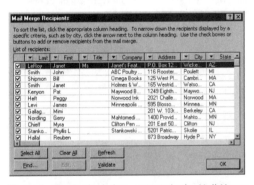

Figure 35 The Outlook data appears in the Mail Merge Recipients dialog.

USING OUTLOOK WITH WORD

WEB PAGES

Web Pages

The World Wide Web has had a bigger impact on publishing than any other communication medium introduced in the past fifty years. Web pages, which can include text, graphics, and hyperlinks, can be published on the Internet or an intranet, making them available to audiences 24 hours a day, 7 days a week. They can provide information quickly and inexpensively to anyone who needs it.

Microsoft Word 2002 has built-in Web page creation, modification, and interaction tools. With Word, you can build Web pages and open links to other Web pages and sites.

✔ Tips

- This chapter provides enough information to get you started using Word to create Web pages. Complete coverage of Web publishing, however is beyond the scope of this book.

- To learn more about the World Wide Web and Web publishing, check these Peachpit Press books:

    ▲ *The Little Web Book* by Alfred and Emily Glossbrenner.

    ▲ *The Non-Designer's Web Book, Second Edition*, by Robin Williams and John Tollett.

    ▲ *Putting Your Small Business on the Web* by Maria Langer.

Continued on next page...

Continued from previous page.

- Web pages are normally viewed with a special kind of software called a *Web browser*. Microsoft Internet Explorer, Netscape Navigator, and Netscape Communicator are three examples of Web browsers.

- To access the Internet, you need an Internet connection, either through a network or dial-up connection. Setting up a connection is beyond the scope of this book; consult the documentation that came with Windows or your Internet access software for more information.

- To publish a Web page, you need access to a Web server. Contact your organization's Network Administrator or *Internet Service Provider* (*ISP*) for more information.

- A *hyperlink* (or *link*) is text or a graphic that, when clicked, displays other information from the Web.

- An intranet is like the Internet, but it exists only on the internal network of an organization and is usually closed to outsiders.

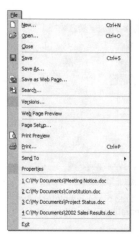

Figure 1
The File menu.

Figure 2
The New Document task pane enables you to create all kinds of Word documents, including Web pages.

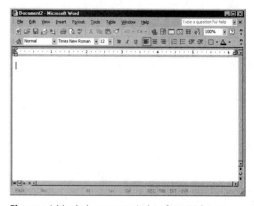

Figure 3 A blank document window for a Web page.

Creating a Web Page

Word offers three ways to create a Web page:

◆ The **Blank Web Page** template lets you create a Web page from scratch, using appropriate formatting options.

◆ **Web Page Templates** let you create Web pages, complete with graphic elements and links, for a specific purpose. Placeholder text helps you organize information on your pages.

◆ The **Web Page Wizard** lets you create a Web site, complete with graphic elements and links, for a specific purpose.

◆ The **Save as Web Page** command lets you save a regular Word document as a Web page. This encodes the document and saves it as HTML.

✔ Tips

■ *HTML* (or *HyperText Markup Language*) is a system of codes for defining Web pages.

■ I explain how to save a regular Word document as an HTML file near the end of this chapter.

To use the Blank Web Page template

1. If necessary, choose File > New (**Figure 1**) to display the New Document task pane (**Figure 2**).

2. Click the Blank Web Page link in the New area. Word creates a blank new Web page and displays it in Web Layout view (**Figure 3**).

3. Enter and format text in the document window as desired to meet your needs.

✔ Tip

■ I explain how to enter and format text for a Web page a little later in this chapter.

To use other Web page templates

1. If necessary, choose File > New (**Figure 1**) to display the New Document task pane (**Figure 2**).

2. Click the General Templates link in the New from template area.

3. In the Templates dialog that appears, click the Web Pages tab to display its options (**Figure 4**).

4. Click the icon for the template you want to use.

5. Click OK. Word creates a new Web page document with placeholder text (**Figure 5**).

6. Edit placeholder text as desired to customize the Web page for your needs.

✔ Tip

- The colored underlined text that appears on Web pages are *hypertext links*. I tell you more about links later in this chapter.

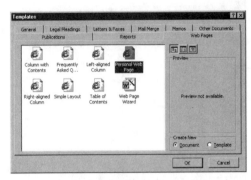

Figure 4 In the Web Pages tab of the Templates dialog, click the icon for the template you want to use.

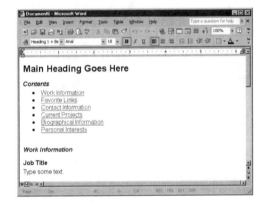

Figure 5 This example shows a Web page created with the Personal Web Page template.

Figure 6 The Start screen of the Web Page Wizard explains what the Wizard will do.

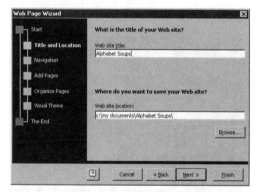

Figure 7 The Title and Location screen prompts you to enter a title for the Web site. The location for the site is entered automatically based on the site title.

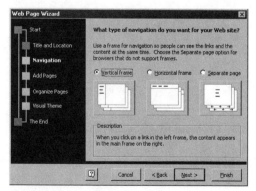

Figure 8 The Navigation screen offers three options for creating navigational links.

To create a Web site with the Web Page Wizard

1. If necessary, choose File > New (**Figure 1**) to display the New Document task pane (**Figure 2**).

2. Click the General Templates link in the New from template area.

3. In the Templates dialog that appears, click the Web Pages tab to display its options (**Figure 4**).

4. Click the Web Page Wizard icon to select it.

5. Click OK.

6. Follow the steps in the Web Page Wizard dialogs that appear (**Figures 6** through **13**) to create the Web pages.

7. When the wizard is finished, the home page appears (**Figure 14**). Edit placeholder text and enter new text as desired on each Web page to customize pages for your needs.

✔ Tips

- If you select one of the two frame options in the Navigation screen of the Web Page Wizard (**Figure 8**), the Frames toolbar appears automatically with the home page (**Figure 14**). You can use this toolbar to create and modify navigation frames.

- When viewing options in the Theme dialog (**Figure 12**), you may be prompted to install a theme before you can preview it. If so, insert your Word or Office CD and click the Install button that appears onscreen to install the theme files.

- Although the Web Page Wizard displays just the first or home page for a site, it creates multiple Web pages. You can use the Window menu to switch from one Web page to another for editing.

- Themes and links are covered later in this chapter.

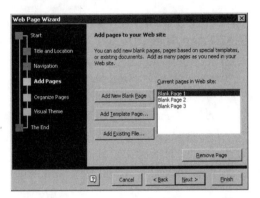

Figure 9 The Add Pages screen enables you to add blank pages, template pages, or existing page files. You can also remove selected pages.

Figure 12 Clicking the Browse Themes button in the Visual Theme screen (**Figure 11**) displays the Theme dialog, which you can use to select a theme.

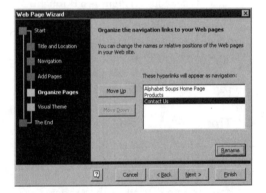

Figure 10 The Organize Pages screen enables you to rename the pages and change their order.

Figure 13 The End screen tells you that Word is finished gathering information and prompts you to click the Finish button.

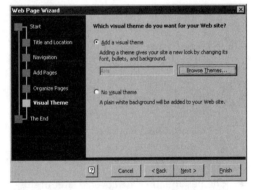

Figure 11 The Visual Theme screen lets you specify whether you want a special look for the pages.

Figure 14 The home page created by the Web Page Wizard with the settings shown in **Figures 6** through **13**.

Figure 15 Select the text that you want to modify.

Figure 16 Whatever you type replaces the selected text.

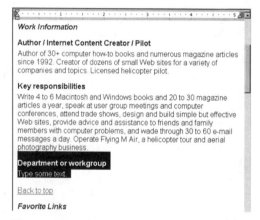

Figure 17 Select the text that you want to delete.

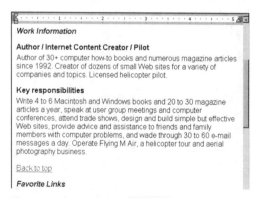

Figure 18 When you press [Backspace], the selected text disappears.

Editing Text

You can add, edit, or delete text on a Web page the same way you add, edit, or delete text in a regular Word document.

✔ Tip

- For more detailed instructions about editing text, consult **Chapter 2**.

To add text

1. Position the insertion point where you want to add the text.

2. Type the text that you want to add.

To modify text

1. Select the text that you want to change (**Figure 15**).

2. Type in the replacement text. The selected text is deleted and the replacement text is inserted in its place (**Figure 16**).

To delete text

1. Select the text that you want to delete (**Figure 17**).

2. Press [Backspace]. The selected text is deleted (**Figure 18**).

Formatting Text & Pages

You format text on a Web page the same way you format text in any other Word document: by using the Formatting toolbar (**Figure 19**), Format menu commands (**Figure 20**) with their related dialogs, and shortcut keys.

Figure 19 The Formatting toolbar includes many formatting options that can be applied to Web pages and Word documents.

Although the font and paragraph formatting techniques are the same for Web pages as they are for regular Word documents, there are two options that are especially useful for Web pages:

◆ **Background** enables you to set the background color, pattern, or image for the page.

◆ **Theme** enables you to set background patterns, graphic elements, and color schemes for an entire page all at once.

✔ Tips

■ For more detailed instructions about formatting text, consult **Chapters 3** and **4**.

■ Formatting techniques not specifically covered in this chapter either work exactly as they do for regular Word documents or they do not apply to Web pages.

Figure 20
The Format menu offers many commands for formatting a document and its contents.

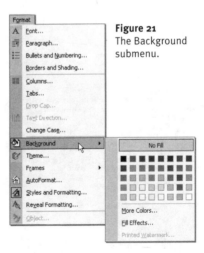

Figure 21
The Background submenu.

FORMATTING TEXT & PAGES

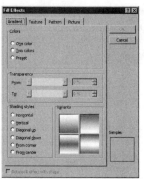

Figure 22
The Fill Effects dialog offers options for Gradient, ...

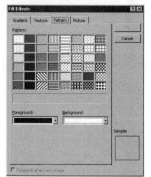

Figure 23
... Texture, ...

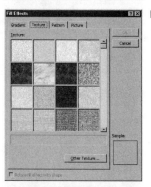

Figure 24
... Pattern, ...

Figure 25
... and Picture for the background.

To set the page background color, pattern, or image

1. Choose Format > Background to display the Background submenu (**Figure 21**).

2. To set a background color, choose a color.

   or

   To set a background pattern or texture, choose Fill Effects. Then set options on one of the four tabs in the Fill Effects dialog that appears and click OK:

   ▲ **Gradient** (**Figure 22**) enables you to set a gradient fill pattern for the background. Select a color option and shading style to create the gradient you want. Other options appear in the dialog depending on the options you select.

   ▲ **Texture** (**Figure 23**) enables you to set a texture for the background. Click a texture button to select it.

   ▲ **Pattern** (**Figure 24**) enables you to set a standard fill pattern for the background. Select the pattern you want, then choose Foreground and Background colors from the drop-down lists.

   ▲ **Picture** (**Figure 25**) enables you to use an image as a background. The image is repeated to fill the page. Click the Select Picture button to locate and select a picture file on disk.

   or

   To remove a background color or pattern, choose No Fill.

SETTING THE PAGE BACKGROUND

To set the page theme

1. Choose Format > Theme (**Figure 20**) to display the Theme dialog (**Figure 12**).

2. In the Choose a Theme scrolling list, select the name of the theme you want to apply to the page. The Sample area changes to show what the theme looks like.

3. Set other options by toggling check boxes near the bottom of the Theme dialog:

   ▲ **Vivid Colors** makes styles and borders a brighter color and changes the document background color.

   ▲ **Active Graphics** displays animated graphics in the Web browser window when the theme includes them.

   ▲ **Background Image** displays the background image for the theme as the page background. Turning off this check box enables you to use a plain background color with a theme.

4. Click OK to save your settings. The page's colors and background change accordingly (**Figure 26**).

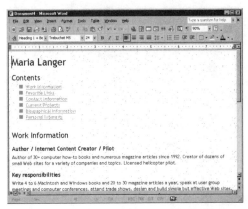

Figure 26 A Web page with the Axis theme applied.

Favorite Links

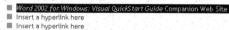

■ *Word 2002 for Windows: Visual QuickStart Guide* Companion Web Site
■ Insert a hyperlink here
■ Insert a hyperlink here

Figure 27 Select the text that you want to use as a hyperlink.

Figure 28
Choose Hyperlink from the Insert menu.

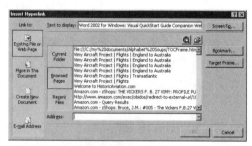

Figure 29 The Insert Hyperlink dialog for inserting a link to an existing file or Web page.

Hyperlinks

A hyperlink is text or a graphic that, when clicked, displays other information. Word enables you to create two kinds of hyperlinks:

◆ A link to a *URL* (*Uniform Resource Locator*), which is the Internet address of a document or individual. Word makes it easy to create links to two types of URLs:

▲ **http://** links to a Web page on a Web server.

▲ **mailto**: links to an e-mail address.

◆ A link to a Word document on your hard disk or network.

By default, hyperlinks appear as colored, underlined text (**Figure 34**).

✔ Tip

■ Word can automatically format URLs as hyperlinks. Simply type the complete URL; when you press (Spacebar) or (Enter), Word turns the URL into a hyperlink. You can set this option in the AutoFormat tab of the AutoCorrect dialog, which I tell you about in **Chapter 4**.

To insert a hyperlink

1. Position the insertion point where you want the hyperlink to appear.

or

Select the text or picture that you want to convert to a hyperlink (**Figure 27**).

2. Choose Insert > Hyperlink (**Figure 28**); press (Ctrl)(K), or click the Insert Hyperlink button 🔲 on the Standard toolbar.

The Insert Hyperlink dialog appears (**Figure 29**).

3. Choose one of the Link to buttons on the left side of the dialog:

Continued on next page...

HYPERLINKS

Continued from previous page.

▲ **Existing File or Web Page (Figure 29)** enables you to link to a file on disk or a Web page. If you select this option, you can either select one of the files or locations that appear in the list or type a path or URL in the Address box (**Figure 30**).

▲ **Place in This Document (Figure 31)** enables you to link to a specific location in the current document. If you select this option, choose a heading in the document hierarchy.

▲ **Create New Document (Figure 32)** enables you to create and link to a new document. If you select this option, you can either enter a pathname for the document or click the Change button and use the Create New Document dialog that appears to create a new document.

▲ **E-mail Address (Figure 33)** enables you to link to an e-mail address. If you select this option, you can either enter the e-mail address in the E-mail address box or select one of the recently used e-mail addresses in the list.

4. Click OK to save your settings and dismiss the Insert Hyperlink dialog.

The hyperlink is inserted.

or

The selected text turns into a hyperlink (**Figure 34**).

Figure 30 Type the URL for the link location.

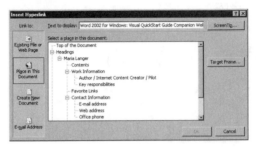

Figure 31 The Insert Hyperlink dialog for inserting a link to a place in the current document, ...

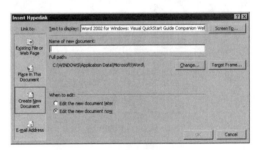

Figure 32 ... to a new document, and ...

Figure 33 ... to an e-mail address.

Favorite Links

■ *Word 2002 for Windows: Visual QuickStart Guide* Companion Web Site
■ Insert a hyperlink here
■ Insert a hyperlink here

Figure 34 Hyperlinks appear as underlined text.

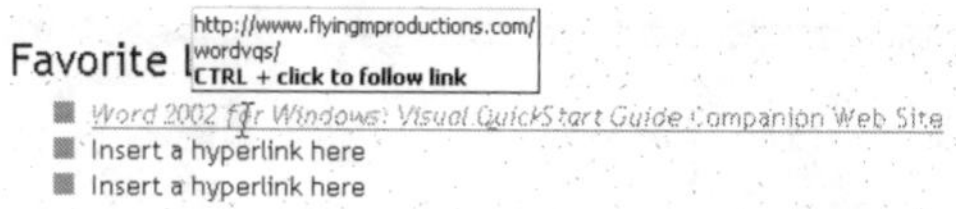

Favorite | http://www.flyingmproductions.com/
wordvqs/
CTRL + click to follow link
- *Word 2002 for Windows: Visual QuickStart Guide Companion Web Site*
- Insert a hyperlink here
- Insert a hyperlink here

Figure 35 Pop-up menus like this one enable you to link to favorite or recent URLs or documents.

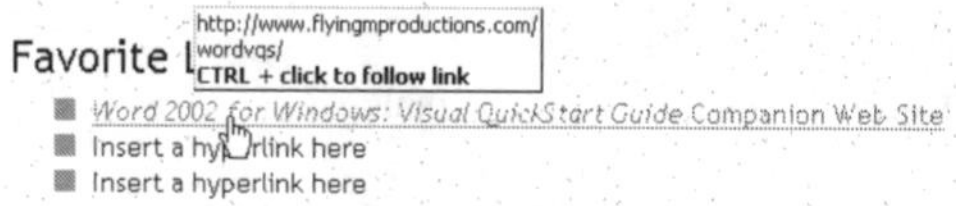

Favorite | http://www.flyingmproductions.com/
wordvqs/
CTRL + click to follow link
- *Word 2002 for Windows: Visual QuickStart Guide Companion Web Site*
- Insert a hyperlink here
- Insert a hyperlink here

Figure 36 When you point to a link, the mouse pointer turns into a pointing finger and the link location appears in a yellow Screen Tip box above it.

To follow a hyperlink

1. Position the mouse pointer on the hyperlink. A box containing the URL for the link and some instructions appears (**Figure 35**).

2. Hold down Ctrl—the mouse pointer turns into a hand with a pointing finger (**Figure 36**)—and click the link.

   If the hyperlink points to an Internet URL, Word runs your default Web browser, connects to the Internet, and displays the URL.

   or

   If the hyperlink points to a file on your hard disk or another computer on the network, the file opens.

   or

   If the hyperlink points to an e-mail address, Word launches your default e-mail application and displays a new message form with the address included in the link.

FOLLOWING HYPERLINKS

To remove a hyperlink

1. Position the insertion point anywhere within the hyperlink.

2. Choose Insert > Hyperlink (**Figure 28**) or press Ctrl K.

   or

   Click the Insert Hyperlink button 🔘 on the Standard toolbar.

3. In the Edit Hyperlink dialog that appears (**Figure 37**), click the Remove Link button.

4. Click OK.

   The link is removed from the text, but the text remains. All hyperlink formatting is removed.

or

1. Drag to select the hyperlink.

2. Press Backspace.

   Both the text and its hyperlink are removed from the document.

✔ Tip

■ You can also use the Edit Hyperlink dialog (**Figure 37**) to modify the link, as discussed earlier in this section.

Figure 37 The Edit Hyperlink dialog.

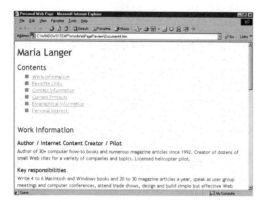

Figure 38 The Web page appears in your default Web browser's window.

Working with Web Page Files

Word offers several options for working with Web page files.

◆ Preview Web pages with your default Web browser.

◆ Save Web pages created with a Web page template.

◆ Save Web page files as regular Word documents.

◆ Save regular Word documents as Web pages.

◆ Open Web pages stored on your computer, another computer on the network, or the World Wide Web.

✔ Tips

■ The name of a Web page file should not contain any spaces and should end with the .htm or .html file name extension to be properly recognized as a Web page file. If you're not sure which extension to use, ask your network administrator or ISP.

■ When copying Web pages to a directory on a Web server, be sure to include the Web page file and its associated image files.

■ Using the Open and Save As dialogs is covered in **Chapter 2**.

To preview a Web page

Choose File > Web Page Preview (**Figure 1**).

Word runs your default Web browser. The Web page appears in the browser window (**Figure 38**).

To save a Web page

1. Choose File > Save (**Figure 1**) to display the Save As dialog (**Figure 39**).

2. Use the dialog to enter a name and select a disk location for the file.

3. Make sure Web Page is chosen from the Save as type drop-down list (**Figure 40**).

4. Click Save.

   Word saves the file. Each picture within the file is also saved as an individual JPEG or GIF format graphic file in a folder named for the Web page (**Figure 41**).

To save a Web page as a regular Word document

1. With a Web page open, choose File > Save As (**Figure 1**) to display the Save As dialog (**Figure 39**).

2. Use the dialog to enter a name and select a disk location for the file.

3. Make sure Word Document is chosen from the Save as type drop-down list (**Figure 40**).

4. Click Save.

To save a regular Word document as a Web page

1. With a Word document open, choose File > Save As Web Page (**Figure 1**) to display the Save As dialog (**Figure 39**).

2. Use the dialog to enter a name and select a disk location for the file.

3. Make sure Web Page is chosen from the Save as type drop-down list (**Figure 40**).

4. Click Save.

   Word saves the document as a Web page. Each picture within the file is saved as a JPEG or GIF format graphic file in a folder named for the Web page (**Figure 41**).

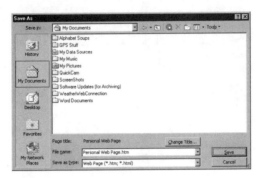

Figure 39 The Save As dialog for a Web page.

Figure 40 Use the Save as type drop-down list in the Save As dialog to choose the format in which you want to save the file.

Personal Web Page_files   Personal Web Page.htm

Figure 41 A saved Web page and folder containing image files, viewed in Windows Explorer.

Figure 42
Use the Set Page Title dialog to change the title for a Web page.

✔ Tip

- You can change the *title* of a Web page—the text that appears in the title bar of a Web browser—by clicking the Change Title button in the Save As dialog (**Figure 39**). Enter a new title for the document in the Set Page Title dialog that appears (**Figure 42**) and click OK.

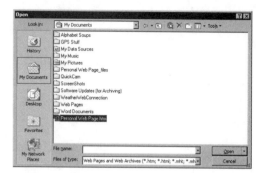

Figure 43 The Open dialog.

Figure 44 The Files of type drop-down list in the Open dialog.

To open a Web page

1. Choose File > Open (**Figure 1**).

2. Use the Open dialog that appears (**Figure 43**) to locate and select the file you want to open. Then click Open.

   Word opens the Web page you indicated, whether it is on your hard disk, another computer on the network, or the World Wide Web.

✔ Tips

- You can choose Web Pages and Web Archives from the Files of type drop-down list (**Figure 44**) so only Web pages appear in the Open dialog.

- To open a Web page on the World Wide Web, your computer must be connected to the Internet. Word will initiate a connection if it needs to.

- Double-clicking the Finder icon for a Web page created with Word will open the document with your default Web browser—*not* Microsoft Word.

OPENING WEB PAGE FILES

SETTING WORD OPTIONS

The Options Dialog

Microsoft Word's Options dialog offers eleven categories of options that you can set to customize the way Word works for you:

- ◆ **View** options control Word's onscreen appearance.

- ◆ **General** options control general Word operations.

- ◆ **Edit** options control editing.

- ◆ **Print** options control document printing.

- ◆ **Save** options control file saving.

- ◆ **User Information** options contain information about the primary user.

- ◆ **Compatibility** options control a document's compatibility with other applications or versions of Word.

- ◆ **File Locations** options specify where certain Word files are stored on disk.

- ◆ **Security** options enable you to set file encryption, file sharing, and privacy options for a file.

- ◆ **Spelling & Grammar** options control spelling and grammar checker operations.

- ◆ **Track Changes** options control the track changes feature.

✔ Tip

- ■ Word's default preference settings are discussed and illustrated throughout this book.

To set options

1. Choose Tools > Options (**Figure 1**) to display the Options dialog (**Figure 2**).

2. Click the tab to display the category of options that you want to set.

3. Set options as desired.

4. Repeat steps 2 and 3 for other categories of options that you want to set.

5. Click OK to save your settings.

✔ Tips

■ I illustrate and discuss all Options dialog options throughout this chapter.

■ If Microsoft Word is installed on your computer as part Office XP, you can use the Save My Settings Wizard to save your options settings on your computer, another network computer, or the Microsoft Web site. This makes it possible to restore your settings if they should become corrupted or changed by someone else. Choose Start > Microsoft Office Tools > Save My Settings Wizard to get started.

Figure 1
To open the Options dialog, choose Options from the Tools menu.

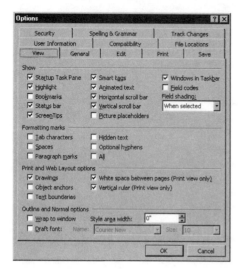

Figure 2 The default settings in the View tab of the Options dialog.

Figure 3
Smart tags enable you to perform tasks with certain text.

View Options

The View tab of the Options dialog (**Figure 2**) offers options in four categories: Show, Formatting marks, Print and Web Layout options, and Outline and Normal options.

Show

Show options determine what Word interface elements appear on screen:

◆ **Startup Task Pane** is the New document task pane that appears when you run Word from the Start menu.

◆ **Highlight** displays text highlighting.

◆ **Bookmarks** displays document bookmarks by enclosing their names in square brackets. If displayed, the bookmarks do not print.

◆ **Status bar** displays the status bar at the bottom of the window.

◆ **ScreenTips** displays information or comments in boxes when you point to buttons or annotated text.

◆ **Smart tags** displays purple dotted underlines beneath text for which there is a smart tag. Pointing to the text displays a pop-up menu you can use to perform tasks with the text. **Figure 3** shows an example of a smart tag that appears when you type in a date.

◆ **Animated text** displays animation applied to text. Turning off this option displays animated text the way it will print.

◆ **Horizontal scroll bar** displays a scroll bar along the bottom of the window.

◆ **Vertical scroll bar** displays a scroll bar along the right side of the window.

Continued on next page...

Continued from previous page.

→ Here's·some·text·to·show·off·all·the·non¬printing·characters.¶

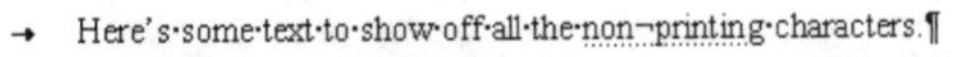

Figure 4 Formatting marks revealed!

◆ **Picture placeholders** displays graphics as empty boxes. Turning on this option can speed up the display of documents with a lot of graphics.

◆ **Windows in Taskbar** displays a Taskbar icon for each open Word document window.

◆ **Field codes** displays field codes instead of results.

◆ **Field shading** enables you to specify how you want fields shaded. The options are:

▲ **Never** never shades fields.

▲ **Always** always shades fields.

▲ **When selected** only shades a field when it is selected.

Formatting marks

Formatting marks options determine which (if any) formatting mark characters appear on screen (**Figure 4**).

◆ **Tab characters** displays gray right-pointing arrows for tab characters.

◆ **Spaces** displays tiny gray dots for space characters.

◆ **Paragraph marks** displays gray backwards Ps for return characters.

◆ **Hidden text** displays text formatted as hidden with a dotted underline.

◆ **Optional hyphens** displays L-shaped hyphens for optional hyphen characters.

◆ **All** displays all formatting marks. Turning on this option is the same as turning on the Show/Hide ¶ button ¶ on the Standard toolbar.

Figure 5 When you turn on the Draft font option, you can choose a font and size.

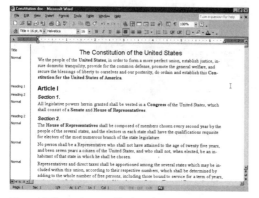

Figure 6 The style area displayed in Normal view.

Print and Web Layout options

Window options determine which elements are displayed in Print and Web Layout views.

◆ **Drawings** displays objects created with Word's drawing tools. Turning off this option can speed up the display and scrolling of documents with many drawings.

◆ **Object anchors** displays the anchor marker indicating that an object is attached to text. An object's anchor can only appear when the object is selected, this check box is turned on, and nonprinting characters are displayed. You must turn on this option to move an anchor.

◆ **Text boundaries** displays dotted lines around page margins, text columns, and objects.

◆ **White space between pages** displays the full top and bottom margins of pages in Print Layout view.

◆ **Vertical ruler** displays a ruler down the left side of the window in Print Layout view.

Outline and Normal options

Window options determine which elements are displayed in Outline and Normal views.

◆ **Wrap to window** wraps text to the width of the window rather than to the right indent or margin.

◆ **Draft font** displays most character formatting as bold or underlined and displays graphics as empty boxes. If you turn on this option, you can set the font and size to use for the draft font (**Figure 5**). Using this option can speed up the display of heavily formatted documents.

◆ **Style area width** enables you to specify a width for the style area. When set to a value greater than 0, the style area appears along the left side of the window and indicates the style applied to each paragraph in the document (**Figure 6**).

General Options

General options (**Figure 7**) control the general operation of Word:

◆ **Background repagination** paginates documents automatically as you work. (This option cannot be turned off in Page Layout view.)

◆ **Blue background, white text** displays the document as white text on a blue background—like the old WordPerfect software.

◆ **Provide feedback with sound** plays sound effects at the conclusion of certain actions or with the appearance of alerts.

◆ **Provide feedback with animation** displays special animated cursors while waiting for certain actions to complete.

◆ **Confirm conversion at Open** displays a dialog that you can use to select a converter when you open a file created with another application.

◆ **Update automatic links at Open** automatically updates linked information when you open a document containing links to other files.

◆ **Mail as attachment** sends the current document as an attachment to an e-mail message when you choose File > Send To: Mail Recipient (as Attachment). With this check box turned off, the contents of the current document are copied into an e-mail message rather than sent as an attachment.

◆ **Recently used file list** enables you to specify the number of recently opened files that should appear near the bottom of the File menu. This feature is handy for quickly reopening recently accessed files.

◆ **Help for WordPerfect users** displays Word instructions when you press a Word-Perfect for DOS key combination.

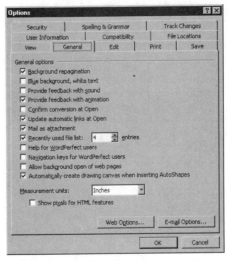

Figure 7 The default settings in the General tab of the Options dialog.

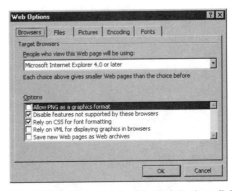

Figure 8 The Browsers tab of the Web Options dialog.

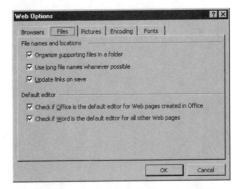

Figure 9 The Files tab of the Web Options dialog.

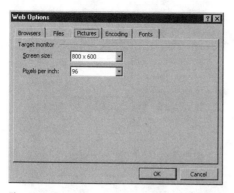

Figure 10 The Pictures tab of the Web Options dialog.

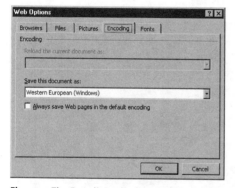

Figure 11 The Encoding tab of the Web Options dialog.

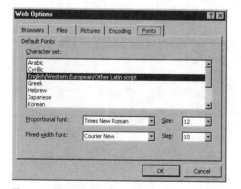

Figure 12 The Fonts tab of the Web Options dialog.

◆ **Navigation keys for WordPerfect users** changes the functions of [Page Up], [Page Down], [Home], [End], and [Esc] to the way they work in WordPerfect.

◆ **Allow background open of Web pages** enables you to open HTML documents in the background while you work with Word.

◆ **Automatically create a drawing canvas when inserting AutoShapes** creates a drawing canvas on the drawing layer of a document when you draw an AutoShape.

◆ **Measurement units** enables you to select the measurement unit used throughout Word. Options are Inches, Centimeters, Points, and Picas.

◆ **Show pixels for HTML features** changes the default unit to pixels in dialogs while working with HTML features.

Web Options

Clicking the Web Options button displays the Web Options dialog (**Figures 8** through **12**), which has five different tabs of options for creating and working with Web pages. Although these options are advanced and far beyond the scope of this book, here's a quick overview of each.

◆ **Browsers** options (**Figure 8**) control various compatibility and formatting options for the Web pages you create.

◆ **Files** options (**Figure 9**) control file naming and locations and the default editor for Web pages.

◆ **Pictures** options (**Figure 10**) control the file formats of images and the resolution of the target monitor.

◆ **Encoding** options (**Figure 11**) control how a Web page is coded when saved.

◆ **Fonts** options (**Figure 12**) control the character set and default fonts.

E-mail Options

Clicking the E-mail Options button displays the E-mail Options dialog (**Figures 13** through **15**), which has three tabs of options related to e-mail. The options are advanced and beyond the scope of this book, but here's a quick look at each.

◆ **E-mail Signature** options (**Figure 13**) enables you to enter and save text that can appear at the bottom of every e-mail message you write.

◆ **Personal Stationery** options (**Figure 14**) enables you to specify the themes and font appearance used in e-mail messages you write.

◆ **General** options (**Figure 15**) enables you to set HTML options for e-mail messages you send.

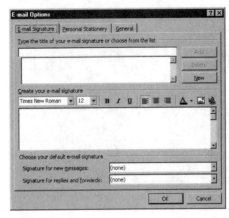

Figure 13 E-mail Signature options in the E-mail Options dialog.

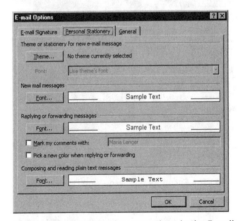

Figure 14 Personal Stationery options in the E-mail Options dialog.

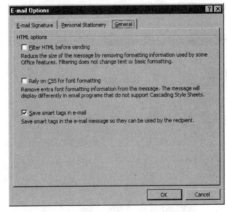

Figure 15 General options in the E-mail Options dialog.

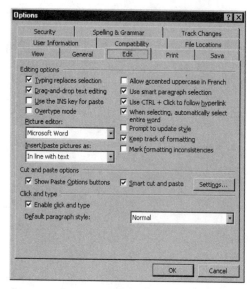

Figure 16 The default options in the Edit tab of the Options dialog.

Figure 17
Use this drop-down list to determine how pictures are inserted or pasted into your documents.

Edit Options

Edit options (**Figure 16**) control the way certain editing tasks work. There are three categories: Editing options, Cut and paste options, and Click and type.

Editing options

Editing options set the way text is edited:

◆ **Typing replaces selection** deletes text when you start typing. If you turn this check box off, Word inserts typed text to the left of any text selected before you began typing.

◆ **Drag-and-drop text editing** allows you to move or copy selected text by dragging it.

◆ **Use the INS key for paste** enables you to press Ins to use the Paste command.

◆ **Overtype mode** replaces characters, one at a time, as you type. This is the opposite of Insert mode.

◆ **Picture editor** is the program you use to edit pictures within Microsoft Word.

◆ **Insert/paste picture as** enables you to determine how pictures are inserted or pasted into your document. The default is In line with text, but you can select a different option from the drop-down list (**Figure 17**).

◆ **Allow accented uppercase in French** enables Word's proofing tools to suggest accent marks for uppercase characters for text formatted as French.

◆ **Use smart paragraph selection** includes the paragraph mark when you select a paragraph.

◆ **Use CTRL+Click to follow hyperlink** requires you to hold down Ctrl while clicking a hyperlink to follow it.

Continued on next page...

EDIT OPTIONS

Continued from previous page.

- **When selecting, automatically select entire word** selects entire words when your selection includes the spaces after words. This feature makes it impossible to use the mouse to select multiple word fragments.

- **Prompt to update style** tells Word to display a dialog when you format text containing a style and then choose the style again. The dialog enables you to update the style to match the new formatting or reapply the style.

- **Keep track of formatting** tells Word to record formatting commands as you type so you can apply the formatting again.

- **Mark formatting inconsistencies** applies a wavy blue underline to formatting that is similar but not exactly the same as other text in the document. To use this option, you must also enable the Keep track of formatting option.

Cut and paste options

Cut and paste options set the way the cut, copy, and paste commands work.

- **Show Paste Options button** displays a button beneath pasted text which offers additional options for the text.

- **Use smart cut and paste** adds or removes spaces as necessary when you delete, drag, or paste text. This feature can save time when editing text.

Click and type

Click and type options control the way the click and type feature works:

- **Enable click and type** turns on the click and type feature.

- **Default paragraph style** enables you to select the default style for click and type entries in a document.

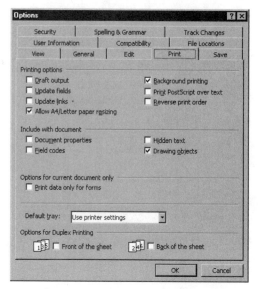

Figure 18 The default options in the Print tab of the Options dialog.

Print Options

Print options (**Figure 18**) control the way documents print. There are four categories: Printing options, Include with document, Options for current document only, and Options for Duplex Printing.

Printing options

Printing options let you specify how the document content is updated and printed:

◆ **Draft output** prints the document with minimal formatting. This may make the document print faster, but not all printers support this option.

◆ **Update fields** automatically updates Word fields before you print. This feature prevents you from printing a document with outdated field contents.

◆ **Update links** automatically updates information in linked files before you print. This feature prevents you from printing a file with outdated linked file contents.

◆ **Allow A4/Letter paper sizing** automatically adjusts the paper size for documents created with another country's standard paper size (such as A4, which is used in Europe) to your standard paper size (which is Letter in the U.S.).

◆ **Background printing** allows your printer to print Word documents in the background while you continue to work with Word or other programs. With this option turned off, you would have to wait for a document to finish printing before you could continue working.

PRINT OPTIONS

Continued on next page...

Continued from previous page.

◆ **Print PostScript over text** prints any PostScript code in a converted Word for Macintosh document (such as a digital watermark) on top of document text instead of underneath it. This option only works with PostScript printers.

◆ **Reverse print order** prints documents in reverse order—last page first. This might be useful if your printer stacks output face up.

Include with document

Include with document options enable you to print or suppress specific information from the document:

◆ **Document properties** prints the document's summary information on a separate page after the document. This information is stored in the Summary tab of the Properties dialog (**Figure 19**).

◆ **Field codes** prints field codes instead of field contents.

◆ **Hidden text** prints text formatted as hidden.

◆ **Drawing objects** prints objects drawn with Word's drawing tools.

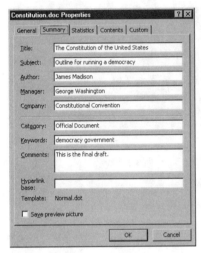

Figure 19 The Summary tab of the Properties dialog.

Options for current document only

As the name implies, options for current document only affect the way the active document prints:

◆ **Print data only for forms** prints just the information entered in fill-in forms—not the form itself.

◆ **Default tray** is the default tray from which paper should be used when printing. (This option is printer-specific and may not appear for your printer.)

Options for Duplex Printing

These options control the order of pages printed on both sides.

◆ **Front of the sheet** prints the first page on the top sheet. With this check box turned off, the first page prints on the bottom sheet.

◆ **Back of the sheet** prints the second page on the top sheet. With this check box turned off, the second page prints on the bottom sheet.

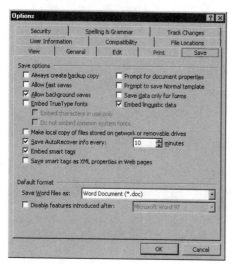

Figure 20 The default options in the Save tab of the Options dialog.

Save Options

Save options (**Figure 20**) control the way files are saved to disk. There are two categories of Save options: Save options and Default format.

Save options

Save options enable you to set file saving options for all files that you save.

◆ **Always create backup copy** saves the previous version of a file as a backup copy in the same folder as the original. Each time the file is saved, the new backup copy replaces the old one.

◆ **Allow fast saves** speeds up saving by saving only the changes to an existing file. If you turn off this check box, Word saves the entire file; this takes longer but results in slightly smaller files that are less likely to suffer from file corruption problems. This option is not available when the Always create backup copy option is enabled.

◆ **Allow background saves** allows Word to save a document in the background while you continue working with it. This option is especially useful for large or complex files.

◆ **Embed TrueType fonts** includes font information in the document so others can view your document with the fonts you applied, even if the fonts are not installed in their system. If you turn on this check box, you can turn on one or both of the options beneath it:

▲ **Embed characters in use only** embeds only the characters that are used in the document. This minimizes the file size.

▲ **Do not embed common system fonts** does not embed the font if it is one of the commonly installed system fonts.

Continued on next page...

Continued from previous page.

◆ **Make local copy of files stored on network or removable drives** makes a copy on your hard disk of any file you store on a network or removable drive.

◆ **Save AutoRecover info every** enables you to set a frequency for automatically saving a special document recovery file. Word can use the AutoRecover file to recreate the document if your computer crashes or loses power before you get a chance to save changes.

◆ **Embed smart tags** saves smart tag information with the document.

◆ **Save smart tags as XML properties in Web pages** saves smart tags in files you save as HTML documents.

◆ **Prompt for document properties** displays the Properties dialog (**Figure 19**) when you save a file for the first time. You can use this dialog to enter and store information about the file.

◆ **Prompt to save Normal template** displays a dialog that enables you to save or discard changes you made to the default settings in the Normal template. With this check box turned off, Word automatically saves changes to the Normal template.

◆ **Save data only for forms** saves the data entered into a form as a single, tab-delimited record that you can import into a database.

◆ **Embed linguistic data** saves speech and handwritten input data with the file.

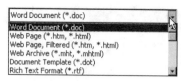

Figure 21 The Save Word files as drop-down list in the Save tab of the Options dialog.

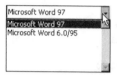

Figure 22
Use this drop-down list to choose the features you want saved with files.

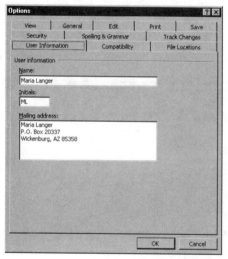

Figure 23 The User Information tab of the Options dialog.

Default format

The Default format options enables you to set the default format for files you save.

◆ **Save Word files as** enables you to choose a default format for saving Word files. The drop-down list (**Figure 21**) offers the same options found in the Save As dialog.

◆ **Disable features introduced after** enables you to select the features you want included with the file. Choose a version of Word from the drop-down list (**Figure 22**) to disable features introduced after that Word version.

User Information Options

The User Information options (**Figure 23**) store information about the primary user of that copy of Word. This information is used by a variety of features throughout Word. The fields of information here are self-explanatory, so I won't go into them in detail.

Compatibility Options

Compatibility options (**Figure 24**) control the internal formatting of the current Word document for compatibility with other applications or versions of Word.

◆ **Font Substitution** enables you to specify a font to be used in place of a font applied in the document but not installed on your computer. (This happens most often when you open a file that was created on someone else's computer.) Click this button to display the Font Substitution dialog (**Figure 25**). You can then select the missing font name and choose a substitution font from the Substituted font drop-down list. The menu includes all fonts installed on your computer. To reformat text by applying the substituted font, click the Convert Permanently button. If the document does not contain any missing fonts, Word does not display the Font Substitution dialog.

◆ **Recommended options for** enables you to select a collection of compatibility rules for a specific application. Choose an option from the drop-down list (**Figure 26**).

◆ **Options** enables you to toggle check boxes for a variety of internal formatting options. These options are automatically set when you choose one of the rule sets from the Recommended options for drop-down list, but you can override them as desired.

◆ **Default** applies the current dialog settings to all documents created with the current template from that point forward.

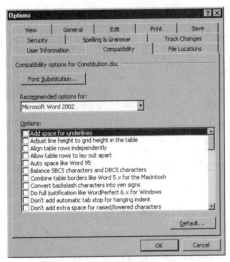

Figure 24 The Compatibility tab of the Options dialog.

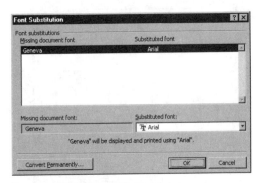

Figure 25 The Font Substitution dialog.

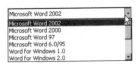

Figure 26 The Recommended options for pop-up menu.

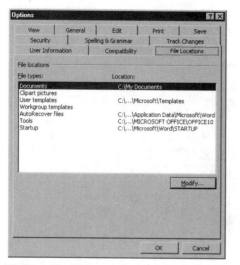

Figure 27 The File Locations tab of the Options dialog.

Figure 28 Use this dialog to set the location of a specific type of file.

Figure 29 The pathname for the folder you set appears in the dialog.

File Locations Options

File Locations options (**Figure 27**) enable you to set the default disk location for certain types of files. This makes it easier for Word (and you) to find these files.

To set or change a default file location

1. Click to select the name of the file type for which you want to set or change the file location (**Figure 27**).

2. Click the Modify button.

3. Use the Modify Location dialog that appears (**Figure 28**) to locate and select the folder in which the files are or will be stored.

4. Click OK.

The pathname for the location appears to the right of the name of the file type (**Figure 29**).

FILE LOCATIONS OPTIONS

287

Security Options

Security options (**Figure 30**) help keep your documents and system secure. There are four categories of options: File encryption options for this document, File sharing options for this document, Privacy options, and Macro security.

File encryption options for this document

File encryption encodes a file so it is impossible to read without entering a correct password. To use this feature, enter a password in the Password to open box. Clicking the Advanced button beside this option displays the Encryption Type dialog (**Figure 31**), which you can use to set advanced file protection options.

File sharing options for this document

File sharing options protect a document from unauthorized modification.

◆ **Password to modify** enables you to specify a password that must be entered to save modifications to the file.

◆ **Read-only recommended** displays a dialog that recommends that the file be opened as a read-only file (**Figure 32**) each time the file is opened. If the file is opened as read-only, changes to the file must be saved in a file with a different name or in a different disk location.

◆ **Digital Signatures** displays the Digital Signature dialog (**Figure 33**), which provides information about signatures attached to the document.

◆ **Protect Document** displays the Protect Document dialog (**Figure 34**), which you can use to limit the types of changes that can be made to the document. If you use this option, you can enter a password that would be required to unprotect the document.

SECURITY OPTIONS

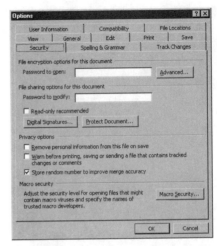

Figure 30 The default settings in the Security tab of the Options dialog.

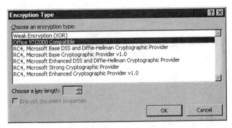

Figure 31 Use the Encryption Type dialog to set advanced document protection options.

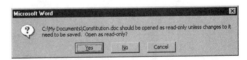

Figure 32 This dialog appears when you open a document that has been saved with the Read-only recommended option enabled.

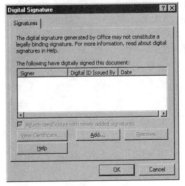

Figure 33 The Digital Signature dialog displays information about digital signatures attached to a document.

Figure 34
Use the Protect Document dialog to limit the types of modifications a user can make to a file.

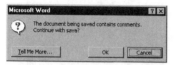

Figure 35 Word can warn you when you save, print, or e-mail a file that contains tracked changes or comments.

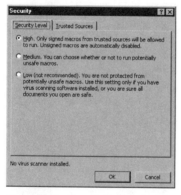

Figure 36 The Security Level tab of the Security dialog.

Figure 37 The Trusted Sources tab of the Security dialog.

Privacy options

Privacy options help protect your privacy.

◆ **Remove personal information from this file on save** removes user information from the file when you save it.

◆ **Warn before printing, saving or sending a file that contains tracked changes or comments** displays a warning dialog (**Figure 35**) when you print, save, or e-mail a file that contains tracked changes or comments. This helps prevent you from sending draft files that may include confidential information.

◆ **Store random number to improve merge accuracy** tells Word to store a random number in the file for use with its merge feature. This increases the accuracy of the merge.

Macro security

The Macro security options enable you to protect your computer from viruses attached to macros that work with Word or other Microsoft Office products. Clicking the Macro Security button displays a dialog with two tabs of settings. Although these advanced options are beyond the scope of this book, here's a quick explanation of each.

◆ **Security Level** (**Figure 36**) enables you to set a general security level for protecting your computer from macro viruses.

◆ **Trusted Sources** (**Figure 37**) displays a list of the sources from which you have accepted files containing macros.

SECURITY OPTIONS

Spelling & Grammar Options

Spelling & Grammar options (**Figure 38**) control the way the spelling and grammar checkers work. There are three categories of options: Spelling, Grammar, and Proofing Tools.

Spelling

Spelling options control the way the spelling checker works:

◆ **Check spelling as you type** turns on the automatic spelling check feature.

◆ **Hide spelling errors in this document** hides the red wavy lines that Word uses to identify possible spelling errors when the automatic spelling check feature is turned on. This option is only available when the Check spelling as you type option is enabled.

◆ **Always suggest corrections** tells Word to automatically display a list of suggested replacements for a misspelled word during a manual spelling check.

◆ **Suggest from main dictionary only** tells Word to suggest replacement words from the main dictionary—not from your custom dictionaries.

◆ **Ignore words in UPPERCASE** tells Word not to check words in all uppercase characters, such as acronyms.

◆ **Ignore words with numbers** tells Word not to check words that include numbers, such as *MariaL1*.

◆ **Ignore Internet and file addresses** tells Word not to check any words that appear to be URLs, e-mail addresses, file names, or file pathnames.

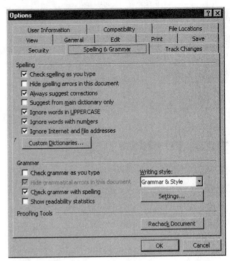

Figure 38 The Spelling & Grammar tab of the Options dialog.

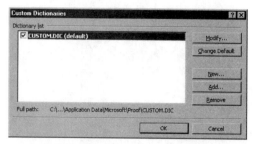

Figure 39 The Custom Dictionaries dialog.

Figure 40
Use this dialog to make changes to a custom dictionary.

◆ **Custom Dictionaries** enables you to create, edit, add, and remove custom dictionaries. Click this button to display the Custom Dictionaries dialog (**Figure 39**), which lists all the dictionary files open in Word. Then:

▲ To activate a dictionary file so it can be used by the spelling checker, turn on the check box to the left of its name in the Custom dictionaries list.

▲ To edit the selected dictionary, click the Edit button to display a dialog like the one in **Figure 40**. You can add a word to the dictionary by typing it into the Word box and clicking Add. You can delete a word from the dictionary by selecting the word in the list and clicking Delete. When you are finished making changes, click OK.

▲ To change the default dictionary (the one that words are automatically added to), select the dictionary you want to be the default and click Change Default.

▲ To create a new custom dictionary, click the New button and use the dialog that appears to name and save the new dictionary file.

▲ To add a dictionary to the Custom dictionaries list, click the Add button and use the dialog that appears to locate and open the dictionary file. This feature makes it possible to share dictionary files that contain company- or industry-specific terms with other Word users in your workplace.

▲ To remove a dictionary from Word, select the dictionary and click the Remove button. This does not delete the dictionary file from disk.

When you are finished making changes in the Custom Dictionaries dialog, click OK.

SPELLING & GRAMMAR OPTIONS

Grammar

Grammar options control the way the grammar checker works:

◆ **Check grammar as you type** turns on the automatic grammar check feature.

◆ **Hide grammatical errors in this document** hides the green wavy lines that Word uses to identify possible grammar errors when the automatic grammar check feature is turned on. This option is only available when the Check grammar as you type option is enabled.

◆ **Check grammar with spelling** performs a grammar check as part of a manual spelling check.

◆ **Show readability statistics** displays readability statistics (**Figure 41**) for a document at the conclusion of a manual spelling and grammar check. This option is only available when the Check grammar with spelling option is enabled.

◆ **Writing style** enables you to select a set of rules for the grammar checker. Use the drop-down list to select an option (**Figure 42**).

◆ **Settings** enables you to customize the rules for the grammar checker. Click this button to display the Grammar Settings dialog (**Figure 43**). Choose the set of rules that you want to modify from the Writing style drop-down list (**Figure 42**), then use the options in the dialog to set the style's rules. You can use the Reset All button to reset all writing style rule sets to the default settings.

Proofing Tools

The Proofing Tools area includes one button: Recheck Document. Clicking this button clears the list of ignored problems so you can recheck a document for errors.

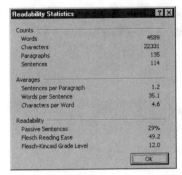

Figure 41 Readability statistics for the Constitution of the United States.

Figure 42 The Writing style drop-down list offers two predefined sets of rules.

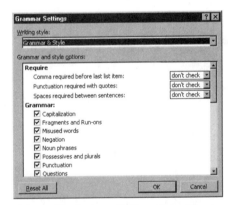

Figure 43 The Grammar Settings dialog lets you fine-tune the settings for writing style rule sets.

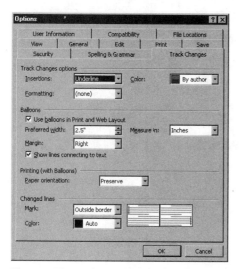

Figure 44 The Track Changes tab of the Options dialog.

Figure 45
Use this drop-down list to specify how you want insertions and formatting to appear.

Figure 46
Use this drop-down list to specify how you want changes to be colored.

Track Changes Options

The Track Changes options (**Figure 44**) control the way the Track Changes feature works. There are four categories of options: Track Changes options, Balloons, Printing (with Balloons), and Changed lines.

Track Changes options

The Track Changes options enables you to control the appearance of the Track Changes feature.

◆ **Insertions** controls the appearance of text that is inserted into the document. Choose an option from the drop-down list (**Figure 45**).

◆ **Formatting** controls the appearance of text which has been reformatted. Choose an option from the drop-down list (**Figure 45**).

◆ **Color** controls the color of change marks. Choose an option from the drop-down list (**Figure 46**). The By author option color codes the changes by reviewer.

Balloons

The Balloons options enable you to display changes in a document's margin.

◆ **Use balloons in Print and Web Layout** displays changes in the margins in Print and Web Layout views.

◆ **Preferred width** enables you to set the width for the area in which changes appear.

◆ **Measure in** enables you to specify whether the Preferred width measurement is in inches or a percentage of the page or window width.

◆ **Show lines connecting to text** displays lines connecting the change notations to the text that was changed.

Printing (with Balloons)

The sole option in this area is a drop-down list (**Figure 47**) for setting the paper orientation when printing pages with tracked changes. Choose one of the options:

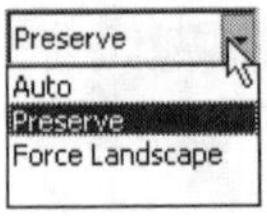

Figure 47
Choose an option from this drop-down list to set the paper orientation for a document with tracked changes.

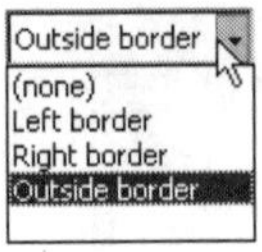

◆ **Auto** lets Word decide what the best orientation for printing the document is.

◆ **Preserve** keeps the orientation setting in the Page Setup dialog.

◆ **Force Landscape** prints the page in landscape mode.

Changed lines

The Changed lines options determine the location and color of vertical lines that appear beside changed lines of text.

Figure 48
Use this drop-down list to specify where a changed line mark should appear.

◆ **Mark** offers a drop-down list (**Figure 48**) for selecting the location of the changed line mark.

◆ **Color** offers a drop-down list (**Figure 46**) for selecting the color of the changed line mark.

MENUS & SHORTCUT KEYS

Menus & Shortcut Keys

This appendix illustrates all of Microsoft Word's standard menus and provides a list of shortcut keys—including some that don't appear on menus.

To use a shortcut key, hold down the modifier key (usually Ctrl) and press the keyboard key corresponding to the command. For example, to use the Save command's shortcut key, hold down Ctrl and press S.

✔ Tip

■ Using menus and shortcut keys is discussed in detail in **Chapter 1**.

File Menu

Ctrl N	New
Ctrl O	Open
Ctrl W	Close
Ctrl S	Save
F12	Save As
Ctrl F2	Print Preview
Ctrl P	Print
Alt F4	Close or Exit

Send To submenu

(no shortcut keys)

Edit Menu

Ctrl Z	Undo
Ctrl Y	Redo or Repeat
Ctrl X	Cut
Ctrl C	Copy
Ctrl V	Paste
Ctrl A	Select All
Ctrl F	Find
Ctrl H	Replace
Ctrl G	Go To

Clear submenu

Del	Clear Contents

View Menu

Alt Ctrl N	Normal
Alt Ctrl O	Outline

Toolbars submenu

(no shortcut keys)

Insert Menu

Ctrl Shift F5   Bookmark

Ctrl K   Hyperlink

AutoText submenu

Alt F3   New

Reference submenu

(no shortcut keys)

Picture submenu

(no shortcut keys)

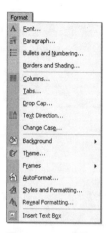

Format Menu

Ctrl D   Font

Shift F3   Change Case

Alt Ctrl K   AutoFormat

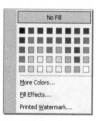

Background submenu

(no shortcut keys)

Frames submenu

(no shortcut keys)

INSERT & FORMAT MENUS

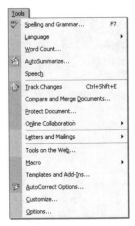

Tools Menu

F7	Spelling and Grammar
Ctrl Shift E	Track Changes

Language submenu

Shift F7	Thesaurus

Online Collaboration submenu

(no shortcut keys)

Letters and Mailings submenu

(no shortcut keys)

Macro submenu

Alt F8	Macros
Alt F11	Visual Basic Editor
Alt Shift F11	Microsoft Script Editor

TOOLS MENU

Table Menu

(no shortcut keys)

Window Menu

(no shortcut keys)

Insert submenu

(no shortcut keys)

AutoFit submenu

(no shortcut keys)

Help Menu

| Ctrl F1 | Microsoft Word Help |
| Shift F1 | What's This? |

Delete submenu

(no shortcut keys)

Convert submenu

(no shortcut keys)

Select submenu

(no shortcut keys)

INDEX

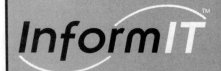